SRI RAMAKRISHNA, THE FACE OF SILENCE

"God has made different religions to suit different aspirants, times and countries. All doctrines are so many paths; but a path is by no means God Himself. Indeed, one can reach God if one follows any of the paths with whole-hearted devotion."

—Sri Ramakrishna

SRI RAMAKRISHNA, THE FACE OF SILENCE

Swami Nikhilananda *and* Dhan Gopal Mukerji
Edited and with an Introduction by Swami Adiswarananda
Foreword by Dhan Gopal Mukerji II

Walking Together, Finding the Way
SKYLIGHT PATHS® Publishing
Woodstock, Vermont

RAMAKRISHNA-VIVEKANANDA
CENTER OF NEW YORK
"As Many Faiths, So Many Paths"

Sri Ramakrishna, the Face of Silence

2005 First Printing

Page 325 constitutes a continuation of this copyright page.

Library of Congress Cataloging-in-Publication Data
Nikhilananda, Swami.
Sri Ramakrishna / Swami Nikhilanda. The face of silence / Dhan Gopal Mukerji ; [both] edited and with an introduction by Swami Adiswarananda ; foreword by Dhan Gopal Mukerji II.
p. cm.
ISBN 1-59473-115-2 (hardcover)
1. Ramakrishna, 1836–1886—Teachings. 2. Hindu saints—Biography. I. Adiswarananda, Swami, 1925– . II. Mukerji, Dhan Gopal, 1890–1936. Face of silence. III. Title. IV. Title: Face of silence.
BL1175.R26N53 2005
294.5'55'092—dc22
[B]
                                                                2005010482

10 9 8 7 6 5 4 3 2 1

Manufactured in Canada
Jacket Design: Sara Dismukes
Jacket Art: White Alabaster bust of Sri Ramakrishna by noted American sculptor Malvina Hoffman (commissioned by Swami Nikhilananda in 1952 and presently installed on the altar of the Ramakrishna-Vivekananda Center of New York, New York City).

SkyLight Paths Publishing is creating a place where people of different spiritual traditions come together for challenge and inspiration, a place where we can help each other understand the mystery that lies at the heart of our existence.

SkyLight Paths sees both believers and seekers as a community that increasingly transcends traditional boundaries of religion and denomination—people wanting to learn from each other, *walking together, finding the way.*

Walking Together, Finding the Way
Published by SkyLight Paths Publishing
A Division of LongHill Partners, Inc.
Sunset Farm Offices, Route 4, P.O. Box 237
Woodstock, VT 05091
Tel: (802) 457-4000   Fax: (802) 457-4004
www.skylightpaths.com

Contents

Foreword by Dhan Gopal Mukerji II   vii

Preface by Swami Adiswarananda   xi

Introduction: Sri Ramakrishna and His God-Consciousness
     by Swami Adiswarananda   1

The Face of Silence by Dhan Gopal Mukerji

     1. Ramakrishna Monastery   17

     2. The Ramakrishna Legend   21

     3. Ramakrishna's Early Life   27

     4. Holy Man   39

     5. Ramakrishna and Other Religions   51

     6. Orthodox Hindus and Ramakrishna   59

     7. Ramakrishna and a Modern Social Reformer   67

     8. Ramakrishna and His Disciples   79

     9. Ramakrishna and His Disciples *(continued)*   97

     10. Description of the Indescribable   105

     11. A Recent Initiation   115

12. Holy Man or Incarnation of God   129

13. Ramakrishna and a Wayward Soul   139

14. Mahaprasthan or Last Journey   147

15. Turiyananda's Conclusion   151

16. Last Impression   161

Sri Ramakrishna by Swami Nikhilananda

1. The Early Years   173

2. Dakshineswar   183

3. Spiritual Longing and God-Vision   189

4. Sadhanas or Spiritual Disciplines   205

5. Contemporaries   239

6. The Coming of the Disciples   249

7. The Final Years   281

Appendix: Dhan Gopal Mukerji and His Intense
    Spiritual Longing   295

Notes   313

Glossary   317

Credits   325

Foreword

The Face of Silence was the first book written in English to make Sri Ramakrishna known outside India. My father saw it as a follow-up to Swami Vivekananda's famous visit to America in 1893.

A further reason the book was important was more personal. My father's first literary success had been *Caste and Outcast*, which told of his arrival in America as a penniless brahmin seeking his destiny. That was followed by *My Brother's Face*, which told of his return to India in 1920, with an American wife, only to find a different India, to which he was now an outsider. The only aspect that was unchanged was the loving face of his elder brother. It was *Caste and Outcast* in reverse.

During the months he and my mother were visiting India, my father was aware that all his life so far had been a search for who he was and where he belonged. In *The Face of Silence*, the reader shares his discovery that the whos and whys of his life have become inextricably enlaced with the glorious name of Ramakrishna. Taken with the two earlier books, *The Face of Silence* made a trilogy of a man's search for his soul. It would dominate a life that ended while he was still relatively young, forty-seven, a few days after receiving the ocher cloth from Swami Akhandananda, the president of the Ramakrishna Order.

The Face of Silence has a life of its own. When it appeared in 1926, it was an immediate literary success, encouraging publishers in Europe to translate it for their readers. Victor Attinger, who had presses in France and Switzerland, urged my father to come to Geneva to participate in the translation to French of all three books. This led to a necklace of events.

By 1928, Romain Rolland, the 1915 Nobel laureate in literature, was living in Geneva. He had been exiled by his native France for opposing World War I. He was seriously depressed. His solace was to have his sister, Madeleine, read the latest publications aloud to him.

She returned from shopping one day with *The Face of Silence* in French. On hearing it, he became excited; he told his sister to find out how he could contact the author. She called old man Attinger who was honored, he said, to tell her, "Mukerji is living here in Geneva." That same day, she called my father and begged him to come and see her brother. My father, who considered Romain Rolland to be "a great soul," was overjoyed to accept.

In Romain Rolland's famous journal, he tells of my father's visit. Rolland questioned him about Ramakrishna, Vivekananda, Vedanta, the new India. My father put him in touch with the monastery at Belur Math and wrote personal letters of introduction to Swami Shivananda, one of the direct disciples of Sri Ramakrishna, and other monks. A few years later, Romain Rolland wrote his great *Life of Ramakrishna* and *Life of Vivekananda,* thus bringing them to the attention of his enormous audience.

On July 28, 1936, Josephine Tantine MacLeod, Swami Vivekananda's devoted follower, wrote from Helsinki to my father's beloved brother, Jadu, in India, on hearing of my father's death. She had received the news of Dhan's death while on her way to Leningrad. She wrote:

> Dhan Gopal has gone to join the great ones he so loved.
> His *nostalgie de Dieu* [love of God] took him over…. The

Russian government has translated all of Rolland's books into Russian—including his life of Ramakrishna and Swamiji [Swami Vivekananda]! It was Dhan Gopal's book *The Face of Silence* that inspired him to write those two great lives—bless them both.

May *The Face of Silence* continue to enlarge our souls.

Dhan Gopal Mukerji II

Preface

Nobel laureate Romain Rolland refers to Sri Ramakrishna's life as nothing less than "the book of life itself." In Rolland's words,

> It is always the same Book. It is always the same Man—
> the Son of Man, the Eternal, Our Son, Our God reborn.
> With each return he reveals himself a little more fully,
> and more enriched by the universe…. The man whose
> image I here evoke was the consummation of two thou-
> sand years of the spiritual life of three hundred mil-
> lion people.

Writers and thinkers have used many epithets in an attempt to describe Sri Ramakrishna: Prophet for the New Age, Prophet of the Harmony of Religions, Godman of Modern India, Spiritual Hero, Savior of the Eternal Religion, the Great Master, a Phenomenon. But perhaps no description is more profound or intriguing than that given by Dhan Gopal Mukerji: the Face of Silence. It was this 1926 biography that was destined to play a key role in introducing the life and teachings of Sri Ramakrishna to the world.

Dhan Gopal Mukerji was one of the earliest émigrés from India to America, and he achieved a great measure of success as a writer. Nevertheless, at one point in his life, feeling at home neither in India nor

America, he faced a crisis of identity—a spiritual crisis that proved to be a turning point in his life. It was Josephine MacLeod, the dedicated devotee of Swami Vivekananda, who introduced Dhan Gopal Mukerji to the life of Sri Ramakrishna and paved the way for his visit to the Sri Ramakrishna Monastery at Belur, India. It was there that Mukerji became acquainted with many of the direct disciples of Sri Ramakrishna, a transforming experience that inspired him to write *The Face of Silence*. The book was widely read and found its way into the hands of Romain Rolland, prompting him to write his *Life of Ramakrishna*. In the preface, Romain Rolland expresses his "gratitude to Mr. Dhan Gopal Mukerji, who first revealed Ramakrishna's existence to me." Thus, within only a few decades of Sri Ramakrishna's passing, his name became known throughout Europe, the United States, and other Western countries.

Dhan Gopal Mukerji tells us that in writing *The Face of Silence*, he was guided not so much to write a factual history of Sri Ramakrishna but rather what he called the "Ramakrishna legend." Mahendranath Gupta (known as M.), the chronicler of *The Gospel of Sri Ramakrishna*, encouraged Mukerji in this approach, suggesting that by themselves facts lacked the power to uplift anyone. "Legend," he said, "is the chalice of truth." Mukerji sought out and talked with many individuals who actually met Sri Ramakrishna and who recalled their experience of seeing the Master. *The Face of Silence* is the story of Sri Ramakrishna and, at the same time, a poetic interpretation that conveys the deeper spirit within that story—the Ramakrishna legend.

For a long time *The Face of Silence* has been out of print. In bringing out this new edition, SkyLight Paths Publishing in cooperation with the Ramakrishna-Vivekananda Center of New York makes available once again a classic work of religious literature that is an important link in the life of the Ramakrishna-Vivekananda-Vedanta movement. We are extremely grateful to Mr. Dhan Gopal Mukerji II, the son of the author, for his dedication to the legacy of his father and for the help and cooperation he has given to this project. His foreword is a most welcome addition to this book.

A second major feature of the present book is the biography of Sri Ramakrishna by Swami Nikhilananda, originally published in 1942 as an introduction to *The Gospel of Sri Ramakrishna*, the swami's monumental English translation of the conversations of Sri Ramakrishna with his disciples, devotees, and visitors. In this biography, the reader will find a historically accurate portrayal of the life of the Master, descriptions of people who came in contact with him, and short explanations of several systems of Indian religious thought intimately connected with Sri Ramakrishna's life. The biography will enable the reader to better understand and appreciate the unusual life of Sri Ramakrishna.

By placing Swami Nikhilananda's historical portrait of the Master side by side with Dhan Gopal Mukerji's poetic interpretation of the Ramakrishna legend, we hope to give the reader a fuller understanding of the life and spiritual significance of Sri Ramakrishna, about whom Mahatma Gandhi wrote, "His life enables us to see God face to face." A prophet for our time, Sri Ramakrishna is a silent force in molding the spiritual destiny of our world.

Swami Adiswarananda
Ramakrishna-Vivekananda Center of New York

Sri Ramakrishna

Introduction

Sri Ramakrishna and His God-Consciousness

Nineteenth-century India met with a spiritual crisis that shook the very foundation of her thousands of years of spiritual existence. India passed under British rule during the middle of the eighteenth century, and soon there followed a torrent of materialistic ideas from the West, which overwhelmed and stupefied the educated community. Anything Indian was looked upon with contempt and anything Western was coveted. The historian Thomas Macaulay remarked, "A single shelf of a good European library is worth the whole native literature of India and Arabia." Nothing was accepted as true and valid unless it passed the test of scientific reasoning. The atheistic and agnostic thoughts of contemporary Western thinkers that had already struck at the root of religious beliefs of the Western mind now began to gain sway over the educated Indian mind. Every new discovery of science in the West was taken to be another step toward the final liberation of humankind from outdated religious beliefs. The existence of the soul within the body was looked upon as an ancient myth and human consciousness as a product of biochemical reactions. Only the principles of biological selection and the survival of the fittest determined the course of human history. All spiritual quests came to be considered a regression to infantile primitivism, and spiritual experiences hallucinations resulting from functional

1

disorders in the brain. Passion for truth was caused by overstimulated nerves. Dispassion was due to an indisposed liver or zero bank balance. Discontentment with the shams of the world was a symptom of a disordered colon.

The traditions of Hinduism were called upon to meet this challenge from the West and prove their worth. The challenge was powerful and the shock severe. Many educated Hindus became skeptics, atheists, or agnostics, and more than a few converted to Christianity. In order to meet the challenge, several religious revival movements sprang up in India, most notably the Brahmo Samaj and the Arya Samaj. Although these new movements were able to give a sense of direction to the people for the time being, none were able to resolve the spiritual crisis decisively. The need of the time was not a new religion but a new spiritual vision capable of withstanding the tests of scientific reasoning.

Advent of Sri Ramakrishna

While India was passing through this state of confusion and loss of faith, an unknown temple priest, oblivious of his surroundings, sitting on the bank of the Ganges on the outskirts of Calcutta, was engaged in an epoch-making spiritual adventure of experimentation and verification that would stem the tide of skepticism and give India a new vision and faith in her spiritual identity. This unknown temple priest was later to become known to the world as Sri Ramakrishna. In keeping with the scientific temper of the time, Sri Ramakrishna wanted to see God not in a dream or a vision but face to face. Through his life, he demonstrated that God, far from being just a metaphysical concept, is a living reality, pervading the entire universe and yet pulsating in the heart of every being, and that spiritual knowledge is not contrary to human reason and common sense.

Sri Ramakrishna's advent fulfilled the spiritual need of India. His God-intoxicated life and burning spiritual realizations infused new life into Hinduism and restored its faltering rhythms to a proper balance. Sri Ramakrishna did not give India a new religion or philosophy, and he did not uphold any particular system of thought to the exclusion of others. His unique message was his all-embracing God-consciousness. When God-consciousness falls short, traditions become oppressive, teachings dogmatic, and philosophies meaningless speculations. The God-centered life of Sri Ramakrishna was like a searchlight focused upon the entire spiritual heritage of India. He stood before nineteenth-century India as the very embodiment of faith and spiritual illumination, in the light of which people saw through the hollowness of contemporary nihilism and skepticism. To a world full of doubt and disbelief, Sri Ramakrishna brought certainty of faith.

The experience of ultimate Truth made Sri Ramakrishna sensitive to the most minute psychological facts. The keenness of his observation, coupled with a power and skill of expression, made it possible for him to describe the indescribable with amazing directness and precision. It was Sri Ramakrishna who for the first time explored the vast and unknown realms of the human soul in all its dimensions. He saw what no eye could see, heard what no ear could hear, and discovered what no mind could comprehend. In his search for Truth, he walked alone and was not understood even by the best Hindus of his time. Through his life, he demonstrated that God is very much real and can be realized. What is necessary is not philosophy or logic, but sincerity of purpose.

What is it that makes Sri Ramakrishna so profound and powerful? Compared with the distinguished and erudite personalities of his time, he seemed to be an ordinary person devoid of position and popularity. Yet in this humble and artless life there was something staggeringly deep and expansive—his God-consciousness. He saw God more intensely than he saw the world and talked with God as a child with its mother. In him there was only God, and he saw God everywhere and in everything.

Romain Rolland described Sri Ramakrishna's life as the fulfillment of the spiritual aspirations of three hundred million Hindus for the last two thousand years. Max Müller designated him as "a real mahatman," or truly a great master. "No one," said Mahatma Gandhi, "can read the story of his life without being convinced that God alone is real and all else is an illusion."

Above all, Sri Ramakrishna is an historical personality. He has been photographed and his teachings have been stenographically recorded. His spiritual states were observed with awe by skeptics, agnostics, and atheists alike; his ecstasies were tested for genuineness by medical doctors; and his teachings have not been obscured, as yet, by doubtful myths.

Yearning for God-Vision

Sri Ramakrishna was born in 1836 and passed away in 1886. His life was an uninterrupted contemplation of God. God-consciousness was the very breath of his life. His fragile and finite human form struggled to contain within it the limitless God of infinite dimension. The yearning for God-vision manifested even in his early childhood. Sri Ramakrishna was born of parents living in an out-of-the-way village of Bengal. His father, Khudiram, was a pious and truthful brahmin, who devoted most of his time to prayer and contemplation and led a life of utter simplicity, completely depending on God for everything. Sri Ramakrishna's mother, Chandramani Devi, was a personification of guilelessness, compassion, and purity. As a boy, Sri Ramakrishna was full of fun and life, yet it was noticed that his mind would very often be transported to the divine realm. Stories of saints and holy persons would set his imagination on fire and create in him an exalted state of mind. He manifested total indifference to the conventional education imparted in the schools. When an elder brother tried to enroll him in a school, Sri Ramakrishna told him, "Brother, what shall I do with this bread-winning education? I should rather acquire that wisdom which will illumine my heart and on getting which one is satisfied forever." Regarding philosophers and theologians devoid of God-consciousness, he would say later on, "They are like vultures that soar high on the wings of their undisciplined intellect, having their attention fixed all the time on the carrion of name, fame, and wealth."

The French writer Maurice Barrès was once asked, "What is the good of the saints?" He replied, "They delight the soul." Indeed, Sri Ramakrishna, even as a child, was the delight of the souls around him. At the age of seven, Sri Ramakrishna lost his father and from then on became more attached to his mother. The event, moreover, gave him a glimpse of the transitoriness of life, and he became more and more absorbed in his spiritual thoughts. He would frequent cremation grounds and other secluded places, where he would become lost in the contemplation of God.

Search for God

At the age of sixteen, Sri Ramakrishna came to Calcutta, where after some time he was engaged as a priest in the Kali temple of Dakshineswar. The fire of his longing for God, which had been smoldering within for many years, now burst into flame. He was not satisfied with merely seeing the image of the deity. He wanted to see the living form of the Mother with his eyes open. Assurances of the scriptures could not satisfy him, and philosophical speculations about God only made him impatient. He wanted the direct vision of a living God. He refused to wait for God's slow-moving grace to come to him in the course of time—he wanted to meet it more than halfway through intense effort. Skepticism would often creep into his soul and fill his mind with disappointment and agony. His worship mainly consisted of the passionate cry and prayer of a child separated from its beloved mother. As outpourings of his soul, he would sing songs composed by seers of God, and tears would then flow from his eyes. Often he would accuse the Divine Mother of being stonehearted and unkind for not granting her vision to him, saying, "Are you true, Mother, or is it a mere fiction of the mind—only poetry without reality? If you do exist, why can't I see you? Life is passing away. One day is gone, followed by another. Every day I am drawing so much nearer to death. But where are you, my Mother?"

The Vision of God

Discouraged, anguished, and in utter despair, one day Sri Ramakrishna was about to put an end to his life, when at that very moment he was blessed with an all-engulfing vision of the Mother pervading the universe. Sri Ramakrishna's first vision of God was the result of his passionate prayer and intense yearning. At the time he was not acquainted with any prescribed form of spiritual discipline.

After his first vision of God, Sri Ramakrishna was taken over by a divine frenzy. He now wanted to have an uninterrupted vision of the Divine Mother. He forgot food and drink, sleep left him altogether, and he subjected himself to various forms of spiritual austerities and practices for self-purification and self-control. Like a true scientist, he knew that the success of an experiment depends on the scrupulous observance of its rules. None could persuade him to deviate, even a little, from the path of truthfulness in thought, word, and deed. His entire nervous system became attuned to such a high state of God-consciousness that any contact with worldly objects or thoughts would cause him excruciating pain and suffering. Whenever he sat for meditation, he was unable to move even slightly until his meditation was completed. He practiced *pranayama* (control of breath) to such an extent that he would sometimes remain without breathing. During his worship, he placed the flowers on his head instead of offering them at the feet of the image of the Mother. The distinction between the Mother in his heart and the Mother in the image had disappeared for him. Sometimes he would cry in agony, sometimes sing and dance around the Mother's image in spiritual exultation.

God-Intoxication and Marriage

Unable to understand Sri Ramakrishna's divine frenzy, the people around him thought he had gone mad. One who does not share the insanity of his neighbors is usually looked upon as insane. Hearing the news of Sri Ramakrishna's madness, his mother felt greatly disturbed and thought that marriage would help him to regain his normal state of mind. Soon the marriage was arranged, and Sri Ramakrishna gave his willing consent to it, seeing in it also the hand of God. When later his wife came to the temple garden, Sri Ramakrishna knelt before her and said, "The Divine Mother has shown me that every woman is her manifestation. Therefore I look upon all women as the image of the Divine Mother. I also think of you as such." Free from all carnal desire, the two souls lived as partners in their spiritual quest. Not even for a moment would either of them think of any worldly relationship. One night while his wife, Sarada Devi, later known to devotees as the Holy Mother, was massaging Sri Ramakrishna's feet, she asked him, "How do you look upon me?" Sri Ramakrishna replied, "The Mother who is worshiped in the temple is the mother who has given birth to this body and is now living in the temple garden, and she again is massaging my feet at this moment. Verily I always look upon you as the visible manifestation of the blissful Mother."

The marriage of Sri Ramakrishna failed to bring his mind to the world; instead it increased his divine intoxication a thousandfold. Now

Sri Ramakrishna embarked on a prolonged spiritual adventure, during which he practiced the disciplines of the different schools of Hinduism in a systematic way and realized that all of them led to the same goal. Later he practiced Christianity and Islam, arrived at the same conclusion, and declared, "As many faiths, so many paths." Different paths are but different opinions, while the goal is one and the same.

Sri Ramakrishna's message of the harmony of religions is founded on his own all-embracing God-consciousness that transcends all limits of sects and denominations. Through his life he demonstrated that God-realization is not dependent upon any religious indoctrination but upon sincerity of purpose and purity of heart. "Truth is one: sages call it by various names." All roads lead to Rome, provided Rome is the destination. Similarly, all creeds lead to God, provided the worshiper is determined to know God.

It is said that when the flower blooms, the bees gather around it of their own accord. Drawn by the aroma of Sri Ramakrishna's transfigured existence, people began to flock to him from far and near. There were men and women, young and old, philosophers and theologians, philanthropists and humanists, scientists and agnostics, Hindus and Brahmos, Christians and Muslims—seekers of truth from all races, creeds, castes, and religious affiliations. His small room in the Dakshineswar temple garden became a veritable parliament of religions. Everyone who came to him felt uplifted by his profound God-consciousness, boundless love, and universal outlook. Each seeker of truth saw in him the highest manifestation of his or her own ideal. Last of all there came a band of young men who were destined to carry his message of God-consciousness to people in different parts of the world. After Sri Ramakrishna's passing, one among them, who became their leader, would be known to the world as Swami Vivekananda. Narendra, as he was then called, represented the modern spirit of scientific reasoning and doubt. A person of brilliant intellect and innate purity, he would not accept anything unless he had verified it by direct evidence. Haunted by an insatiable desire for God-vision, Narendra met many spiritual luminaries of the time and asked each of them a single question, "Sir, have you seen God?" Nowhere did he get a direct reply until he met Sri Ramakrishna. When Narendra asked the same question to Sri Ramakrishna, the direct and emphatic reply was, "Yes, I have seen God. I see him more tangibly than I see you. I have talked to him more intimately than I am talking to you. But my child, who wants to see God? People shed jugs of tears for money, wife, and children. But if they would weep for God for one day they would surely see him." Narendra was overwhelmed at this spontaneous reply. All of his doubt soon disappeared, and he became transformed. Sri Ramakrishna passed his fire of God-consciousness to Narendra, who took the vow of renunciation and service of God in all. Sri Ramakrishna placed the band of young men in the care of Narendra, thus creating an instrument for spreading his message far and wide.

The Message of God-Consciousness

The central theme of Sri Ramakrishna's message is God-consciousness. God-consciousness is the essence of all teachings of all religions. It is the goal of all study of scriptures, philosophical speculation, prayer and contemplation, sacraments and rituals, charity and austerity, and pilgrimage to holy places. To Sri Ramakrishna, the message of all scriptures, of all religions, is that God alone is real and all else is illusory. One must grasp this message and then plunge into oneself for the realization of Truth. The essence of the Bhagavad Gita is given in Sri Ramakrishna's inimitable words: "What is the significance of the Gita? It is what you find by repeating the word ten times. It is then reversed into *tagi*, which means a person who has renounced everything for God. And the lesson of the Gita is: O man, renounce everything and seek God alone."

Different scriptures and traditions describe various obstacles to God-realization. Sri Ramakrishna indicated that all obstacles center on two things—lust and gold. Renunciation of lust and gold is true renunciation. It is the degree of manifestation of God-consciousness that makes the difference between a sinner and a saint. The purpose of all spiritual practices, Sri Ramakrishna indicated, is to become sincere. It is, in his words, "to make our thought, word, and action the same." While God-consciousness, the goal of religion, remains the same for all ages, denominations and paths vary, as they must, to suit the diverse tastes of different seekers.

Sri Ramakrishna's God-consciousness was so intense and so spontaneous that he continually had to make efforts to bring his mind to the consciousness of the outer world. The slightest suggestion—a scene, incident, or conversation—would arouse God-consciousness in him, and immediately he would be taken over by *samadhi*, or total absorption in God. It was as if every particle of Sri Ramakrishna's being was filled with God-consciousness. Sri Ramakrishna saw God in everything, with his eyes both open and closed. Bowing before even a fallen woman, he would say, "You are the manifestation of the Divine Mother. In one form you are standing in the street and in another form you are worshiped in the temple. My salutations to you." Seeing drunkards in a grog shop, he would be overwhelmed with divine inebriation. When in a state of divine ecstasy, he would move around with his clothes under his arm like a child. Seeing someone meditating or hearing the chanting of the holy name of God, his mind would become intoxicated, and he would go into samadhi. Such was the depth of Sri Ramakrishna's divine inebriation that for a six-month period he was totally unconscious of his own body and surroundings. Flies would enter his mouth, birds would perch on his head, and snakes would crawl over his motionless body without his being aware of it. In fact, Sri Ramakrishna's body was preserved solely due to the efforts of a wandering monk who appeared at Dakshineswar at that time. The monk would forcibly bring Sri Ramakrishna's mind to the outer world, sometimes by striking him, and then thrust some food into his mouth.

The sacred texts of Vedanta testify: "The knower of Brahman becomes Brahman"; "He who realizes Truth becomes one with Truth"; "By the vision of the Divine, man himself becomes divine." Sri Ramakrishna's life demonstrates the validity of these scriptural passages. Greatly amazed to see Sri Ramakrishna's continual God-intoxication, Mathur, the proprietor of the Kali temple, lovingly told Sri Ramakrishna, "Father, your body is like an empty shell. Inside it there is nothing but God."

Sri Ramakrishna's God-consciousness was neither an emotional thrill nor an intellectual exultation. It was vivid, direct, and dynamic, a blazing fire of divinity that purified and transformed anyone who came near it. It was grounded on complete renunciation of lust and gold. By touching him or seeing him, the impure became pure, and the pure became purer. For him, the Vedic saying "I am Brahman" was as true as the other Vedic saying "That thou art." The Bhagavad Gita says that the yogi sees the Self in all, and all in the Self. Sri Ramakrishna's life was a demonstration of this truth. Never did a word of condemnation escape his lips. Never did he refuse anyone the solace of his instruction. He was incapable of seeing evil in others, and his whole personality was transfused with love and compassion.

As a result of constant ecstasy and spiritual conversation with ever-increasing numbers of seekers of truth, Sri Ramakrishna contracted a sore throat that gradually worsened—a condition that was later diagnosed as cancer. Even when it became almost impossible for him to swallow anything, he could not send away any sincere inquirer without giving the necessary spiritual help. One moment he would be in great pain, and the next moment he would be filled with divine ecstasy, his face beaming with joy. Samadhi was a constant occurrence. Visitors were puzzled to see this phenomenon and would exclaim, "Good heavens!

It is as if he were possessed by a ghost!" The illness of Sri Ramakrishna's body never touched his soul, which was in constant communion with the God. It only proved the reality and intensity of his God-consciousness.

It was at this time that Pundit Shashadar, a noted religious leader, came to see Sri Ramakrishna and said to him, "The scriptures tell us that a *paramahamsa* like yourself can cure his physical illness by his own willpower. Why don't you try it, sir?" Sri Ramakrishna replied with annoyance, "You call yourself a pundit and you make such a suggestion! This mind has been given to God once and for all. How can I withdraw it from him and make it dwell on this worthless body?" The pundit was silenced. But later Narendra begged him to pray to God for the cure of his ailment, for the sake of the devotees[1], if not for his own sake. To this Sri Ramakrishna said, "Do you think I am suffering like this because I want to? Of course I want to get better! But it all depends on Mother." "Then please pray to Mother," said Narendra. "She can't refuse to listen." So at the earnest importunity of his beloved disciple, Sri Ramakrishna relented. A few hours later, when Narendra asked him, "Well, did you pray to Mother?" Sri Ramakrishna replied, "Yes, at your request I prayed to her. I said, 'O Mother, I can't eat anything through this mouth because of pain in the throat. Please relieve this pain if it be your pleasure.' But Mother pointed to all of you and said, 'Why, are you not eating through all these mouths?' So I felt ashamed and couldn't utter another word."

Toward the last phase of Sri Ramakrishna's life, ecstasy and samadhi became almost constant. He indicated to everyone that his time for departure had already come. He prophesied, "He who sincerely prays to God will certainly come here. He must…. I see that it is God himself who has become all this. It seems to me that men and other living beings are made of leather and that it is God himself who, dwelling inside these leather cases, moves the hands, the feet, the heads."

On August 16, 1886, Sri Ramakrishna began to experience samadhi frequently, and finally, uttering the name of Mother Kali three times, he fell into deep samadhi, never to return to the world of outer consciousness. A thrill passed though his body, making his hair stand on end. His eyes became fixed on the tip of his nose, and his face became lit by a divine smile.

Sri Ramakrishna's material form disappeared from human view; it could no longer contain the blazing fire of God-consciousness. In his invisible spiritual form, Sri Ramakrishna continues to live and inspire sincere seekers of all races and countries to realize God, taste the bliss of God-consciousness, and attain the highest fulfillment of life.

The Face of Silence

by Dhan Gopal Mukerji

To Those Who Pointed Me the Path
Josephine MacLeod
Jadu Gopal Mukhopadhaya
Alice Sprague
Mrs. Sumner Hunt

Belur Math, the monastery and headquarters of the Ramakrishna
Order near Kolkata, India

1
Ramakrishna Monastery

That a holy man, whom many of his followers called an incarnation of God, lived in recent years near Calcutta, is one of the surprises of our time. Not only that. The most surprising thing about the matter is that I should go straight back from America of the twentieth century and find his followers leading their medieval life right in the center of modern progress: monks and nuns living so close to the city of Calcutta, touching it at every vital point, yet maintaining their aloofness from it with perfect ease. However, I must begin this story as it unfolded itself to me—bit by bit.

Through the kindness of a friend I had been invited to come and live in the monastery where Ramakrishna's followers had their home. It looked quite imposing from the Calcutta side of the Ganges whence we approached it on a boat. The tower of a new temple stood out like a white nimbus above clumps of palm trees against the purple of the sunset sky. At its foot was a high stone palisade of graying yellow against which the river dragged its weary low tide. Soon our boat crossed the middle of the river. Now the rest of the monastery buildings raised their yellow heads one by one till the last little white shrine dedicated to the Divine Mother came like a veil of silver into view for a moment.

Suddenly they all vanished as we drew close to the embankment, which rose like an immense precipice, shutting everything from our view.

After we had moored our boat at the foot of the ghat, we climbed the stairs in great haste, for we were afraid to be too late for *arati* (evensong). On reaching the highest step we found ourselves on a large terrace of gray cement whence ran a small path toward the sacred shrine. Beyond the shrine gleamed the fierce green of the tropical gardens already taking on a softening tone of dull gold as the purple dusk stole down from the sky on wings of silence.

Just at that moment someone smote a gong in the shrine. That made us hasten within—for the arati had begun. The shrine was divided into two rooms: inner and outer. We sat near a group of shaven-headed monks who occupied the scarlet floor of the outer shrine. They beat their several cymbals and loudly chanted a benediction. In the room beyond—the inner shrine—a monk in yellow waved a *pancha pradip* (a candelabra of five lit candles) before a picture of Ramakrishna, which occupied the flower-decked altar. Around the altar innumerable lamps— their wicks soaked in ghee (clarified butter)—lifted their fragrant flames to the image of the Teacher. Seen in that circle of light, Ramakrishna's picture afforded one the strangest impression: though he looked full of life, he appeared inert as inertness itself.

"How came he to achieve that state?" I pondered to myself, hoping to inquire into his career fully and critically later on. Just then the clashing of cymbals ceased along with the singing. The monk inside stopped waving the pancha pradip. After setting it down he took up a conch shell and blew into it three times. After the last echo had died down he quietly seated himself before the altar and began to meditate. Following his example, the *sannyasins* (monks) in the outer shrine put away their cymbals, then chanted the thought on which they were to meditate. Now, one by one, they became still. Their bodies became rigid. Save their regular slow breathing that rose and fell in unison there was nothing to distinguish them from statues. Just then came a sound like bees around a faraway hive; the monk in the inner shrine chanted in a low tone, enunciating every word most clearly:

> Whence our words come back broken, and thoughts return like dogs beaten in a chase, that silence over which gathers the dust of all sound. O river of miracles....

That meditation, like a sharp shearing current, cut through my thoughts and flooded the entire room. The faces of each of the monks before me were austere like flint and as purged of desire as burned gold. With eyes shut and mouths tightly closed, they went on fathoming that silence whose depths "cannot be reached even by the plummets of stars!"

That was my first experience of the followers of Sri Ramakrishna. It fascinated me. And as I went on living with them I grew more and more curious to learn everything about their daily deeds. Why did they act as they did? What rules of conduct were they following? Who formulated the scheme of their life? But the men whom I questioned said very little. They urged me "*to live* among them awhile longer."

The smoothness and simplicity that formed the routine of their life had a vivid reality. I could not avoid being conscious of the consecration that gave meaning even to their coming and going. Their faces shone with pure light. They were not troubled by false hopes, nor deluded by fancies. There was a grim but beautiful reality in all that they said and did. Every morning they rose before five o'clock in order to meditate for two hours. Then they went on to their day's deeds such as taking care of the sick, succoring the poor, and teaching the young.

At noon they held a short communion with the Lord, then had their dinner. A siesta followed. At about half past two o'clock they held classes in which erudite scholars discussed and taught Vedanta. The most illuminating interpretations of the Upanishads that I have ever known I heard in the classrooms of this monastery.

Then about four o'clock tea was served. At half past four all the monks went forth to take their favorite physical exercise. When evening came, as I have described, one met them in the shrine where the arati was held.

These ocher-robed men walking across green lawns discoursing gently on God and Ramakrishna were men of action as well. If there was sickness, they looked after the sick of the neighboring locality. If there was famine in any part of India, or inundation or plague, they were there like an eagle to its prey to help the distressed. Once that was over they returned to the monastery to live and to be their own selves. Action never smirched them. Nor did inaction taint them with idleness. In one word, they were free men.

And when I questioned them as to what had freed them from both pleasure and pain, they invariably pointed at the life and sayings of Sri Ramakrishna. "When all the signposts point to the same road," the proverb enjoins, "one is forced to take it." So when the monks repeatedly pointed at the life of Ramakrishna, I had to go and study it. "It is better to examine the source of the fountain," I was told.

But I did not go to a printed page. Early in my youth my mother had taught me, "Do not put a printed page between yourself and life." So in order to study the life of Ramakrishna, I began to look for its chroniclers and not the chronicle.

2

The Ramakrishna Legend

One morning I got a message from the Pundit.[1] He was one of the disciples who had known Ramakrishna intimately. He had taken down many of the Teacher's conversations. How he knew that I was searching for a man who had chronicled Ramakrishna's teachings I cannot tell. Anyway, the moment I received his kind invitation I went off to see him in his house.

The Pundit lived in the depths of the city on Amherst Street. When I reached the house I was surprised to find it so big. It was not beautiful, but large and clean. Its gray walls were pierced by tall windows with long bars of iron. In front of the house, railed off from the street, was a small playground. Once I looked carefully, I saw on the front gate a sign that said this was a school building. But not to be deterred by such bagatelle, I opened the gate, crossed the playground, then pushed open the large green entrance door. I was in the vestibule. Not a soul was there, but I waited. In a short time a brown boy of ten or twelve, bare to the waist, came dashing down a stairway at the other end of the vestibule. I called out to him. The young monkey (as we would say endearingly) answered, "My lord, do you hunger to set eyes on our teacher, the Pundit?"

I said, "I am famine stricken for him."

"Then follow me, O honorable," answered the lad. In a trice he was leading me up the stairs. That a lad of twelve could have the dignity of an elephant was proven to me by my young mentor. He walked so quickly yet so gracefully.

After climbing a seemingly endless series of steps I found myself on the third floor of the house, face to face with a white-bearded man who was seated on a couch at an open window.

The little boy saluted him gravely, then said, "The honored intruder craves to behold your blessed countenance." Then, again saluting the Pundit gravely, he went out of the room as silently as sand shifts in an hourglass.

I felt so awed in the presence of the Pundit that I wished to do something as a token of my homage to him. So I knelt down, brahmin though I was, and bowed to him, touching my forehead to the ground. At that instant I felt and heard a movement soft as a cat leaping. I looked up. There was the Pundit standing by me. Then he shouted in alarm, "What sacrilege! You, a brahmin, prostrating yourself before a non-brahmin!"

I scrambled to my feet and rejoined, "But Ramakrishna has blessed you, which lifts you far above any brahmin." Now I looked at him carefully. He was at least six feet tall and strong chested like a gorilla. His face was that of a white-bearded tiger. He had strange brown eyes, bordering on amber, and a magnificent Grecian nose with delicate, almost effeminate, nostrils. Above that, as if by sinister contrast, rose his large brow and shaggy white mane that crowned his head with a sort of tousled halo. His height was all the more intensified by the long line of his snow-white robe falling in sheer straight lines down to his feet. He took me by the hand and seated me next to him on the couch. He went on talking to me while my eyes wandered from wall to wall, studying the room. It was the usual whitewashed, bare-walled affair—the beams showing from the ceiling like ribs of a famine-stricken man. Besides the couch on which we sat, there was not another piece of furniture in the room. It was very hot that afternoon in May. Through the large iron-barred window one could see roofs of houses and a dusty metallic sky vibrating with heat. Having examined our setting, I now paid full attention to my host. As he spoke I noticed in his words the tenderness which lay like a bloom on his voice. He was saying, "I have written down all that I heard the Guru Maharaj [Sri Ramakrishna] say. But the mouth from which these words dropped like stars from heaven, how can I give you a sense of that? A mouth that was the cavern of Immortality!"

"Why do you say that?" I asked.

"If for no other reason," Pundit rejoined, "save this: whatever he said came true. His words of prophecy have all been fulfilled. No doubt Immortality lurked behind his thoughts. He was not erudite and did not speak with any dramatic force. He spoke as the common people speak, simply and directly. Yet his speech was not diseased with perishable qualities. It conveyed to his listeners the sharp tang of the imperishable. Though he is dead, his words keep on fulfilling their promise. Now let me ask you a question—you who bristle with a thousand questions. What do you wish to learn of Ramakrishna?"

"What do you mean, my lord?" I begged.

"I mean, do you seek the Ramakrishna history, or the Ramakrishna legend?" the pundit elucidated. Since I had not come prepared to answer this question, the Pundit had to wait till I thought the matter over. At last I was able to answer, "I seek just enough facts to enable me to gather all the trustworthy legends together."

"Good!" shouted my host with joy. His mane and beard seemed to tremble with pleasure. "Ramakrishna legends have not been gathered together. They contain more of the truth about him than all the authentic facts that I have written down. Legend is the chalice of truth. Facts are so veracious and so dull that nobody is uplifted by believing in them."

"But history is most necessary and most trustworthy," I exclaimed.

"Yes, it is necessary. Because on and around history will grow legend. As raw material for legend there is nothing finer than history. That is why I have written the Ramakrishna chronicle. Five hundred years from now my work will find its fulfillment when a great poet will use it to create the Ramakrishna legend as deathless as my Master himself."

"Are there many Ramakrishna legends extant now?" I asked.

He nodded and said, "Yes, some. Go to Dakshineswar and all the surrounding villages. Call on their oldest inhabitants; then ask them questions. There are two old people living yet who saw him just at the time of his first illumination. They say that when he left the Kali temple and passed by them that day, there was such a light on his face that they could not bear to look at him. Go, visit those people. Whatever I know of the Holy One is committed to writing; it won't disappear tomorrow. But those old folks may die any time now. Listen to them, gather the music of their reed flutes while they are yet able to pipe about the Lord."

"My lord, is there anything else that I need to do while I go in search of the legends?" I pleaded for advice.

"Why should you do anything? Let the Lord who is within you speak out. Do not do anything. Only bear in mind that you will hear nothing unusual or miraculous. Ramakrishna was the simplest of the simple. He said nothing to stir people to heroic deeds. Though eternity dwelt in his speech, it did not put out such symbols of time as the sun and the moon. He did not do anything that can be of theatrical interest to a storyteller, though his touch revealed God to many men."

"His touch revealed God to men!" I exclaimed in amazement.

The Pundit answered gravely, "Whenever he spoke of God a light unknown on earth would come on his face; then, if he touched anyone with his hand or foot, that person would see the whole world bathed in radiance and *Ananda* (Bliss) for at least three to four days. He would behold all faces bright as the stars, all places bright as if they had put on the full moon for a dress, and all the dark spaces of the night would be as vivid as the morning sun. In these six days that I was illumined, life was one. There was no death. Day and night were not marked by any difference: *Anandarupa*—the light of bliss—shone on all hours and all things. And the heart of all existence sang but one song: 'Words cannot speak of this *Abam Manasogocharam* and the mind cannot come near it. I am the light of silence eternal. I am bliss, I am bliss!'"

The Pundit stopped. The memory of his first spiritual experience filled his face with radiance. His eyes were filled with tears that shone like gems. Words and questions that had occupied my mind now fled as dogs before a tiger. I took the dust from the Pundit's feet. Then I rose to go in search of those other men and women who had seen and known Ramakrishna in order to gather from their living lips the story of his life.

3

Ramakrishna's Early Life

According to the legends, Ramakrishna was born in the spring of 1836, in the famous Chattopadhyaya family of the brahmins of Bengal. At birth he was named Gadadhar, which was later abbreviated into Gadai Chattujjay.

His parents gave him the usual education of a brahmin boy of the 1840s. It consisted of studying in Sanskrit such books as the Gita, the *Ramayana*, and the *Mahabharata*, besides a thorough training in meditation. Though he showed an exceptional aptitude in learning meditation, Ramakrishna proved himself but of average intelligence when it came to studying philosophical works. He could not stomach any metaphysics. However, he so loved books on sacred matters that he devoured hundreds of ballads and poems that dealt with the lives of the saints and gods of Hinduism. In fact, there was no one else his age who could recite from memory such a volume of religious poetry and lore of mysticism.

Since he was so earnestly devoted to matters of religion, his family decided to dedicate him to the priesthood. Before he was sixteen years old, he was made an acolyte in the Kali temple of Rani (Queen) Rasmani who was one of the most able rulers that feudal India has known. It was her spiritual acumen that directed her two sons-in-law to appoint Ramakrishna her family chaplain by the time he was eighteen years old.

Dakshineswar Temple Garden

The legend has it that the rani and her entire household became aware of their young priest's spiritual powers from the very first day he came to their temple. And during her lifetime as well as that of her sons-in-law, they guarded and cherished him with the utmost care and appreciation. Even at the present time, nearly forty years after his death in the village of Dakshineswar, one is told tales of the friendship that Rani Rasmani's household showed to Ramakrishna the very day he came there as an acolyte.

No doubt from the very start the kindness of the royal household made Ramakrishna feel at home in Dakshineswar. The place itself was very beautiful and spacious. The temple stood in the heart of a garden that spread for acres along the shore of the Ganges. Hundreds of boats—red, blue, white, and green—drifted by toward Calcutta, only six miles down the river. Even now, with the temple grounds fallen into neglect, one feels the majesty of the place. The gray turrets and domes of the shrines, the palatial halls and corridors, and the long, dark inmost sanctuary lit by scores of torches, where the white-vestured priests sit meditating on silence, give a feeling of nostalgia for the unknown. In the garden the plants, grasses, and weeds gleam like flames of emerald under the fierce Indian sun. Then if one looks farther to the north, one sees the forest of Panchavati with the far-spreading branches of its immense trees, which afforded Ramakrishna the necessary solitude for his meditations.

All the stories about him make it abundantly clear that in the impregnable isolation of Panchavati, Ramakrishna not only had his most vital spiritual experience, but that he went thither from the very first to find relief from the strenuous and intricate task of administering a royal chapel. He did so with greater frequency as his work at the Kali temple defined itself more and more clearly. The potential holy man in him realized that he was expected to be a prince of the church. Suddenly he said to himself, "This temple is too rich. Its income is fabulous. It

wears out the soul of the ministrant priest. It gives him no time to meditate on God."

In other words, Ramakrishna came from a simple, poor, and very
religious brahmin home in the country to take care of a famous palace
of worship, as if he were a mighty potentate of the medieval church.
What was expected of him by the people of the surrounding countryside was not holiness and mysticism, but elegance, dignity, and spiritual diplomacy. "They expected him to flatter the rich and feed the poor,"
says one of his younger contemporaries. He continues,

> But, alas! They counted without the mystical nature of
> their priest and the symbolism of the goddess whom he
> worshiped. It is certain that Kali, the symbol of time and
> eternity, of death and immortality, made so deep an
> impression on the young Ramakrishna that he had no
> illusion or desire to become a prince among priests.
>   That grim image, whom he worshiped daily, drew
> forth from his soul the man that he really was—a mys-
> tic, not a theologian. He devoted more time to prayers
> and meditation than was prescribed by the usual obser-
> vances of the priesthood. He paid a minimum of atten-
> tion to rituals by insisting that in the inner shrine stood
> the Goddess Kali, not as a dead fact, but as a living sym-
> bol of man's spiritual experience.

Kali is the symbol of time, and beyond time, immortality! She is the
mother of the universe as well as its destroyer. Out of her all things come,
and into her all return. Her image, that of a dancer, is hewn out of black
marble, for time is invisible: it has no color. And yet, because we cease-
lessly experience the succession of time's moments, the symbol of time
lies in the art of dancing, which is a succession of movements. Moments
of time are but movements of people. When people see with their eyes
they behold only space, but when they dance they experience time.
Hence Kali, the symbol of our experience of time, must be an image

of the dance. And she must also wear a garland of human heads around her neck, for those are the epochs of human history that time wipes out of existence. Beside those weird ornaments, she has four hands, which are emblems of the three features of time: the past, the present, and the future. The first two hands, holding a sword and a human head each, mean that man, the latest embodiment of human destiny, is being wiped out by death. Her other two hands are raised to indicate hope (the future) and memory (the past). Such is Kali. But that is not all, for, behold, Kali is stepping on Shiva, the snow-white god, under her foot. He is the symbol of immortality, for he is the god of renunciation, whom she cannot vanquish. Suddenly the frenzied movements of her dance are arrested, for Shiva is unconquerable. She who has conquered all, cannot conquer the god of renunciation. Hindus understand Kali perfectly. Even children learn to pray to her thus:

> Show me thy face of compassion which has been hidden by the dust of illusion. O Goddess, thou face of immortality, reach me through and through with thy deathless compassionateness.

The stark clarity of the symbolism of Kali, that nothing abides but renunciation, made Ramakrishna see through the pageantry of rituals and rites. How could he see the meaning of her presence and yet remain a prince of the church? Though not yet out of his teens, he understood her message and set out to shape his sacerdotal duties accordingly. First, he gave up his silken vestments and gold-embroidered silver chadars. He refused to eat from plates of gold, waited on by a dozen servants. Last, he moved from his sumptuously furnished residence into the little room near the servants' quarters where he lived for the rest of his life. Having done that, he set out to simplify some of the most ornamental services of the temple. No more did he put on himself the dhoti, the ceremonial garlands of pearls, the vestment of scarlet silk, and the chadar of gossamer blue shot with bits of diamonds like stars. He refused to wave censers of gold before his deity and gave up reading to the people from a book held between gold-embossed covers. As he whittled down the intricate pictorial rituals, he concentrated more and more on learning and teaching his congregation the inner meaning of their worship.

Of course the visitors to the temple began to complain of his iconoclasm. They appealed to Rani Rasmani to have the young priest summarily discharged. But she said to them, "Why should we dismiss him because he worships Kali in his own way; he is a priest, he ought to know what is proper better than we do. As long as he wears the garb of industriousness, as long as purity dwells in his speech and morality in his deeds, it is idle to criticize him."

Hardly had that deputation returned home when another, made up of the most respectable people of the outer neighborhood, waited on the rani. They complained, "O Rani, mirror of truth and protector of religion, please dismiss your priest Gadai Chattujjay for he seems to be somewhat mad."

This time the "mirror of truth" answered, "He is not insane. He is afflicted with the superior madness of a saint."

Now for the space of a year or so Ramakrishna was left alone, though he acted as strangely as he pleased. He soon formed the habit of praying to the Goddess Kali at unusual hours. At night or during the afternoon siesta, when the doors of the inner shrine were shut and when the deity was supposed to take her rest, one could hear the young priest crying and praying within: "O Mother, give me wisdom. Make me see your loving face that you hide under that mask of stone."

At last the frenzy of his praying began to annoy the respectable people of Dakshineswar again. But instead of complaining to the rani, they grumbled among themselves. They said, "This is outrageous. There is a time for sleeping and a time for praying. No respectable priest disturbs his deity with talk when he should be asleep in bed. He acts more and more fantastically! What are we to do?"

Hriday, a nephew of Ramakrishna's who was his constant companion, tells some very revealing stories about the Master's eccentricities. First of all, though a brahmin of the brahmins, Ramakrishna would eat what was leftover from the plates of the outcast beggars who dined at Dakshineswar, because the golden rule of Hinduism says that one must see God in everyone. This violated the caste rules in which he had been brought up and which all Hindus accept. Yet the most orthodox people about the place willingly shut their eyes to his strange conduct. One day when he was offering rice and sweets, the liturgic offerings, to Kali, a cat crept into the shrine and mewed for food. Ramakrishna instantly turned to the wretched animal and fed it, saying, "Ah, Mother, you have come disguised as an animal; since you are in all beings, I offer it to you. Eat; stop your mewing."

No doubt all these incidents show that Ramakrishna, after a time, compelled acquiescence, if not respect, from all the people. And they also verify his consistent standard of living: he put into practice what religion teaches.

But what people saw him do in public was nothing compared with what he strove for in private, which is illustrated by the story of his overcoming the desire for wealth. He prayed to Kali to give him the right conception of money. He did not rest with praying. He constantly meditated on the following sentence from the scriptures: "gold is clay; clay is gold." Sometimes to prove it in conduct, he gave away the gold and silver offerings that were brought to him by rich pilgrims. Thus he prayed and practiced for nearly a year, yet reached no solution of the problem of money. He prayed and meditated for hours every day. As he says himself:

> I was most deeply perplexed by the problem of money.
> Our religion teaches that gold and dust are one. Since

> I took my religion seriously, month after month, every
> morning, I held a coin and a little clay together in my
> hand and meditated, "gold is clay and clay is gold,"
> yet that produced no spiritual experience in me. Noth-
> ing proved the truth of that statement. I do not remem-
> ber after how many months' meditation, one day I was
> sitting on the riverbank very early in the morning. I
> prayed to the Mother to give me light. Lo! Suddenly I
> beheld the whole world in the radiant vesture of gold.
> Then it changed into a deeper luster—the color of
> brown clay more beautiful than gold. With that vision
> deep down in my soul I heard, like the trumpeting of
> ten thousand elephants: "clay and gold are one to thee."
> Now that my prayers were answered, I flung both gold
> and clay into the Ganges.

From that day Ramakrishna lived unafraid of money, or the lack
of it. His attitude toward it was perfectly balanced. He never said such
shallow things as "lucre is filthy"; nor did he say "money is power." With
wealth, as with every other of life's problems, he held, and then taught
his disciples that one must rise above the "opposites"—two aspects of
the same thing. He used to say to his disciples, "To neglect money, or
not to give any account of it, is just as erroneous as to hoard it like a
miser. Money buys a few things, that is true, but the ladder to heaven
is not made of gold."

There is a story in India that one day one of Ramakrishna's young
apostles went shopping. He considered bargaining with the shopkeepers too materialistic, hence beneath his dignity. So he made his
purchases and returned to Dakshineswar. When he opened his bag
and showed Ramakrishna the small size of the goods he had bought,
the Master wanted to know why he had paid so much for so little. The
young holy man answered, "I did not drive any bargain." Then he gave
his reason for it, "I did not drive a bargain, my Lord, for that is not
spiritual."

But Ramakrishna replied, "What, you think because you neglect to learn the art of bargaining, God will make you a holy man? Fie! A holy man is he who has contempt for nothing. While in the bazaar of life you must learn to master its laws. Do not confuse holiness with idiocy. Your spiritual life makes you most compassionate. It also makes you infinitely more vigilant than those who live in the world. Brahma, God, is Bliss Infinite, no doubt, but he is also infinite Intelligence!"

Though the pleasure of recounting such incidents as this is very great, we must resist that temptation and go back to the Kali temple where we left Ramakrishna practicing the religious austerities of his teens. We have already noticed that so much religious earnestness in one so young appeared utterly eccentric, if not mad.

At last he did something that proved to the worldly that he was too insane to be a priest: He flagrantly neglected his duties at the temple. Sometimes he secluded himself for days at a stretch in the woods of Panchavati. Were it not for his nephew Hriday who acted as his substitute, the business of Kali worship would have collapsed. This happened nearly a dozen times. Now all the people of Dakshineswar, with the exception of the rani's household, were convinced beyond any doubt that their priest had truly gone mad. A very large deputation waited on the rani. They demanded that Ramakrishna be sent away, but again Rani Rasmani refused to act according to their request. She answered, "I am certain he is the coming Teacher. We must be patient with this lion cub of spirituality for treating our temple as his native desert."

Those words of Rasmani's convinced everyone that they must expect nothing from the rani save more advice to endure Ramakrishna's eccentric actions. Instead of being vindictive, the people of the countryside felt so sorry for Ramakrishna that some of them traveled a hundred miles into the interior in order to break the melancholy news to his mother. She was told, "God has cracked your son's mind." But that wise lady was not perturbed by the news, though she was a little puzzled.

Sri Sarada Devi, The Holy Mother

In order to see him with her own eyes she came to Dakshineswar. One look at him convinced her that he was far from mad. Just the same, she was afraid that he would give up the world and take the vow of celibacy, and a monastery was the last place where she wished to see him. In order to prevent his becoming a monk she urged him to marry. "Marriage," everybody counseled, "will put an end to all this God-madness." The timeworn, threadbare Indian method of keeping a man from going mad about the Infinite has been to wed him swiftly to a young woman. This stratagem was tried on Buddha too. Though it never succeeds in bringing about the desired end, parents take to it as a hangman to the noose.

However, after a time Ramakrishna announced to his mother that he was quite willing to marry a young girl whom the Divine Mother had shown to him in his meditations. They followed the directions he gave them: about sixty miles away the bride dwelled with her parents. There, to the amazement of the matchmakers, they found the eligible brahmin girl, as Ramakrishna had said. Her name was Sarada—the world's desire. In proper time and place, Ramakrishna was married to her.

He brought his wife home to Dakshineswar. Then he did a thing that only a saint addicted to superior madness would do. He said to her, "Do you see that tower? It is big and spacious. You will find everything there that you need. Go, and meditate and pray to God to give me illumination. Why should you do it? Because it takes two women to make a man holy—his mother and his wife. My mother has brought me thus far, now it is your task to be my other mother, not my wife, and to take me across the river of delusion to the house of heaven." The little wife did as she was told. She went and lived in that tower. It was high and its windows looked onto the Ganges in the west and to the gardens and the temple in the east. North and south of that tower were tall trees. To that seclusion she banished herself. With the exception of her girlfriends, she saw no one. Her husband she saw rarely, except during those hours when he performed the common rites of the temple. Those were very hard years for her. No less hard for him, as he was meditating and praying day and night. The legend runs that he never slept during this period.

Ramakrishna was pressing closer and closer to the ultimate mystery. Like a true Hindu wife, Sarada was glad and proud to help him walk the path of renunciation and holiness. Yet her own life was not full enough, and she suffered moments of loneliness. It was during one of those moments that she came to Ramakrishna and said, "My Lord, I want children."

Ramakrishna answered, "Your children will be many, and they shall come from the ends of the earth. I already see them coming to you, though some of them speak languages that you do not know!" The ring of authority was so great in his voice that the Holy Mother [Sarada] bowed before it. She went back to her life of prayers and devotion in the tower.

About fifty years later when some English and American devotees came to pay their homage to the Holy Mother, she said aloud, "His words have come true. I have children, whose language I do not understand."

4

Holy Man

At last when he was about thirty years old, Ramakrishna had his first illumination. It came to him early one morning. After he had finished the morning rites of the temple, he sat down before Kali and said to her, "Mother, either I receive illumination today, or I shall take my life tomorrow. I have prayed and meditated a dozen years now. I have practiced all the austerities prescribed by each and every teacher that came my way. I have lived according to the teachings of our holy books that you have revealed to men. Yet, Mother, you do not grant me the vision of your face. If you do not show it to me tomorrow, I will take this life that you have given me."

Then he sat still and meditated. "Those who with steadfast love seek me shall find me," says the Lord in the Gita. Ramakrishna repeated that line to himself with the most fervent sincerity. And whenever his mind tired of repeating it, he prayed, "Break my heart, Mother, but end my doubts. Show me your face of immortality."

Suddenly her arms of stone moved. Her lips changed into two burning petals of light. Thence the light spread all over her face. Now her hair caught fire and glowed like a circle of infinite flame, as if the very sun had come down from heaven and stood behind her. Now the light danced and coursed down her body, down, down to the Shiva lying under her feet, but it did not stop there. Like eagle wings the conflagration spread over the whole shrine in an instant. Even small things like the bells, the candles, and the flowers danced, possessed by the unearthly radiance.

Wherever Ramakrishna looked, he saw light, light, light.

"I have found you, I have found you." Crying, he dashed out of the temple. Wherever he went he saw nothing but light. The Ganges curved at his feet like a sickle of gold. The shore on which he stood was but a rock of solid flame. The trees in the distance, the boats and their boatmen in the middle of the river, the birds coursing through the sky, and the very sky itself sang possessed of the divine light. "I have found you, I have found you!" He cried with the *rishis* of old:

> Harken unto me, ye sons of Immortality. I have found him, the Person Supreme! Even the gods—those dwellers in the highest spaces—are humbled now that I have found him, the sun-clad One!

According to some observers, Ramakrishna stayed in that state of ecstasy for nearly two weeks, while others testify that he had the experience only for a few days. But they all agree that during that time he neither ate nor drank. He praised God continually. He said to one and all, "I see the Divine Mother in you. Can't you see her? There she is in your eyes, in your voice, in your heart—the fathomless river of bliss." Sometimes as he spoke, the light that shone on his face would become so bright that people had to hide their eyes lest they be blinded.

As everyone knows, news spreads very rapidly in the East. Within a fortnight of his attaining illumination, hundreds of people came to Dakshineswar to see the Holy Man. Though Rani Rasmani had been dead many years now, her sons-in-law, who had stood by Ramakrishna, felt blessed at the fulfillment of his search and, ready to serve him to the best of their ability, extended their hospitality to all who journeyed to their Kali temple. No matter how large the number of pilgrims, they were all fed and given shelter in the royal mansion. "You are welcome," they were told. "Do not thank us. We but seek to acquire merit by serving our Holy Man."

Weeks passed into months, bringing in their train many more pilgrims. Ramakrishna instructed and blessed each one in the name of the Mother. He ceased to avoid people. On the contrary, he welcomed them now. He put an abrupt end to all his so-called eccentricities. He stopped praying to Kali during forbidden hours and performed all his priestly duties at the temple with the regularity of a clock. Even the most intricate rituals could no longer tax his patience. Now he lived under the public gaze without ever running away to the seclusion of the Panchavati woods.

Eyewitnesses say that at this time such a power emanated from him that no one could pass by without stopping to salute him. Whether in the streets or in the temple, people were bound to stand still a moment if their eyes fell on Ramakrishna. "Though he compelled attention, his face bore no expression but one of humility." And the strange attraction that emanated from him never ceased.

Soon he began to attract people from remoter parts of India. Flocks of pilgrims came to obtain *darshan* (vision of his face). "For," they reasoned, "a sight of the face of an illumined soul washes away the sins of a lifetime."

Of course none of them knew the exact nature of Ramakrishna's recent experience. It is doubtful if he himself had realized fully the limits thereof. He was full of Ananda; he cared for nothing else.

One morning a very strange man came to see him. He was of the west country, and judging by his appearance, the man was an advanced teacher. But since Ramakrishna was busy performing the rites of the temple, the newcomer had to wait until the afternoon, when he joined the group of pilgrims who had come to be instructed by the young Master.

It was nearly ten o'clock in the evening when the assembled multitude dispersed, leaving Ramakrishna alone to meditate on the riverbank. Now Totapuri, for that was the teacher's name, approached him.

Ramakrishna said to him, "Why have you not gone away with the other pilgrims? If you want a bed here, the royal mansion will accommodate you for the night."

The teacher answered, "I have not come to beg for hospitality. I want speech with thee. My friend, thy soul has climbed the first flight of stairs that lead to the House of Silence. There are two more flights to mount."

Ramakrishna, not at all surprised, said, "What are they?"

The teacher propounded, "Thou knowest the story of Rama and Hanuman. When that incarnation of God said to Hanuman, 'How dost thou perceive me, O my beloved devotee?'—what did Hanuman answer?"

"Hanuman said," replied Ramakrishna, "'When I feel you, my Lord, I am your son and servant. When I think you, I am a part of you. But when I realized you—I am you.'"

"You have felt your Mother. Now it is for you to think and realize her. Do you not wish to attain oneness with God?"

"What will happen to me if I attain oneness?" asked Ramakrishna.

The teacher said, "Then all this thou-and-me conception of God will come to an end. You will lose your self—your me-ness."

Ramakrishna smiled with mischief. "But I can lose my me-ness by going to sleep or through a fainting fit."

The teacher, who was apparently without a sense of humor, retorted, "But that is not samadhi [oneness]. In sleep or in a fainting fit the me-ness remains though it is not articulate. The instrument, the brain, through which it articulates itself, is disturbed. That is all. All the desires and passions are present as the food is present in the recently dined, well-fed man, who has suspended digestion for some moments. When a man is asleep or lying in a swoon, his heart goes on beating. The pulse does not stop, nor does the circulation of the blood. These are signs and symbols of me-ness. In samadhi, all these functions of man stop. The other signs of me-ness in sleep are just as interesting in their total difference from those of samadhi. A man recovering from a sudden loss of consciousness or coming out of sleep is the same man, filled with the same desires, passions, and ambitions that he took to bed. He is no better coming out of an unconscious state than when he went in."

Ramakrishna interrupted, "But what would I gain by attaining oneness?"

The teacher answered, "A man who enters that state is bound to lose all his me-ness—his petty desires, lusts, hopes, and weaknesses. When he emerges from it he is a bridge to Immortality! He is filled with joy, compassion, and discrimination. While in samadhi, though his heart and pulse do not beat, yet he is not dead. In fact his life is keen as the sharpness of a razor. His experiences have grown sharper and more inclusive. For all the worlds—matter, mind, and spirit—live in him. Within him all the experiences of reality find their nest. He becomes *Tat* [That][1] in which all beings find their homing place. After he has had samadhi, a man feels himself not a part, but all of God. He has become the backbone of the universe, nay, the very measurement of immortality!"

The teacher spoke those last words with great conviction. It moved Ramakrishna. But he was very cautious. He asked, "What do you wish me to do?"

The teacher said, "I would have you learn higher meditation. You are an advanced seeker. I will initiate you into Advaita Vedanta—the science of attaining identity."

"But," objected Ramakrishna, "I cannot do anything without the Divine Mother's consent."

The teacher paused a few moments, then said cryptically, "Then go and get it from her."

Ramakrishna went away silently while Totapuri sat on the riverbank and meditated.

In the meantime, inside the shrine, Ramakrishna communed with Kali. After an hour or so he heard her command: "Yes, my son, go and learn of him."

He returned and told Totapuri that he had obtained the Mother's permission. The teacher, though struck by the innocent simplicity of the young man, perhaps smiled at his apparent superstition in addressing the image in the temple as Mother. A great Vedantin, he did not believe in a personal God, nor did he believe in the efficacy of prayer, or devotion to a creator. But he said nothing to Ramakrishna on that point, thinking that under his training the disciple would come to know the truth and spontaneously brush aside his superstitions.

Later on, the teacher informed Ramakrishna that he must be initiated with proper ceremony into the secret mysteries before beginning to learn the truths of Vedanta or practicing its disciplines. He must give up the insignia of his present state of life, such as the sacred thread and tonsure that marked him as a brahmin. He must begin a new life. Ramakrishna agreed.

Totapuri then went to the deepest part of the woods of Panchavati and took up residence there. Every day for some hours Ramakrishna came to receive his preliminary instructions. As soon as that was over, the teacher set the date for initiation. Again, Ramakrishna went into the Kali temple and communed with the Mother. And again she commanded him to follow his teacher and attain oneness.

At last, on the auspicious day, Ramakrishna renounced his position as the priest of the temple and went forth into the woods of Panchavati.

On the altar that Totapuri had already built, they lit the sandalwood fire.

Now Ramakrishna was ordered to perform his own funeral ceremony. One must cremate all of the finite consciousness in thought and

speech before one can be taught Advaita, the science of identity. So there
he stood in the dense forest facing his guru across the altar. He chanted,

> I renounce my father, my mother, and my wife. I
> renounce my learning and my knowledge. I renounce
> my name and my station. I renounce my feelings, and
> I renounce my thoughts. O fire, thou symbol of immor-
> tal purity. O ye trees, the very emblem of all life, O thou
> sky, thou witness of God's silence—witness with my
> guru that into this burning pyre I fling my earthliness
> and my me-ness! I proclaim my Self homeless in time.
> I proclaim my Self homeless in space. And I proclaim
> my Self homeless in the heavens. I proclaim my Self
> homeless in all save the God Eternal, Infinite, and Silent.
> Burn me, O fire, till I am no more.

Totapuri took him by the hand and walked around the fire seven
times. Now Ramakrishna flung into it all the insignia and symbols of
his caste and station. Then he meditated a long while, facing the fire.
He was asked to renounce his name, Gadadhar Chattopadhyaya, that
his parents had given him. That too he renounced.

Totapuri took him by the hand again and led him into a small
hut. There he and Ramakrishna sat down to meditate on "I am God. I
am infinite Bliss. I am infinite Knowledge. I have no name, no form. I
am the One! I am he."

Hour after hour passed. The day turned into night, yet the two meditated. The moon rose higher and higher. The night declined. The sun
rose again. Yet the two holy men went on meditating.

When the sun had set the second time and the moon had risen
again, suddenly Ramakrishna shouted, "I cannot go beyond this point."
The teacher asked, "Why can you not?"

The disciple cried out, "I see the Mother before me. I want to worship her as her servant. I do not wish to attain identity."

"Why this weakness? Are you to remain a child forever? Begin again."

Again they chanted the mantra of oneness and plunged into meditation. Regarding his second attempt Ramakrishna later told his own disciples:

> I failed to bring my mind to Brahman—the Absolute. I had no difficulty in withdrawing the mind from all earthly objects, but I could not obliterate from my consciousness the all too familiar form of the Blissful Mother who appeared before me as a living reality and would not allow me to pass beyond. She was all name and form! Again and again I tried to concentrate my mind upon the Brahman, but every time the Mother's form stood in my way.
>
> In despair I said again to the guru, "It is hopeless. I cannot raise my mind to the unconditioned state and come face to face with my Self—the Absolute."
>
> The teacher said sharply, "What! You cannot do it? But you must." He cast his eyes about the dimly lighted room and finding in a corner a piece of broken glass, he took it up and pressing its point between my eyebrows said, "Concentrate thy mind on this point!" Then with a stern determination I again set to meditate. I felt an appalling pain between my eyes, and in the heart of that agony the gracious form of the Mother danced like a flame! I used my discrimination now. As a sword cuts to pieces a body, so with my discrimination I severed her in two. Nothing obstructed me now. I at once soared beyond name and form, above pain and pleasure, and I found myself at one with the Absolute. Before that supreme ecstasy the senses and the mind stopped their functions. The body became motionless like a corpse. The universe rolled away from my vision—even space itself melted away. Everything was reduced to ideas that floated like shadows on the dim silence of the mind. Only the faint consciousness of "I, I" repeated itself in dull monotony. My soul became the Self of Reality, and all idea of dualism of subject and object was gone. My Self knew no bounds. All life was

one infinite bliss! Beyond speech, beyond articulate experience, and beyond thought! To even call that state freedom is to limit its meaning.

From that day on Totapuri called him Ramakrishna Paramahamsa—the Lord and Master Supreme. Following his example, all India now calls him by that name. A few weeks after that great event, Totapuri went away as he had come, unknown and unseen by the multitudes. He had fulfilled his task. But Ramakrishna always voiced his gratitude to him, whom he called Nangta (the unclad one).

It was about this time that people saw Ramakrishna's appearance alter. First the expression of his face changed. It grew to look like a mask, save his eyes where dwelt a new light that was deeply tranquil, "but fierce with love." And, by contrast with the expression of his "young eyes," the rest of his face looked all the more aged. People said, "He has ceased to live in his face; now you can see in his eyes that he lives only in his soul." Not only his face but also his strong, athletic body, so agile and quick, now clung to him like a blanket—something that he washed and cleansed and carried about. That is exactly what one feels when one looks at the photographs of Ramakrishna in the shrine of the monastery.

From then on, he had two distinct appearances, one inner and the other outer. "Physically," says Saradananda, "he was unconscious of earthly matters: half the time he was unaware whether he wore anything or not. His disciples saw to it that his clothes were all on him. Though he bathed and cleansed his body regularly, to an outsider he looked like a man utterly careless about it." He was so detached from his body that it was not even a burden to him. He dwelt in it as a log floats on the tide. Better still—he lived in his body as the fire abides in the wood. Yet whenever he spoke of the Lord, its very pores grew radiant. "Holiness exuded from him as fragrance from flowers."

"Neither you," said another who knew Ramakrishna, "nor any other man who never saw him and heard his words can conceive by looking at any of his photographs the flame that he was. In a photograph you see only his ashes, not the conflagration of spirituality that is spreading from soul to soul throughout Hindustan. Even if you saw him sitting at ease he would look as inert as that picture. But if you took the name of God in his presence, then he would lose his body. You express surprise? But how else can I put it? If you can imagine a man wrapped in the raiment of ecstasy, of such luster that he was all light and no flesh, then you have truly beheld him. Yes, sometimes he became so radiant that all of us had to hide our faces before his presence. It appears peculiar to those who know not the ways of God-consciousness. But it is quite natural that the mere taking the name of God may inspire a soul to spiritual ecstasy. Ramakrishna could be kindled even by a chance word, the sight of a face, the shifting of the tide of the Ganges, and many such common, everyday occurrences."

At this time, his attitude toward his wife changed. Now he requested her to come out of her secluded tower and live near him. From that time, she looked after him and his disciples. This was not an easy task. She had to keep house and also instruct. She took care of his female disciples as if they were her own *chelas*. She watched over the preparation of food for Ramakrishna and his "sons." One afternoon, for instance, his first disciple, Brahmananda, failed to commune with the Lord as well as usual. That worried the Master considerably. He wanted to know what had gone wrong. After a few moments' cogitation, he remarked suddenly, "I know—it is his food!" He rushed to the foot of the tower and called out to the Holy Mother, "What did you put in his dinner? My boy's soul is full of sloth. It looks as if he has eaten forbidden food. What did you put in it?"

She answered from the window of her tower, "My Lord, thinking that it would do his body good, I put in some extra dabs of butter. I am sorry."

At this admission, Ramakrishna roared with laughter. He was glad to know that it was the extra butter, and not rank materialism, that was weighing down the soul of his disciple.

Along with feeding and caring for Ramakrishna and his disciples, Sarada took lessons in meditation from the Master. Legend has it that when he started to train her in *advaita* yoga—science of oneness—he found that she had already advanced very far on the path of *sadhana* (realization) through her own exertions. It did not take her long to attain illumination under his guidance. As soon as that had happened, Ramakrishna taught her all he knew. There was nothing that she failed to master. Though she was silent and averse to publicity, her fame soon spread among the Hindu women. Some came to her with their problems; some came to confide to her their secret longing for realization; and many came to her to grant them boons, for they believed that she had the power to do miracles. The upshot of the matter was that around her grew a nucleus of brave and deeply religious women who started to reform Indian society from within.

When Ramakrishna died, the direction of all his disciples fell into her hands. All of them say that she was their mother as Ramakrishna was their father. The common people explain the matter beautifully: "Ramakrishna left an eagle's nest full of eaglets. It was his widow, the Holy Mother, who watched and protected them till they had learned to fly."

Since her life is uniquely interesting, no one can write of it in a few hundred words. Though she died in 1920, it was not until later that the chroniclers succeeded in assembling all the materials for her biography. They all agree that her life story is nearly as interesting a spiritual document as that of Ramakrishna's.[2]

5
Ramakrishna and Other Religions

Now that Ramakrishna had become a master, like bees to the flower many earnest religious souls came to receive instructions from him. They came from all walks of life. Social reformers, university students, brahmins, rajahs, artisans, peasants, Buddhists, Christians, and Muslims all flocked to Dakshineswar. Many came out of curiosity, but there were some who came to embrace the new religion of the new Teacher.

After they had conversed with him, his visitors realized that Ramakrishna had nothing new to say. In fact, what he did say sounded simple to the point of being commonplace. But one and all felt that what he said was nothing compared to what he withheld. "It was his being," says one of those visitors, "that gripped us. His realization was tiger strong. As in the jungle when the tiger goes about, even the leaves stop trembling in his presence, so did we feel in the presence of the Master. And after we had gone home, we realized what he had done to our souls. For days afterward we were not the same human beings."

We have already noted that among the visitors to Dakshineswar there were Christians and Muslims. They came to see what "the heathen Ramakrishna" was like. Of course, many of them saw in him nothing but a religious man. But there was a Christian who perceived in him a great teacher. He went further than that; he said to Ramakrishna, "You verify to me the teachings of my own religion."

"What is your religion, my son?" asked the Master.

"Christianity, my Lord," answered the gentleman.

Ramakrishna explained, "Yes, *Yata mat tato path*—as many souls, so many pathways to God. But I have never studied your particular religion. Now I will do so."

From that day on, for two years Ramakrishna studied Christianity. Since he did not know English, he had the New Testament read to him in translation many times over. Gradually it had such an effect on him that he began to meditate on the Christos. He lived like a Christian anchorite, all alone in the famous woods of Panchavati. Then one day, after many months, he came out and proclaimed, "I found God at the end of the road of Christianity. So if anyone follows Christ he will reach God. I have verified it."

Another time a Muslim visitor said to him, "You are the most devout Muslim I know!"

That roused the Master. He decided to spend some time studying Islam. Forthwith he had himself converted to that religion. Again he retired into Panchavati to meditate on what had been taught him from the Qur'an by his Muslim teacher. Months passed. Then he came out of his seclusion and proclaimed, "That road too leads to the palace of the same King. Religions differ in their appearance, but not in their essence. No matter which path you take it will usher you in the end into his presence: the end of all! As the many-colored rivers tear and claw their way to the ocean and are lost in its steady emerald level, so all the religions, turgid with dogmatism, lose themselves in the serenity of God. Since religions are but means to finding God, why quarrel about their respective merits and defects? That will take you nowhere."

By now the entire countryside became aware that Ramakrishna had become a universal holy man. An English Christian missionary who had heard all kinds of reports came to investigate him. The legend has it that he came with an interpreter. This sun-ripe, red-faced man from Europe had no sooner sat down in the presence of the Master than he was told, "I salute Lord Jesus Christ as an incarnation." The abruptness of that statement filled the missionary with embarrassment. He asked, "What do you know about him?"

Ramakrishna: "Why, I have seen him in my meditations. His protection spreads like an umbrella over your head. All you Christians are safe from the sun of materialism and the rain of sin under that umbrella."

Missionary: "Are there others under whom people can be safe? Are there other umbrellas?"

Ramakrishna: "No doubt. There are those who are under prophets that went before Christ. There are other incarnations of God who are continually looking after their believers. They are just as real as your Lord."

Missionary: "You are wrong. There is only one Son of God."

However, some time later an Indian Christian named Prabhudaya Misra came to see Ramakrishna. Misra was a Christian holy man. His reputation was that of a saint.

No sooner had he seated himself before Ramakrishna than he propounded, "It is the Lord who shines through every creature."

The Master answered very slowly, "The Lord is one, but is called by a thousand names."

"But I believe Jesus is God himself."

"Do you see any visions?" questioned Ramakrishna.

The Christian holy man answered, "I used to see effulgence. But later I beheld Jesus. No word can describe his beauty. There is no woman, man, or anything else on earth to equal that beauty when the Invisible breaks the folds of the visible and reveals himself."

Ramakrishna sat silent. No one spoke. Misra kept as still as the rest.

After what seemed hours, Misra felt the force of the Master's being. He rose to go. He said, "I feel the same power behind you as I perceived in my own Savior's face. Can you tell me if there is any difference?"

Ramakrishna said, "It is the one flame: eyes of men see it in different colors."

Misra exclaimed, "I would like to surrender everything to you, and follow you."

Ramakrishna forbade him. "No, no. Follow your own unique path. The light that you see now will be dimmed by the greater brightness that it will shed further ahead. Go on; stop not till the end is reached."

It must be borne in mind that Ramakrishna cannot be identified with any sect. He did not preach a religion. He lived a life that verified the inner reality of all religions. And, what is more important, all people must develop from their own unique heritage a full spiritual life of their own. Though Ramakrishna inherited Hinduism, he developed a unique soul-experience whose magnitude went beyond the limits of any one religion. He lived so that by his example a Muslim was heartened to be a better Muslim, a Christian a better Christian, and a Buddhist a better Buddhist. This was not the outcome of a wishy-washy eclecticism, but a realization achieved after years of spiritual experiments that he made with all those religions. Not only did he master the inner meaning of the great religions, but also that of the small denominations. For instance, Ramakrishna experimented with and experienced the soul-illumination promised by several minor sects of India. He spent some months as a Vaishnava—a worshiper of Vishnu the preserver of the world. Another time he got someone to initiate him into the mysteries of Rama-pantha. One of the great medieval Rama-panthi (Rama worshiping) saints was Tulsidas whose *Ramayana* (a mystical work) is sung—thousands of lines at a time—by Hindu mothers to their children, by minstrels to their audiences, and by mystics to their disciples.

After experiencing the ecstasies promised by Vaishnavism (Vishnu worship) and Rama-pantha (Rama worship), Ramakrishna said, "I went by two different roads, but found myself at the end before the same king." Yet he maintained that he who calls God Rama must go on doing so, as must those who call God Vishnu, Jehovah, Christ, or nirvana.

Then one of his disciples asked him, "If all those names mean the One Person, why not use one name only? Why should sects insist on their little names?" In answer, the Master told a story.

> When Rama, the incarnation of God, was in difficulty, his servant and devotee Hanuman, the monkey, sought to extricate his Lord. But he could not do so unaided by Garuda, the thunderbird, friend and servant of Vishnu. After having rendered his aid, Garuda prayed to Rama to appear in the form Garuda knew. Lo! Suddenly Rama became Vishnu. After his adoration of Vishnu, Garuda flapped his lightning wings and flew away into the silence of the sky. Then suddenly Vishnu changed into Rama and asked Hanuman if he could worship the Lord appearing as Vishnu.
>
> Hanuman said, with tears in his eyes and love in his voice, "*Shrinathe Janaki Nathe*—I know that the two forms are of the One Beloved, yet to me the form of Rama is everything. It is Rama's feet that are my home; it is Rama that is the chalice of my salvation. Oh! my Beloved, avert not from mine eyes thy face of Rama!"

Thus did Ramakrishna answer his disciple, "Unto each soul its own image of God."

According to a legend, to those who cared for his opinion of the seven great religions of the world, Ramakrishna said, "The scriptures are right. God incarnates among men irrespective of time and place. Whenever righteousness is stoned to death and the unrighteous rule the earth, he is born among men, as a man, to bring about the victory of truth, love, and wisdom. Buddha, Jesus, Mohammed, and Krishna were such incarnations."

When asked, "Are we likely to have incarnations of God in the future?" Ramakrishna replied, "Yes. Who are you to shut the door of the future in the face of the oncoming God? The future is surprise-wombed. If rascals and demons can be foaled of that womb, why not God? He will come again and again irrespective of sex and age whenever men need him!"

The same legend gives an example of Ramakrishna's interpretation of some passages of the New Testament. Some of his visitors took exception to the beatitudes that extolled the mourners and the poor in spirit.

They said, "We do not know what they mean mystically, but from the intellectual point of view the mourners are a wretched lot. So are the poor in spirit." The Master answered,

> But if you look at it from the point of view of realization, it is the truth. Suppose you mourn for God day in and day out. Imagine a mother cat whose kitten has been taken out of her basket and put elsewhere by a mischievous boy. Does she not wail and mourn till her voice reaches her lost one who, in turn, answers her. And in a short time they find each other. So is the mourner of God. He has lost his infinite child. He must wail and cry till the child of Silence cries and reveals himself to the seeker. Untold human beings have found God that way.
>
> Similarly the poor in spirit. They say to him, "You are infinite. You have made me nothing. I will accept no riches or glory, save the boundless wealth of beholding you." If they sincerely go on thinking and praying, they will find him in a short time. And suddenly their nothingness will become the all-inclusive Nothingness of God. God is like the hollow in a cup. It is the hollow that can be filled with water. Call him Nothing:

behold he contains everything. Then if you call him Everything, he suddenly slips out of your definition, like a songbird from a broken cage, proclaiming his eternal homelessness in things.

Oh, no, you must not stop with an intellectual criticism of what any incarnation of God said about the poor in spirit. You must meditate on it till you tear to pieces what he said and find under it—with the eye of realization—what he meant. The incarnations of God never speak one language: they always use two—that of sound and silence, vision and realization.

It is a pity that the commentaries that Ramakrishna made on the New Testament, the Qur'an, and other holy books have not been preserved.

6

Orthodox Hindus and Ramakrishna

When he was about thirty-six years old, Ramakrishna settled down to elucidate his religious experiences to those who wished to hear him. Now that he had had his supreme realization, he hoped to train some earnest souls besides his own wife.

But earnest souls are rare in this world. And those who came to him at first were either social reformers, or orthodox brahmins and hidebound ritualists who wanted him to help them in their pet practices. They were not lukewarm believers, but they emphasized the letter more than the spirit of religious rites. Ramakrishna castigated them mercilessly. He pursued the same course with the social reformers who sought to drown the soul's hunger for God in a turbid philosophy of humanitarianism. If the bigoted begged Ramakrishna to lead a crusade for orthodoxy, the emancipated sought to enslave him to their cause of freedom. Small wonder then that he who had the whole truth offered no encouragement to the votaries of half-truths.

He said again and again, "Religion is a road to lead you to God. A road is not a house; you don't live on the edge of it like shopkeepers vending your wares, each praising his own and denouncing his neighbor's products. Get to the end of the road and behold the Endless. For he alone can extinguish the fire of your quarrels."

One might think that his severe judgments would keep people from coming to him. On the contrary, they flocked to see Ramakrishna in ever-increasing numbers.

First of all, let us see what Ramakrishna had to say to the pious Hindus whose religious sincerity was above reproach and whose orthodoxy had not yet dimmed the light of their souls. Such a one, according to a legend, was Ishan Mukherjee, a very rich, good brahmin. Ishan was a wholehearted believer in karma-yoga—realizing one's salvation through deeds. All his life he had served his fellow men. If there was a hospital to build or an orphan asylum to maintain, the community found in Ishan a ready and wholehearted supporter of the scheme. His benevolence was untiring. He was an orthodox brahmin in the true sense of the word: he lived not for himself but for those who needed him. His fellow men considered him one of the Lord's elect.

But the man himself was not quite sure of that. So in order to find out how one really earns salvation, one afternoon he sought the counsel of the Holy One of Dakshineswar. He found Ramakrishna seated on the ghat discoursing to a small group of men, while beyond, on the Ganges, boats drew their bulging sails of turquoise and ocher against the scorching gold of the sunset sky.

Ishan bowed to the Master and took the dust from his feet. After that a hush fell on the gathering.

Since Ramakrishna alone had the privilege, he at last broke the silence: "What brings you here, O brahmin?"

Ishan said, "Search of salvation, my Lord. I do all that the *shastras* [scriptures] prescribe. I observe all the rituals. But the knowledge that I seek is not in books. It abides in the tiger-mouth of a realized soul."

But Ramakrishna, the same legend continues, did not answer at once. Seeing that the hour of arati was fast approaching, he got up and went to the Kali temple. The others too left. But Ishan remained. He began saying his prayers. The sun set. The boats, the river, and the farther shore slowly sank into the inky stillness of the night. Suddenly, like a flock of birds, the stars preened their silver wings in the dark sky.

It was about an hour later when the moon had begun to rise that Ramakrishna returned from the Kali temple. He said to Ishan, who was waiting for him, "Rituals and routines of worship, if they do not make the heart sing with joy, are of no earthly use. The flower falls from the tree as the fruit appears. So must fall away rituals and prayers like shackles from a liberated soul. Salvation to the soul is what freedom is to a prisoner."

"But is there no salvation in karma—the doing of good deeds?" questioned Ishan the brahmin.

Ramakrishna answered, "There is salvation through every path, whether of deeds, knowledge, or love."

Ishan quoted, "The scriptures say, 'He who with steadfast love loves me (God) will know me. He who with obdurate knowledge pursues me, the seed eternal blossoming in all beings, will find me the end of all knowledge. And he who acts so that he desires no earthly fruits of his actions will find me the fulfiller of all deeds.'"

Ramakrishna answered, "Yes, Ishan, the scriptures are right. But how many men can act for the sake of doing the perfect deed without any hope of earthly results? Also scholarship—like a lamp—if it does not contain the flame of longing for the infinite knowledge of the infinite God, cannot give freedom to a soul. The same is the case with the love of God; like a bird if it is not voiced with an excruciating longing for him, it will not sing the perfect melody of salvation. Knowledge, deeds, and love—each one of them has to be selfless in order to find the Self of God."

Ishan commented to himself, though not in silence, "No matter what path a soul takes, it is strewn with the thorns and pebbles of selflessness."

"No matter what means a soul adopts—deeds, knowledge, or love—it must be kept under the tiger-claw subjection to the end: the Endless," emphasized Ramakrishna.

Ishan wailed, "Then what am I to do?"

Ramakrishna began quietly, "Have you noticed the steady flame of a lamp? The slightest stir in the air will make it flicker. Just as delicate is the task of seeking God. No matter how selfless your deeds—outwardly they may appear perfect—but if within you stirs the slightest feeling of self or desire, it will destroy your realization of God as the wind blows out the candle."

"But how is one to be free of desire to that degree?"

Ramakrishna answered, "Stop listening to the flattery of the priests. Do not for a moment think that your deeds are going to do anybody any good. Begin at the beginning. Purify your deeds of any taint of self by purifying your thoughts. More than that—purify your dreams too. Desire steals into men even when they are asleep. I have experienced it myself. Though I purified my conscious moments of all taints of self in the early days of my spiritual activity, I could not free my sleep from its clutches. Desire would steal into me through my dreams. It took years, but at last I succeeded in achieving total purity. You will not advance your soul toward God to the extent even of a child's footprint if you do not become selfless in dreams as well as in your thoughts. The way most people act, to know and love God is a scandal. They think he is hungrier than a common beggar at their door, easy to satisfy with a handful of any kind of offering. Oh, no; he cannot be fooled by little sacrifices when desire for earthly results stalk through men's thoughts and dreams like herds of elephants through a jungle. And do you think you can satisfy God by presenting him with a fraction of your self? He, being infinite, will not accept anything but the infinite in you."

"So," interrupted Ishan, "it is not enough that we are pure in our waking moments. We have to be free of desire while lying unconscious in our sleep. How can one attain such unalloyed purity?"

Ramakrishna answered, "Pray and meditate. Only undertake those actions that fall within the limits of your purified thoughts and dreams. Eschew any action that is tainted in the slightest by self. Give up building hospitals, houses for the helpless, and other charitable institutions. Seek not to flatter yourself with gigantic deeds. Undertake duties as small in size as your self-surrender to God. Then as your selflessness and purity grow—and things of the soul grow very fast—it will pierce its way through the material world and benefit others as the Ganges sprang through the hard rocks of the Himalayas and watered thousands of miles with her beneficence."

"Is there anything else I can do? Need I study books? Need I practice love of God?" asked Ishan all in one breath.

The Master was amused by his breathless hurry. "Because you want God, why should you give up harmless amusements? Read all you want, love all you can. But see that you grow more selfless through it all. And when you become one with him you will find that he exceeds all books. He is infinite knowledge, and all love. If your God realized through deeds excludes knowledge and love, then he is a false God. The true God includes all. There is only one thing that he excludes, and that is desire for results whether here on earth or in heaven. Renounce all earthly results; give up even the hope of the felicity of heaven."

"Why, my Lord?" questioned Ishan with trepidation.

Ramakrishna replied, "You are a reader of books. You ought to know what the scriptures say on such matters."

Ishan pondered a while, then said that there was a stanza in the Gita that condemned good actions if done for results here or hereafter: "'*Yami Mam puspitam bacham ...*' The purport of it is that men who are full of desires and look upon heaven as their highest goal are not going to attain salvation. I have read that, my Lord. But I do not know what it truly means. Does it really mean something?"

Ramakrishna replied, "If you give up the desire for hospitals here, why should you wish to have a palace in paradise? If the leprosy of desire ruins all here, far worse will be its havoc in heaven!"

"I do not understand, my Lord," exclaimed Ishan.

Ramakrishna explained, "If you defeat your soul's end by doing good deeds with earthly results in view, you will do it endless harm if you act in order to be rewarded hereafter. Selflessness is not only the road out of earthliness but also out of heaven. Does God abide in one and only one place? No. He cannot be chained either to heaven or to earth. And if you fasten your soul's claws on him, you will have to give up the selfish joys of paradise too."

"Then what happens to the acts of beneficence we do on earth? Are they at all permanent? What happens to them if they do not bring us nearer heaven? Can we do any good to anybody?" asked Ishan in amazement.

Ramakrishna answered, "Those who do lasting benefits to their neighbors are men selfless as God. God is infinite and endless, hence his creation has no end. Persons who have renounced their little selves and have attained the Self of God are the ones whose creations cannot perish. No man can achieve deathless deeds if he is attached in the slightest to anything less than the *purusha* [infinite]. When your self is all burned up and God has taken possession of you completely, then every act of your life will be immortal. Whether you seek *jnana*-yoga, realization through knowledge, or karma-yoga, realization through deeds, you must have a dire longing for God at its foundation. Without that foundation the house of knowledge is a perpetual labyrinth of deception, and the temple of deeds is but the tabernacle of self-adulation. Therefore, go tonight: lift yourself like an offering to the Self of the universe. With that act of surrender you will begin to build the palace of immortal acts. With those hands of yours doomed to death you shall erect the citadel of deathlessness."

Ishan was deeply moved by the Master's last words. He slowly bowed and took the dust from the Master's feet. In deep silence he walked into the moonlit night.

7

Ramakrishna and a Modern Social Reformer

Unitarianism bears the name Brahmoism in India. If translated literally it means One-Godism, and people who profess it call their society Brahmo Samaj, or the Society of One God. It was a movement that began a little before Ramakrishna was born and that had its full tide during his lifetime. One of the greatest Brahmos, Keshab Chandra Sen, was a devoted friend of Ramakrishna. His conversations with Keshab Sen and his attitude toward Brahmoism provide another view of Ramakrishna's religious outlook.

But let us begin with a history of Brahmoism and its founder, Rammohan Roy. During the early years of the British rule in India, a very great man rose among the Hindus. His name was Rammohan Roy. He was six feet tall and strong as a tiger. His mind was correspondingly vigorous. In fact, until Dayananda, a Punjabi holy man, and Ramakrishna, India had no man like Rammohan Roy. In the early 1820s, he, a youth of twenty-four, saw a *sati*—a widowed relative of his was burned to death with her husband's corpse. A brahmin of fiery temperament and a scholar of great repute, he started then and there the movement to abolish sati. Since I have explained the origin of sati in my book, *Caste and Outcast*, I shall not go into it here. But it was Rammohan Roy who began the first tremendous attack against it. He proved that no such custom is sanctioned by the scriptures of Hinduism. Since he was a keen Sanskrit scholar, he went from temple to temple and from one Sanskrit Tol (college) to another, rousing the teachers' and priests' horror by expounding to them the utterly irreligious nature of sati. They all agreed that "sati is a social custom several hundred years old; it has had nothing to do with our scriptures and creed."

At the height of his fight against sati, Rammohan had the good fortune that the then British governor general of India also wanted to abolish sati. Since the British sovereign power alone had the authority to pass a law, all the Indian reformers, headed by Rammohan and his associates, sought its help. Before Rammohan was a man of forty, sati had been abolished from India.

Having discovered that a firmly established social and supposedly religious custom like sati had no foundation in the Hindu scriptures, Rammohan was determined to further explore the origins of Hindu society and religion. He not only studied in India, but went as far as Tibet in search of exact and accurate Sanskrit texts. In those days, Tibet was symbolic of no man's land. After a sojourn of half a dozen years there, he returned to India. He found Western missionaries attacking Hindu religion as a heathen affair of no consequence. In order to know the basis of their criticism, Rammohan learned Latin and Greek and read the Bible in those languages. He also studied Arabic in order to read the Qur'an in the original. And he brought to bear on those scriptures—Muslim and Christian—the light of the Upanishads and the Vedas, with the result that in regard to all the religions, one sentence of the Upanishads burned like a steady flame:

Ekam Sat
Vipra Bahudha Vadanti

There is only one God, it is men who have given him
   many names

He came to the conclusion that all religions preach the same inner experience.

Jesus says, "The kingdom of God is within you."

Mohammed says, "He dwells within your very souls and ye see him not."

The Upanishads say, "He is the dweller within you."

The Neo-Platonists say, "*Hominum interiore habitat veritas.*"

After he noticed the resemblance among all the religions, Rammohan set down their differences as nonsense and at once started to preach Brahmoism—the religion of one God who is above the battling claims of religions and priests. This Indian brand of Unitarianism owes nothing to external sources. Its indebtedness, all of it, lies at the door of Rammohan Roy. Soon after launching his movement in India, he went to Europe to discern in its dark night of Christian fanaticism some dawning light of tolerance and brotherhood. Unfortunately soon after his arrival in Europe, Rammohan died. Thus ended the life of India's first missionary to the West.

At his death the leadership of Brahmoism passed to Keshab Chandra Sen. I have already intimated that Keshab was very fond of Ramakrishna. The difference between Keshab and his predecessor, Rammohan Roy, lay in two things. First of all, Keshab knew little Sanskrit and less Arabic. But he was a master of English. In fact, his eloquence in English equaled that of Gladstone.[1] He absorbed many of the bourgeois Victorian English ideas. He had none of Rammohan's gaunt and eagle-eyed scholarship or Eastern upbringing. The latter studied Western thought only after he had been nurtured and formed by the old, austere brahmanic training. And when, at a mature age, he came into contact with Western philosophy and religion, he was all the better equipped to resist whatever weaknesses they had. He praised only their authentic beauty and strength.

By the time Keshab was in his early teens, English universities and their English curricula had been established in India, so he was formed and strengthened by Western learning. In other words, Keshab did not drink much of his mother's milk—he was nursed at the breast of a stepmother. So, from the start, Keshab was a bellicose Western ameliorist and a pietistic Hindu. His Unitarianism was not a religion derived from a scholar's insight. On the contrary, to him Unitarianism was a banner of revolt. It was for him to carry that banner high. Hence, he became a fiery lecturer and a passionate social reformer. His religious experiences remained primarily emotional. He wanted to sweep away idolatry and renew the original worship of the one God of the Upanishads. Next, he wished to abolish the caste system, seclusion of women, and early marriage.

Judging by his portraits, Keshab Sen was a tall man with a light complexion. He had a large oval face, dark brown eyes, and an extremely sensitive, but rather weak, mouth. He often dressed in English style, and his most impassioned lecture—in it he reached his high-water mark of eloquence—was on Jesus the man. Those who heard Keshab on Jesus say that in one lecture he did more for Christianity in India than all the missionaries put together.

Now try to imagine the impression that Ramakrishna made on Keshab. It must have been a negative one, for Ramakrishna was neither an iconoclast nor a reformer of society. I wonder if Keshab came in the company of that other Unitarian, Mazumdar, the author of *The Oriental Christ*. It was Mazumdar, I think, who was the first Unitarian to say about the holy man of Dakshineswar, "Before I met Ramakrishna I had a poor conception of religion—I spent my time rampaging about reforms. But now that I have known him, I know what a true life of religion consists of."

Attracted by such words of praise from a fellow Brahmo of importance, Keshab at last paid Ramakrishna a visit. He came prepared to find a superstitious, backward Hindu. Then, lo and behold! "Here was a man who was the true son of Immortality." A man who had little intellectual training, no contact with any European books or people, yet who could converse so well on important spiritual matters. Whence did he derive his knowledge? Keshab was shocked and surprised. He could not believe that while Rammohan Roy had been wrestling with the scriptures of all the religions to elicit their real meaning, here was this Ramakrishna battling to wrest from the lips of the Divine Mother the secret of life and death. The cult of tolerance that Rammohan Roy found through intense reasoning and study, Ramakrishna had lived these many years! What a surprise indeed! Was it the two halves of one reality that he was seeing? Was Rammohan the scholar of unity and brotherhood and Ramakrishna the exemplary life of it? Such was the effect produced by Ramakrishna on Keshab.

It was not very long before the two men became great friends. Here I shall give some of Ramakrishna's characteristic talks with Keshab, for that alone can illustrate how the holy man respected and emphasized the uniqueness of his friend's character. Ramakrishna aimed to strengthen Keshab in his own light and not to change him.

On their first meeting, Ramakrishna said to Keshab, "I hear that you have had a vision of God. I wish to learn of it from your lips."

Thus began a long discussion that ended with this story from the Holy One: "Everyone conceives God in the light of his own experience. Some men saw a chameleon going up a tree. One of them followed it to the top, then climbed down. He proclaimed to his friends, 'That lizard is green.' Then another man went up the tree to see the animal with his own eyes. He came down and reported, 'That animal is red.' The third man did likewise and reported the lizard to be blue. Thus started an altercation that threatened to be bloody. A passerby came along; noticing those persons raising such a tumult, he inquired as to what was the matter. They told him their trouble. He said, 'Oh, that chameleon! He lives on the tree under which I sleep. He does not wear the same color long—sometimes he is blue, sometimes green, and sometimes utterly colorless.' So is God," concluded Ramakrishna. "He is of infinite appearances."

After that story, suddenly, like a bolt from the blue, he said, "Keshab, your tail has dropped off." Then he explained, "You must have noticed how tadpoles are doomed to swim in the water until their tails drop off; and in a trice they become frogs. As the tail is to a tadpole, so is ignorance to man. Only he who has dropped his ignorance hops upon the shore of God-consciousness. I feel that you are such a man. You live in the world, yet you can enjoy divine bliss."

After their first meeting, Keshab came to see the Master frequently. But in spite of their growing intimacy during the early stages of their friendship Ramakrishna had the feeling that the Brahmo leader was not inclined to put much trust in "the superstitious holy man." Whenever Keshab asked his opinion on religious matters, Ramakrishna generally prefaced his remarks thus: "Keshab, of course I will say what comes to my mind. But you can cut off its head and tail and accept what is agreeable to you."

Though in the course of time the Holy One came to love Keshab dearly, he could not stomach the characteristics of many of his followers. What was most jarring to Ramakrishna was their copying the Protestant service. He described what he found there:

> I went to Keshab's religious service. After a sermon on the glory of God, the leader said, "Let us commune with him."
>
> I thought, "They will now go into the inner world and stay a long time." Hardly had a few minutes passed when they all opened their eyes. I was astonished. Can anyone find him after so slight a meditation? After it was all over, when we were alone, I spoke to Keshab about it. "I watched all of your congregation communing with

their eyes shut. You know what it reminded me of? Sometimes in Dakshineswar I have seen under the trees a flock of monkeys sitting stiff and looking the very picture of innocence. But their thoughts belied the picture they made: they were thinking and planning their campaign of robbing certain gardens of fruits, roots, and other edibles. Oh yes! They were thinking of swooping down on those unprotected gardens in a few moments. The communing that your followers did with God today is no more serious than were those monkeys trying to look innocent of mischief!"

There is a line in a song of the Brahmos: "Think and worship him every moment of the day." On hearing it, Ramakrishna stopped the singer and commented, "Change that line into 'Pray and worship him only twice a day.' Say what you really will do. Why fib to the Infinite?"

There was one particular habit of Keshab's that Ramakrishna criticized the most, namely, ornate praise of the many glories of the Lord. One day, unable to bear the catalog of God's glories enumerated by Keshab, Ramakrishna blurted out, "Why do you give such statistics about his powers and the attributes that he possesses? Does a son say to his father's face, 'Oh, my father, you own so many houses, so many horses, so many cows, gardens, and grottos'? Does that take in any father? It is natural that a father should feed, protect, and put all his resources at the disposal of his sons. We are his sons. That he should be kind, beneficent, merciful, and forgiving is natural and not a matter of surprise. If you think of him and his estate as such a matter of surprise, you can never be intimate with him; you cannot draw close and demand of him the vision of his face. Don't think of him so that he must necessarily be remote from us. Conceive him as your nearest, then he will reveal himself to you! Don't you think his attributes that you dilate on make you idolatrous?"

"I do not see the connection between the two," protested the great reformer. "Idolatry is worship of stones, images, icons, and other inanimate forms. God cannot abide in them. He is formless."

"But Keshab," pleaded Ramakrishna, "God is both. He is in form and formlessness. Images and other symbols of him are as valid and vivid as your strings of divine attributes. Attributes of him are chill, hard forms. They are not different from what you call idolatry."

According to the legend, Keshab retorted in a spirited fashion, "I cannot agree with you. When it comes to flat idolatry and other sordid accretions that have come to be called Hinduism, I consider you to be in the wrong." Keshab always spoke at length. "Child widows, caste system, *purdah* [seclusion of women], worship of sticks and stones, and soulless priestcraft are abominations that must be swept out of existence. Must man, who is God on earth, bend the knee to trees and totems? Is that religion? Do you dare call it spiritual? No, dear Master, the storm that I am raising must cleanse the foul sky of Hinduism so that our children can be called human beings and not dumb beasts who are driven from pillar to post by the cunning of priests and the greed of innumerable Gods."

"But Keshab," commented the Master, "the foul sky, as you call Hinduism, cannot be cleansed by a storm of invectives. That may change the appearance of things, but it is beyond its power to improve reality. Real improvements are wrought by blessings. Can you let loose upon us a food of blessings that will touch and transfigure every shore of our life?"

"What do you exactly mean?" asked Keshab.

"You are a scholar; you can instruct us as to what incarnations of God did when they were on earth. Please tell us," requested Ramakrishna.

Keshab readily agreed: "If you take Lord Buddha, in him you find an apt illustration of your point. He never lost his temper, nor did he criticize his opponents. On the contrary, he blessed one and all that came to him. In fact his vast sympathy, boundless love, and austere morality, no matter whom they touched, made him a better and finer human being. Is that what you call the blessings of a God-man which change the world? Is that what *being* means?"

"What other name can we give that power in an incarnation of God?"

"Ah, dear Master," ejaculated Keshab, "your snare has caught me. I feel that you are right. Only God in us can bring out the God that is in others."

"Keshab, your speech ravishes me!" exclaimed the Master. A glint of exaltation danced in Ramakrishna's eyes. He ceased speaking.

Palpable silence fell upon the audience. It lasted a long time. The air grew pregnant with a strange presence. Ramakrishna's face slowly altered and threw away its usual masklike expression. Instead, as a smoking brazier begins to burn, an intense glow spread over his whole countenance. Slowly his lips parted. No matter how commonplace his thoughts, they sounded invincible now. An indescribable sweetness hung over every word he uttered:

> Men think that to criticize is to give life. A eunuch's denunciation of barrenness does not produce a child. To create is to be like God. One must be all essence! When you are filled with the essence of all existence then whatever you say becomes true. Poets have praised virtue and truth: Has that made their readers virtuous and truthful?
>
> On the contrary, when a selfless person lives among us, his deeds become the very heartbeat of virtue. The being of such a one hovers over the world on wings of benediction. He becomes the chalice of holiness. Whatever he does to others improves even their meanest dreams. Men in their amazement pay their homage by calling him an incarnation of God. Like God, whatever he touches becomes true and pure. He becomes the

father of reality. What he creates never flounders in time. That is what I expect you to do, Keshab. Silence the dogs of invectives! Let the elephant of Being trumpet its blessings on all! You have that power; will you use it? Or shall you squander this lifetime by abusing people? Shall men say that Keshab spent his days in the tavern of talk, drinking the wine of eloquence? On the contrary may you *be* so that they will say "He dwelled among us like a tiger of truth. Wherever he went, errors trembled like leaves in the jungle, and sin fled before him like a herd of goats. He was so full of blessings that even his feeblest gestures showered love on all. His words were immortalities. He did not humble us with criticisms; for he heightened us with God."

Instead of hurting Keshab, all these criticisms made him love Ramakrishna, showing how noble the leader of the Brahmo Samaj really was. Month after month they met and discussed everything between them—Christ, Buddha, Zoroaster, Mohammed, and other incarnations of God who had blessed all humankind.

At last Keshab fell ill. Ramakrishna went to see him very often, and talked about the Lord for hours at a time. One day, perceiving that Keshab would not live long, Ramakrishna intimated to him the approaching end.

With tears in his eyes he said, "Keshab, the master gardener treats the *basra* [rose] plant severely because it produces the best of flowers. The master trims it, sometimes takes it out, root and all, then exposes it to the sun and frost. You are going to be replanted. For the Gardener wants magnificent blossoms from you!" Then Ramakrishna left his bedside. When the news of Keshab's death reached him, the Holy One said: "I have lost one so intimate to myself that I feel as if half of me had perished."

It is fitting that this chapter should close with a statement of Ramakrishna's belief in immortality.

One day a friend of his, Mani Mallik, lost his son. He came to Ramakrishna for some consolation soon after the obsequies were over. The reception room was full of people to whom Ramakrishna was talking. But no sooner had Mallik appeared in his mourning dress than the utterly unrelieved whiteness of it fell on that assembly like the crash of a bolt. However, after Mallik had seated himself, Ramakrishna began to talk, which helped to put all his listeners at ease. Then he stopped. A peaceful hush followed. As the humming of insects disturbs the morning air, the assembly heard a soft murmur fretting the silence that had fallen. It was Mallik, who was telling Ramakrishna his sorrow in a very low tone of voice. The Holy One, perceiving that the crowd was trying to catch Mallik's words, rose to his feet and began to sing and dance:

> Oh soul, lift the lance of truth,
>   Don your coat of mail!
> For behold! death the enemy
>   Has pierced your citadel.

Thus he went on, singing, dancing, and speaking. There was no doubt now that he was acting a mystery play in which the human soul goes to war and conquers death. When that was over he sat down by Mallik and said, "It is a terrible pain you are feeling, but it is not the sorrow inflicted by the sword of truth, but of a body for another like itself. But these physical forms suffer as long as they live—and no more. The soul, that scimitar of truth, never suffers.

"Once I saw a man die. It was my own dear nephew, Akshay. I watched him carefully. Suddenly the sword was removed from its scabbard, which lay there dead. But that made no difference to the sharp blade. What I saw gave me joy. I laughed and danced. After the body was cremated the next day, standing on that veranda yonder I felt as if someone was wringing my heart as a man wrings a water-soaked towel. Then I said, 'But, Divine Mother, if I who have renounced the world feel so much pain, how much more suffer those who live in it!' Ah! thus I tasted a fraction of what you are feeling now, my friend. But you, if you cling to God, will not go under in your deepest sorrow. Behold the small vessels on the Ganges. They are upset by a small wave, but a barge glides over the largest waves with ease. Oh! great barge of the soul, load your-self deeply with God, then you will not be shaken by sorrows even mountain-high. It is the scabbard—the body—wailing for the body, not the sword—the soul—tempered with the immortality of God."

It was not the words only, but the man who spoke them, who moved Mallik so that he rose to go, saying: "I knew I had to come to you, for no one else could have quenched my pain."

Ramakrishna went on, "Those who are attached to earthliness fear death. But he who is not cross-eyed through earthliness sees no death. Many times with mine eyes straightened by meditation I stood on the border contemplating the two mansions: life here and life beyond. There was no death separating the two. So lose your earthliness and your attachment to things; then suddenly you will find life as one. There is no such interruption as death."

8

Ramakrishna and His Disciples

Though Ramakrishna's contacts with the multitude were very interesting, it is impossible to grasp the unique significance of his message without studying the choice and training of his disciples.

Unlike the prophets of the past, Ramakrishna had no taste for evangelism. Time and again he is reported to have said, "Those days are gone when a teacher's inspired speech made people see God. We have to build on other foundations now. We must live such an intense inner life that it will become a Being. And Being will send forth untold torches of truth. Rivers rise and rush because their sire, the mountain, sits still. It took God ages and ages to make mountains, but generations and leagues have been bathed, fed, and sustained by their streams ever since. Let us make a Being—raise a mountain of God in our midst—no matter how long it takes, and when it has been reared it will pour rivers of compassion and light on all men for all time."

With that philosophy in mind, let us now examine the way Ramakrishna trained some of his disciples. Courtesy forbids our exploration of the lives of his disciples still living. We shall confine ourselves to the study of the life events of those who are dead. Regarding two of them, Brahmananda and Turiyananda, our knowledge is fragmentary, for they died recently [1922], and the materials of their life stories have not yet been gathered together. That compels us to concentrate on the lives of Vivekananda, Premananda, and Latu Maharaj. About these three not a great deal is known since they—being monks who had renounced this world—have left us only as much of their own temporal history as they could not destroy. Anyone who has read Vivekananda's life of Ramakrishna is perfectly aware that he says nothing of the intimate and eventful moments between himself and his Master. The same holds true of the other disciples of Ramakrishna. In none of their memoirs does one find any record of the writer's own spiritual experiences. That is what makes the writing of their lives a difficult, if not arid, task.

However, we must gather all the meager details that have been left us by those holy men. First of all, bear in mind that Ramakrishna, who was hospitable and generous to the whole world, was extremely strict in the choice of his disciples.

They were chosen mostly from young university men who came from diverse castes. Almost all of them knew at least one foreign language and had a thorough knowledge of Sanskrit. Once, when asked why he accepted such young men, the Master said, "They are not yet caught in the net of desire, nor caged in wealth. They are wholly unattached. Their character is good.... Then why do you assume that I choose my chelas? The Divine Mother brings them to me. It is she who draws them. I but train those whom she chooses. It is she who makes me examine their secret habits, their tastes and distastes. At night while they are asleep, I commune; the veils fall from around them, and she, the omniscient, points out to me not only what they are but also the degree of spiritual progress each one of them makes daily. When you see with your soul's insight, you see the self of men and women as you see through glass the things resting in a case beyond your touch and taste. Thus do I make sure of my disciples' characters long before I initiate them."

The following incident proves that Ramakrishna was aware of everything about the spiritual life of his apostles. Saradananda and others testify that one night, while the Master was asleep, Vivekananda, Kali Tapasvi [Swami Abhedananda], Saradananda, and two others went to the woods to meditate. Before starting to do so, Vivekananda said to Kali Tapasvi, "Keep your hand on my shoulder while I meditate in the new way that the Master has taught me."

In about half an hour, Kali Tapasvi's hand began to shake as a rope is shaken by a strong wind. When it was all over, they all said to Vivekananda, "Anyone who touched you felt a shock like that of an electric battery."

No sooner had they reached the Master's apartment upon their return home than, out of the darkness, they heard him calling. They lit a lamp and went to see him. He said to Vivekananda, "Hardly had you gathered spiritual treasure than you squandered it. Spirituality grows in the soul as a child in the womb. You cannot experiment on its coming to earth until the time is ripe. When will you learn that whenever you act foolishly I know all about it? Always ask me before starting your childish and rash experiments."

Not only did Ramakrishna examine his disciples thoroughly before accepting them, but he also kept watch on every phase of their life. He accepted for training both householders and unattached persons, yet he insisted on a final public declaration on the part of all disciples as to the exact nature of their obligations to other human beings.

"For," he told his disciples, "let no one suffer want and destitution because you, my son, wish to become a holy man." And he never gave initiation to anyone whose dependents—father, mother, wife, or children—withheld the necessary permissions. Even now the same procedure is followed in the monastery. No one is accepted for the monastic life who is not voluntarily given up by his family. For they say that a man who is fleeing from the responsibilities of this world is too weak to be exposed to the more dangerous responsibility of finding God.

The case of Ramakrishna's first disciple, Swami Brahmananda, illustrates this most amply. When he met the Master he was a rich brahmin boy of twenty-two. Even at that early age he proved so brilliant and gifted that every potential career in life was open to him. Just at that juncture, some of his curious college friends urged him one day to accompany them to Dakshineswar to see the holy man.

"He came to see what I was like," Ramakrishna said years later. "He must have heard strange stories about here," meaning himself. "But fortunately, instead of finding in me a God-chattering monkey, he saw my self. He came again, alone. In a few days he gave up everything and stayed here like a ram tethered to his post. His people followed. They wanted to know what sort of company he was keeping. They were satisfied after a look at me. But they did not wish the boy to be a monk, for they wanted him to marry and settle down. I was questioned about it. That worried me a bit. But I was sure of the lad's soul, so I wished to see the young lady they had chosen for him. One day the little mother was brought to me. One look at her convinced me that she would help and not hinder his soul's reach for God. I told the blessed little mother who and what she was marrying. She seemed to know all that. As a sound is lost in the silence of heaven, my worries vanished at once. In a short time Brahmananda married. Now look what a holy man he is! His wife never claimed him. She realized God by giving him freedom to attain holiness."

After Brahmananda, about five more young men—four of whom are yet living—became Ramakrishna's disciples. Vivekananda was the fifth. In order to know what the ocean tastes like, we need but put one drop of it on our tongue; so, in order to learn the way Ramakrishna brought up his disciples, let us study the case of Vivekananda, for he was typical of all of them; besides, he is not unknown in Europe and America.

From childhood, Vivekananda was brilliant, brave, and versatile. He was one of the *kshatriya* (warrior) caste and had had a religious upbringing. His forebears lived a very strict orthodox life. His father and grandfather carried religious practices as far as the scriptures enjoined. There was no radicalism in his blood. Heresy in religious matters was unknown to him. But, alas! In his middle teens, Vivekananda developed a strong tendency toward agnosticism. He believed, with the ancient Sanskrit philosopher Charvaka, that "God does not exist: He is an invention of the priests." Then from Charvakism he went forward and accepted the Vaiseshika doctrine (atomism) of Kanada. Later, Kapila's Samkhya all the more confirmed in him his notion that, though one must lead a strictly moral life, one need not believe in God.

Vivekananda, whose ancestors were fighters, had no sooner convinced himself of agnosticism than he went to war for it. But in order to fight successfully, one must have followers and friends. The orthodox Hindu society furnished him with none. Then, instead of despairing, he went ahead and joined the Brahmos under Keshab Sen, whose zeal for social reform Vivekananda shared. Thus, before he was twenty years old, he became known as an iconoclast who was a fanatical puritan. All of his contemporaries affirm that he had no respect for anything save the true and the moral. Vivekananda took special delight in going out of his way to attack the pretensions of learned holy persons and brahmins. He was a sort of agnostic bull in the china shop of religion.

One day, in the company of Keshab Sen, Vivekananda came to Dakshineswar. The late Bhupendranath Basu, an eyewitness of that visit, describes the meeting of Ramakrishna and Vivekananda:

> Vivekananda and I were studying the law at the time, when one day he invited me to go with Keshab and others to Dakshineswar. Of course I, too, was eager to see with my own eyes what sort of a holy man Ramakrishna was.

Swami Vivekananda

On our arrival at the Kali temple, we found a very strange looking man whose eyes were like a hawk's. They saw and recognized your worth at a great distance. The only thing I remember of that interview is this: Just as we were getting ready to take our leave, the Master said, "Keshab, though you lecture a great deal, your fame will not reach very far. But this lad," he pointed at Vivekananda, "will be famous across the seas." Everyone present laughed at Ramakrishna's remark. We thought he was making fun of the fame and fortune which Keshab had won. But about a decade later, when I read the reports of Vivekananda's lectures in England and America, I often thought of what the Holy One had said of him at their first meeting.

Instead of pleasing Vivekananda, the prophecy of Ramakrishna offended him. For to him, at the time, it sounded like officiousness and fakery. He hated palmists, fortune-tellers, and soothsayers. However, in spite of the strong dislike that he had for the Master, he felt drawn to him more and more strongly as day succeeded day. Something within him prodded his obstinate intellect to give the holy man another chance. At last, with the desire to find out for the second and last time what sort Ramakrishna was, Vivekananda called on him once more. During his journey to Dakshineswar he felt disturbed. He said to himself, "Why am I going to see this fool of God? I know God does not exist. Then why do I go?… " So on all the way!

On his arrival in Dakshineswar, he found Ramakrishna sitting on his couch, all alone. That relieved Vivekananda. He said to himself, "Now he will not embarrass me by making silly prophecies about my future in the presence of a crowd."

Hardly had Vivekananda said those words to himself when the Master irritated him anew with his words of greeting: "I am so glad you have come. I have waited for you many years."

With an expression of chill effrontery on his face, Vivekananda sat on the edge of the couch. For a while neither of them spoke a word. One can imagine those two faces studying each other. The Master looked old. He was old beyond his years, while the youth before him had a face massive and strong as a "young Buddha of bronze."

The latter, panoplied with beauty and youth, and the former, destitute of everything save the invisible God, sat scrutinizing each other. Suddenly, without a word or the slightest sound, Ramakrishna lifted his right foot, slowly moved it forward, and brought it into contact with Vivekananda's body. No sooner had that happened than …

"That instant," said Vivekananda,

> before my wide open eyes, the walls of the room reeled and fell; then the furniture, possessed by some demonic force, dashed itself on the floor, then sank into a void. All around me was nothing, nothing! And suddenly the lean-mouthed universe set to devour my "me-ness." Then I thought to myself, "To lose one's ego is to die!" Death was so near that I could touch it! Frightened by that sinister realization I shrieked for help: "Oh you! What are you doing to me? I want to live. Do not let me die yet, for my father and my mother are living."
>
> At those words of mine, that madman laughed aloud, gently rubbed my chest with his hand, and said, "Let us stop now; it is not necessary to see it all in one flash. Later you shall know the rest." After these words, as if by wizardry, the furniture, walls, room, and myself all arranged themselves as before.
>
> Later that day I wondered if it was hypnotism or mesmerism that had been practiced on me. The very fact that none of the events of my latest experience squared with the symptoms of either left me all the more troubled. I came to no conclusion save that there are hidden mysteries that our intellectual insolence can never uncover. That experience of mine convinced me that

Ramakrishna was not mad. A madman cannot pulverize into dust one's senses and intellect. Thinking and cogitating about my experience, I spent the rest of the day with him hoping that he would throw some more light on it. At last the sun set, and since I had to get home soon, I bowed to his feet, then rose to depart. But Ramakrishna would not let me go without extracting from me the promise that I would come to see him again soon.

Vivekananda was in no haste to see him again, though his heart yearned for it. He spent many days thinking over his recent experience. It fascinated as well as frightened him.

No matter from what standpoint he examined it, he could not find a satisfactory explanation for his experience. And to crown all his perplexities, a voice within his soul said, "Go to him. He alone can make it clear." As time passed, that cry grew more and more insistent. Nothing could still it. At last, like a river to the sea, he obeyed the urge of his soul, and called on Sri Ramakrishna again.

"The third visit that I paid him," said Vivekananda, "proved most startling. On my arrival I found him strolling in the garden. He asked me to join him. From the garden we sauntered to the riverbank. Thence, walking in a leisurely fashion, we went indoors. He sat on his couch and I seated myself on its edge as I had done before. Just then, he touched me again. This time … "

Vivekananda never divulged the story of his last experience. What happened then may have meant too much to him. It was not to be profaned by being told, at least by him. But years later Brahmananda, M., and Saradananda—all three—asked Ramakrishna about it, and the Master explained, "When Vivekananda lost his temporal 'I,' I asked him some questions about himself. I questioned him particularly about the full amount of realizations that he had already accomplished. Why had he come to earth? He gave me answers that were clear. And they brought me certainty, for all those things I had learned about him in my meditation. All the same, it was good to get his verification. I concluded this, also: that the very next time, if in meditation he comes upon the exact story of his Self, he will at once spit away his body and soar back to his home. For he is a fully realized soul."

About nineteen years later, when Vivekananda died in the monastery, he died in the supreme meditation. His death occurred about seventeen years after the death of Ramakrishna. I have seen the room where Vivekananda meditated; I have also interviewed those who kept constant watch on him during the days before his death. They told me what Ramakrishna said of Vivekananda years before.

After this latest experience, Vivekananda gradually drew nearer the Master and took lessons in meditation and other practices. Even then he hesitated to renounce the world and take the vow of a sannyasin— a mendicant holy man. Time and again he said to Ramakrishna, "Please tell the Divine Mother to provide for my family so that I can take the begging bowl."

Ramakrishna answered, "I cannot. *You* go and pray to her."

Bhupendranath Basu tells another story that explains one of Vivekananda's hesitations:

> Every now and then, Vivekananda would vanish from the lawyer's office where he and I were working at the time. Sometimes our employer sent me searching after the truant. I went to Ramakrishna's place and many other haunts of his but never could find him anywhere. At last one day I asked him about his doings. He vouchsafed me no answer. But God-quest, like murder, generally gets found out.
>
> One day, after I had left our law office, I walked home through another part of town. This was a dangerous slum district; not a single member of our caste deliberately went

there. As I was going along, taking in with each glance the terrible poverty of the people, lo, suddenly, I saw a man in ocher-colored robes begging at the door of a filthy hovel. I could not believe my eyes. How could these destitute people give alms to anybody? What kind of a beggar is it that begs of the lowest? As I drew near, I noticed that the sannyasin was blessing the poor old woman who had given him a handful of rice. Then, as he turned to go, I saw his face. It was Vivekananda. Now that we were face to face, he asked me to follow him. We walked briskly away, and in a short time reached the riverbank where we sat down on the upper steps of a ghat.

Vivekananda said, "You can see that my dress explains everything. I want to be a sannyasin. Ramakrishna draws me so that I would consider it heaven if I could enter his order tomorrow. But I am not sure of myself. I do not wish to offer him a weak character. It is not easy to be a monk. You know our family—its prestige of caste and wealth. Though we are poor now, we were not so twenty years ago. A great deal is expected of us. I feel terribly proud. It is my pride that stands in my way. Can I, my father's son, become as humble as a sannyasin? Can I sink my pride so that I can live by begging? In order to find all that out, I put on the monk's garb and beg in the slums. I get very little from them, materially. But, spiritually, what they are giving me is more than abundant— they are enabling me to lose my pride. I feel very humble now. Probably I shall be able to renounce all and become a worthy disciple of my guru.

"Another thing I have found out that gives me courage is that I can go without food for a number of days. Not only is my mind free of pride, but my body can stand starvation. I feel that I can ask Ramakrishna to give me initiation. I have already mastered the science of meditation and can perform all the austerities of yoga. But I have not dared to ask for the final initiation until I have made quite sure of myself."

Now that he had conquered his own weaknesses, Vivekananda was tormented by the problem of providing for his family. In spite of many discussions between him and Ramakrishna, neither of them prayed to the Mother. Apparently they did not wish to ask God to provide for his family. Here again Vivekananda's pride stood in his way: though he could beg of men, he could not beg of God.

One day he took up the matter with his own mother. That austere and proud lady brought up in the strictest discipline of the *ancien régime* said to her boy, "Since when did a member of our family give up God for the fear of poverty? Your own grandfather renounced wife, children, wealth, and position the moment he heard the Secret of secrets knock at the door of his heart. Did I not pray to God long before you were born that you should be a man of religion? Now that the Infinite stands at the gates of your life, you want to turn him away! None of your ancestors would have done such a thing. What right have you to be afraid of poverty for me?"

Vivekananda bowed his head and walked toward Dakshineswar determined to end all his troubles by taking initiation from his guru. But on his way he cogitated, "I must provide for my dependents. Brave ancestors are all very good. But am I my ancestor? No, until Ramakrishna says that my family are provided for, I shall let God alone." Thus soliloquizing, he tramped the road. All this while, his longing to receive the full and final illumination from his Master was growing so that it became irresistible. By the time he had reached the Holy One's presence, he was a man of decided will.

Ramakrishna apparently had sensed all that, so he said sweetly, "The Lord is stronger than any one of us. What have you allowed to trouble your thoughts?"

Vivekananda answered with vehemence, "My Lord, I must renounce the world. But the hungry for whom I am responsible must be guaranteed security from starvation. Will you not speak to the Divine Mother?"

Ramakrishna said, "I will not disturb her with such trivialities. But I say that your dependents will never lack necessities." That boon from the Master cleared the last obstacle from the path of his initiation.

Now he was initiated and given the name Vivekananda, for that was not the name his parents had given him. They called him Narendra. The names that are given to newly initiated holy men are found in meditation by their Masters. They are not of haphazard choice. Vivekananda's name means "the bliss of discrimination." Why was he given that name? As a youth, he was so kind that he wanted others to enjoy the same benefits from Ramakrishna as he did. He would bring all sorts of people to the Holy One and urge the Master to afford them the beatific vision. Ramakrishna would wail with patient suffering: "How can I give every waif this vision when they do not bring it with them? Why do you not use your discrimination?" No doubt Vivekananda was a man of discrimination in his mind and soul. It was his heart that needed to be purged of sentimentality. It was during the four or five years of his training before his initiation that his heart, though tender as ever, grew keen with discrimination. And when he was initiated, the name that was revealed to him by his guru was Vivekananda—discrimination that is bliss.

For the last time the Holy One enjoined him against sentimentality: "Do three things in conduct. Never lose your taste for God. Respect all sincere devotees of God, no matter where or when. And do not try to be sentimentally kind to others—you, smaller than an insect, how dare you humiliate one of his creatures by your pity? The thing that you must do is to *see and serve every living being as the absolute God*." That was Ramakrishna's golden rule: "See and serve every living being as the absolute God."

After his initiation, Vivekananda had to work much harder than before. He had to practice and master still higher concentration—a science that only an initiate can explain. Fortunately, he has left us some of its results in his *Raja-Yoga*, a book quite well known in America.

After he studied and mastered all that Ramakrishna had to teach, Vivekananda was sent on a pilgrimage to many yogis who lived scattered all over India. It was during this voyage of discovery that the young initiate met Pavahari (the "Air-Eater"), one of the greatest teachers of Yoga in modern times. Pavahari simply charmed Vivekananda, for he was a virtuoso of Yoga. He could do all that Ramakrishna did. No doubt Vivekananda was glad to get a verification of his own Master's authentic powers from another source. He stayed a long time with Pavahari. But, in the end, he found the great yogi wanting in one respect. Despite all his powers, Pavahari lacked compassion. He was not willing to live in the world of weak and suffering men in order to help them. He did not believe that other human beings needed his help.

Pavahari said, "When they need my help, they will come to my cave on the mountaintop. I will not go down to live in the marketplace in order to teach them. If they want to be lions, men must go and live in the desert."

That sentence opened Vivekananda's eyes. He saw at once that Pavahari was not an absolute guru. Pavahari had not attained the spiritual stature of Ramakrishna. No sooner had he realized this than he left Pavahari's cave. He came to Dakshineswar and gave a full report of his year's pilgrimage to Ramakrishna. He asked him, "Why does the air-eater hoard his knowledge in a mountain cave? Why does he not squander all he has upon the world as you do?"

Ramakrishna smiled at his ingenuous disciple, "But I hoard it here. I do not go to many places preaching. Do I?"

"No. But you are so eager to give help. And you live here where everyone can see you," responded Vivekananda.

The Master explained, "The air-eater has more regard for the purity in which knowledge of God should be kept. It should be guarded from the profane and the ignorant. His taste is good. But I am without taste."

"There must be a deeper reason than that," said Vivekananda. But Ramakrishna smiled again and refused to talk.

Now that he had traveled and studied all that the other teachers of India had to offer, Vivekananda was ripe for the next stage of his development. After teaching him some more, Ramakrishna said, "Now, debate with all the scholars and yogis who come to see me. Test what you have been taught by pitting it against what they know. You have got the gold, now put it through the fire of criticism."

Day after day Vivekananda met in fierce mental contests pundits and holy men who came to Dakshineswar. All of their debates were carried on in Sanskrit. And the chief rule that the contestants followed was that every quotation that anyone made should be correct and from memory. No one was allowed to quote from a printed page.

After his success as an intellectual debater had been thoroughly established, one of the visitors urged Ramakrishna to put an end to such nonsense. He said, "What can your disciples gain by humbling other men's intellect? Take the case of young Vivekananda; he never loses a debate. One of these days he will grow conceited and quarrelsome like a serpent raising his head at everybody."

Ramakrishna answered, "He is building up his mental muscles during these exercises. He will have to wrestle with the pundits of distant lands after I am gone. I must see to it now that he is properly trained and equipped. As for conceit, he is a realized soul, it will never touch him. He is not unripe."

Soon afterward Ramakrishna sent Vivekananda on his second pilgrimage. This time he crossed both the length and breadth of India. There is hardly a district that he did not visit. Wherever there was a

railway line, he went by train, but to points that were beyond, he journeyed on foot.

Vivekananda was averse to going on his second pilgrimage. He
prayed to Ramakrishna, "I do not wish to wander. I want to be near you.
It is you whom I love. From you I have obtained my salvation; from you
I have learned all that is worthwhile. Oh! please, do not send me away.
Let me stay near and learn from you."

"But you must," answered the guru firmly. "You must go and visit
the common people's homes. For they live by a secret that never dies.
Soon after my death, a day will come when you will have to preach to
multitudes far and near. At that hour you will find the result of all this.
Through your voice will be heard the clamor of a thousand spiritual
realizations."

Again, with a blessing on his lips and a begging bowl between his
hands, Vivekananda set forth on his pilgrimage, this time "to learn from
the lowest of the lowly and those who are lost altogether—and holy."

Though Vivekananda traveled unknown—for who would care to
know the name of a holy man—he left indelible marks of his personality on many minds. "Very few failed to feel the presence of that stal-
lion of spirituality foaled by father Ramakrishna."

The late Mahratta Sanskrit scholar and patriot Tilak[1] once met him
on a train. Tilak said, "I saw him sitting on the seat next to myself. He
looked like a Buddha. But I despised mendicants, no matter what they
looked like. In order to amuse myself by humiliating him, I decided
to talk to this ignorant faker on metaphysics in Sanskrit. For I was sure
that he had never heard of philosophy, and, as for Sanskrit . . . So I began.
To my astonishment he answered me in the language of the gods. But
that was not enough to convince me of anything, so I started a discussion of Vedanta with him. As our debate progressed I was struck more
and more by two things: the lucidity of his mind and the dignity of
his style. When the train reached my town, Poona, I invited him to come

and stay in my house. Though he spent a week with us, I never asked him for his name. After all, why bother a man who has renounced the world with such a worldly thing? About ten years after he left me, I read in the newspapers the cabled reports of some lectures on Vedanta given in America by one Vivekananda. After reading and rereading several quotations from his speech, I said to myself, 'It is my young holy man. It bears the stamp of his mind.' Then on his return to India I met him again. Of course it was Vivekananda."

Whatever success the "young holy man" won, we know now that it was already anticipated by Ramakrishna. The very best that came out of Vivekananda was what he acquired, as he himself admits, at his Master's feet. "If I have said anything that is original, noble, and good, I owe it to him. And if you ask me about the price I would pay for knowing him: if there is a hell, I am willing to live there three thousand years for every year that I spent in the company of Sri Ramakrishna."

When Vivekananda returned from his second long pilgrimage, the Master remarked, "Now that you have suffered the hardships of deserts and jungles, and now that you have seen almost all there is to see, stay by me. Help me to train and bless all who come here. We must soon finish our joint work, for the time is fast approaching for me to go."

9

Ramakrishna and His Disciples *(continued)*

I have already intimated that one of the most important disciples of Ramakrishna, Turiyananda, died recently [1922] in Benares. I had the privilege of being with him before his death. Since he was quite aware of his approaching end, Swami Turiyananda did his utmost to tell people everything that he knew of Yoga, Vedanta, and Sri Ramakrishna. Though a very reticent man, at the time he spoke without any reserve. Because he traveled very little, those who wished to see him had to go to the Benares Monastery where he lived. In the monastery, as well as all over the holy city, people called him Kesari, the maned one. His face, so full of compassion, was also grim as a lion's: not an atom of superfluous flesh, not a single line of worry. Wherever he went, people knew him as a son of God.

One day, another young man and I took a walk with him. He walked a little ahead, while we followed at a distance of half a dozen yards. In a few minutes a peasant came by. He stared at the holy man as they passed each other. Then, when he saw us and noticed in our gaze that we had seen him staring at the maned one, he stopped short and asked, "Who is that man ahead of you?"

We questioned him, "Why do you ask?"

The peasant paused a moment, then said, "No man can hold his head so high as yon man. Even a king cannot hold his head thus, nor a merchant prince. Only the son of the Real King holds his head so high. He is a Brahmajnanin!"

Such was the majesty of Swami Turiyananda. It was purely spiritual and so communicated itself without any effort even to the commonest peasant.

It was one of the common folk who told me of Turiyananda's early life. He was born, I learned, in an orthodox brahmin family of Bengal. His father, who was one of the ablest Sanskrit scholars of his time, trained the boy in Vedanta and Yoga. Before he had passed his teens, Turiyananda knew Patanjali yoga by heart. As for the Mimamsa philosophy, he knew both the Purva and the Uttara so well that he used to take over his father's class any time the gentleman happened to be away from home. As for the Upanishads and the Sankara Bhashya, even in his old age I heard him recite and explain chapter and verse from memory for more than two hours at a stretch. He amazed groups of pundits who came to consult him, not only with the accuracy of his quotations but also with the ravishing clarity of his interpretation. Once someone asked him: "Where did you acquire so much knowledge and such powers of convincing people?"

The maned one replied, "My father taught me almost all of it, and Sri Ramakrishna fulfilled the rest."

From childhood on, Turiyananda showed such religious zeal that his entire family expected him to be a holy man. So when he came home one day in his twentieth year and announced to his family that he had found his guru, no one was surprised. He said further, "This afternoon some classmates of mine took me to Dakshineswar to see Ramakrishna. As usual the Master was surrounded by a group of listeners. I had to wait till those who had come before me finished questioning him. However, when my turn came, I asked the Master, 'Can any man know God?' He answered, 'If God is willing.' That answer of Ramakrishna's set me thinking. Why is it that all the men of the past who had seen God said the same thing? For instance, Sankara, who was proud to the verge of insolence, said, after his realization, 'I am a part of thee, and through thy compassion I can be one with thee.' Chaitanya and others spoke the same way. At present Ramakrishna proclaims the selfsame truth. I have studied and practiced Yoga to the utmost. But that will not suffice. Now I must go to Dakshineswar to be trained by him in the art of rousing God's compassion."

After his first interview, encouraged by his family, Turiyananda paid some further visits to Ramakrishna. It was during one of those visits that he met Vivekananda. Soon they became deeply attached to each other. From then on, they studied many ancient Sanskrit works together. Whether in the Upanishads or the Yoga texts, whenever they failed to understand anything, they went to Ramakrishna for elucidation, for his were the only answers that satisfied them completely. One day, when he had solved a very difficult problem raised in a text, they exclaimed, "Sir, you who never read these books, how do you know what they mean?"

Ramakrishna answered, "I belong to the great house. The place that I have been to, your books have not yet reached."

On another occasion he remarked, "If you know the creator, his creation is automatically caught like a fish in the net of your knowledge."

Blessed and thrilled by the words and companionship of Ramakrishna, Vivekananda said to Turiyananda as they were walking home, "Tell me what you think of the Master."

Turiyananda answered, "I cannot begin to tell. But let me quote the ancient Sanskrit:

> If the Himalayas were an inkwell,
> And the ocean itself was the ink,
> Then if the endless forests gave all their leaves

For the muse herself to write,
Yet her lightning pen
Could not begin to describe his glory."

Turiyananda gave an indication of the spiritual stature of Rama-krishna. There is no doubt that Turiyananda was one of the univer-sally accepted holy persons of our time. He spoke very little, but when he gave his opinion it was in no uncertain terms. I have heard him speak of Ramakrishna with the awe and worship that other men give to God.

Within several years of his first visit to Ramakrishna, Turiyananda took the begging bowl and became a novice, a *brahmachari*, and soon afterward was given sannyas, initiation. It was then that his original name, Hari, was given up, and Ramakrishna named him Turiyananda. Turiya is a difficult word to translate. It is a cosmic state next to the final identity with God. Anyone who has attained this state can cross over and realize samadhi, identity, at will. Since we shall return to the life-work of Turiyananda in a later chapter, I would now speak of that unique disciple of Ramakrishna whose name was Latu Maharaj.

I have already said that Turiyananda was a scholar. But his contempt for scholarship without realization of God was boundless. And his admi-ration for realization without any scholarship was passionate. That is why he held such a high opinion of Latu, who was an untutored young servant of a merchant prince from the West Country. It was in the com-pany of his rich employer that Latu came east on pilgrimage. While pass-ing through Calcutta, the merchant, in order to acquire merit, did all the charities enjoined by his religion. But, as if that were not enough, he said, "Is there no other thing that I can do in order to acquire further merit?" He repeated this question to men and women he met. At last, in sheer exasperation, one of his servants informed him, "There is a holy man in Dakshineswar to whom you have not paid homage."

So the next day the merchant and his servants set out for Dak-shineswar. They went up the river in the most gorgeous boats. One can visualize the scene: the gold-turbaned merchant in the pure white tunic of pilgrimage, his white beard combed and perfumed, his dark eyes keenly watching all things and all persons from his boat, whose turquoise sails, blown by the southern wind, pulled over the tawny waters. Behind him followed his servants, dressed in purple, blue, and red, seated in three other white boats, one of which contained Latu who held a plate of solid gold covered with gems. This was the offering to be made to the Holy One. At the moment, little did he realize that the Master wanted his soul and nothing less. As they went up the river bordered by green banks that glowed like emerald in the hot morning sun, they passed bathers performing their morning ablutions and swiftly moving barges laden with fruits piled in pyramids. Mountains of oranges and mangoes gleamed under bellying sails the color of jade.

At last they reached Dakshineswar. They climbed the spacious granite steps of the ghat like jeweled insects crawling up the side of a giant structure. On reaching the top, they turned to the left, away from the shrine of the Mother. The goddess was secondary to them today. They wanted to see him, the living teacher. They walked toward the garden. After they had gone a hundred yards or so, they heard through an open doorway the low but resonant voice of the Master. The sound of it was unmistakable. They waited till he finished talking. Now there was silence within. So they ventured to enter, the merchant first and Latu following with the offering plate. There, in the cool darkness of the room, they felt refreshed. They waited and watched. At last their eyes grew accustomed to the shadowy interior. Now they could see. A tall, old man, not attractive looking, was seated on a long couch, leaning against a snow-white pillow. His clothes were almost fallen away from his body. But he was not aware of it. Near his feet sat shaven-headed men in rapt attention. Nobody said a word at the intrusion of the strangers. The merchant bowed and made some appropriate remarks. Then Latu walked forward and put the offering at the Master's feet. The precious stones gleamed at him, but Ramakrishna saw none of them. Lo! His gaze was fixed on Latu's face. That face—long expected—was there in its utter innocence. Latu did not yet know what had happened. As soon as the day's ceremony was over, he and his master went away to sell the gems and the gold plate in order to give their proceeds to the poor, for that is what the Master had commanded them to do.

In two days, Latu was back. Ramakrishna was discoursing, seated on his couch in the same room, and about half a dozen of his disciples were listening to his talk. The moment Latu entered the room, the Master stood up, tall as a tree, saying, "Why? Why do you come back?"

Latu, with tears streaming down his cheeks, said, "I missed you, Lord, in the past, but in this incarnation do not let me lose you." Then he fell and buried his face between the feet of the Master. Latu's conversion was immediate, spontaneous. He had no storm and stress of book-learning to go through. As Turiyananda is reported to have said, "Many of us waded through the murky waters of scholarship, toiling laboriously against the tides of conceit in order to cross over to the other side where the Lord was. But this fellow, Latu, like Hanuman the monkey, leaped over all that and in one bound reached the feet of *mukti* [salvation]. What insight! What spiritual certainty! Oh! Latu was superior to us all. He reached his Master unsoiled by the conceit of scholarship and unscarred by the cutting current of doubt."

During the latter part of his life, after Ramakrishna's death, Latu lived in the *math* (monastery) in Benares, very near Turiyananda. In this place there was a hospital where the poor were taken care of by the monks and the nuns.

But Latu was suspicious of doing good. He had a feeling that if men and women did good without attaining insight into the secret of life, they were being caught in a routine from which no authentic good could accrue. One day, a conceited young fellow said, "I agree with you—doing good is a snare."

Latu answered, "But holy men like Turiyananda and Vivekananda have fallen into it. That means it is a snare worth being caught in."

Latu was convinced that we do good by becoming all the goodness of God. He did not believe in healing through prayers. He always went to a doctor when he was sick and had no morbid love of pain. But at last one day, walking barefooted, he was scratched by a piece of sharp tin lying on the road. He limped his way home to the monastery and went to the hut of Turiyananda. "Well," he said, "I hear the flute playing at last. I must go to the tryst with him."

Turiyananda, when he saw the wounded foot, at once sent for a doctor and put Latu to bed. "But," Latu repeated, "it is no use this time. I hear him fluting for me. The doctor cannot prevent my keeping that tryst." In spite of all the efforts the doctors made, gangrene set in. Within a fortnight Latu had walked "between rivers of light and reached the homeland of his beloved."

Thus ends the story of Ramakrishna's unscholarly disciple. He went into meditation and stayed in samadhi the last four days of his illness. He never lost consciousness. "Until he spat away his body," as the monks say, "he remained in complete identity."

10

Description of the Indescribable

What did Ramakrishna mean by "seeing God"? What does samadhi mean? What are the stages of development through which one attains the state of samadhi?

During my course of gathering the Ramakrishna legends, it became more and more necessary to learn of the nature of the spiritual experience that held his disciples to his side. Why is it that such strong healthy young persons never wearied of him? What made them stay near him with so much devotion? What wonders did he show them? How came they to be blind to the attractions of this world? Did Ramakrishna offer them a greater and deeper attraction?

All those questions I put before Swami Turiyananda in Benares. He said in answer,

> Ramakrishna showed us the face of the Eternal. After that we stayed on with him hoping that through his compassion and by training, we would see him again. Once a disciple, always a disciple. Think of the possibility of being thrown into samadhi—a thing for which men and women toil a hundred incarnations—by one single touch of his finger or foot! How could we leave his side, we who were so greedy like all youth to taste bliss Absolute again and again. He enabled us to stare

into the eyes of God at least once; that naturally blinded us to this world. We see nothing here, and whatever we do see is filled with the brimming light of Tat [That]. No matter what we see or feel, it says, "You are he. You are he—*Tat Tvam asi.*" That is what Ramakrishna did to us. After such an event we were tethered to him as the bird is to the sky—it may go very far in many directions, yet it will remain under the many-branched sky.

It is a well-known fact that his chelas often pressed Ramakrishna to describe the indescribable. But he maintained, "God-consciousness cannot be explained through words. Only experience, not phrases, can reveal to you the full magnitude of the Invisible."

But, in spite of that, the devoted group of disciples urged him to speak particularly of his own experience of samadhi, oneness with the Absolute, Brahman.

Ramakrishna asked to be excused. "I cannot see why I should explain it to you whom I have trained and helped to attain that experience. If it can be put into words why do you not do it?" he said.

"But, my Lord," the disciples said, "we cannot live in it as long as you can. You who have stayed in samadhi six, seven days at a time are the one to explain it. In the presence of Silence, how dare we speak?" But Ramakrishna only smiled at their barefaced compliment. Then a very keen-witted young man tried another way of making him speak. "But, my Lord, how do we know that every one of us attains the same experience, when our paths are different. For instance, when I meditate and quicken all my being with the thought of oneness, my spiritual energy does not act the same way as that of another."

"Ah, that is a comparison of the way men's intuition acts," replied the Master. "That is easy to describe. Here," meaning himself, "I experimented on all the ways in order to verify them. But no matter how my spiritual energy acted, at the end it rose to the seventh valley and there I beheld ... "

That instant Ramakrishna passed into samadhi. His breathing stopped. His heart ceased working. His pulse beat no more. Were it not for the even temperature of his body, there would be no way of distinguishing him from a corpse. Of course there was nothing alarming about it; his apostles had seen him in that state very often, for days at a time.

At last, when he came out of samadhi, he resumed his discourse: "Oh, my sons, I try to explain it to you. But the experience is so great, words cannot render it. You must plunge yourself into the waters of that experience. For there is no other way of fathoming it. Your mind and intellect, swift though they are, cannot overtake the lightning-steed of God-consciousness. Those two only raise the dust of words in which they get lost."

"But, my Lord, you said that the ways in which the soul-sight [dharma-eye] rises in a man you can explain."

"Yes," agreed Ramakrishna. He continued,

> Though what the dharma-eye sees is indescribable, the paths it travels are within the reach of words. And though the end is the same, the ways of reaching it are diverse. The rishis [sages] of old have enumerated at least five different ways that the soul-energy of men rises to God when they kindle themselves with prayers and meditation. For instance, sometimes a man's soul-power moves, as the rishis say, like the hop, hop, hop of a toad. Sometimes it runs as a snake glides up a hillside, in flashes and curves. Then, there is still another way. Each cell of your body and every pulse of your heart beat slowly: the regularity of the rhythm with which your intuitions catch fire is slow and inevitable as the march of a row of ants from one food center to another. The fourth way is the way of a bird or birds. You know how birds fly off one tree and move through the air as though they were wandering aimlessly.
>
> Yet they alight on a distant tree that has been in their mind all the while. Similarly, your soul-energy rises and

alights on the Divine when thoroughly quickened by persistent devotion. Each atom of your being seems to fly up on the wings of all-piercing light. It may wander about aimlessly at first. But if you keep on meditating and praying, those wings will bring you to the house of oneness.

The fifth way is quite different from the others. The sages have called it the way of monkeys. You can sometimes see monkeys sitting still, like so many rocks. Then, suddenly, they start leaping and bounding, and they do not stop until they have reached their destination— somebody's mango garden. So acts your spiritual sight. You sit still and meditate day after day, yet nothing happens. But you keep on thinking of oneness with your body, heart, mind, and soul. Let not even a particle of you flag. Concentrate hard until, in the course of two or three years, suddenly your insight leaps from plane to plane, scaling the steepest precipices with the ease of a hawk, then plunges into advaita—oneness with infinite intelligence.

Now Ramakrishna closed his eyes and sat still. Slowly he passed into samadhi. Again his listeners had to wait a long time. It may sound incredible, but the patience with which they waited on their Master surpasses all measurement. On this occasion, nearly an hour passed before Ramakrishna came out of samadhi and resumed his discourse.

"In addition to the different ways a soul climbs to oneness, you must watch for the planes of consciousness that you must traverse. No matter whose meditation—whether of Lord Buddha or of a common man— it must take him across six different valleys, or planes of consciousness, in order to reach the seventh and last. Whether your soul's intuition hops like a toad or flies like a bird, it must behold the seven valleys."

"Is the experience of each one of those valleys the same, no matter how a soul reaches it?" asked one of the disciples.

"Yes," answered the Master. "It is identically the same."

The same disciple questioned him further: "And did you commence your meditation the same way every time? Was your method at all different from what we do?"

Ramakrishna replied,

> There is no difference at all between them. I sat still, as my guru advised me, and purified my thoughts and feelings of all the dross of separation. In my mind, in my heart, in my soul, in every cell of my body I sought his presence. I knew that I was not separate from him. He was in *me*. Hence, I quickened every bit of myself to elicit the hidden Self. "Come forth, O thou sword of immortality, from this thy scabbard." Thus I prayed for days, weeks, and months. At last my insight hopped—hop, hop, hop—it leaped over the embankment of this world and into the waters of the first of the seven valleys. A light utterly unknown, like another sun, shone upon what I perceived. All the things of this earth that I looked upon wore the vesture of Beauty. Everywhere I glanced, beyond and around, beauty and spirituality leaped out of matter like tigers from dark dens. Now I was aware that this was the home of the senses. The sight of so much wonder filled me with terrible appetites. "Possess, possess," they cried. I was seized with an overpowering desire to taste and own all the beauty that lay about me. Just at that moment another cry broke out in me: "Beware, beware of the sinister temptation of this valley!"
>
> No sooner heard than done. I set out to quicken my meditation. I meditated harder and prayed more intensely for release from the first valley. At the end of some months my prayers were answered. The world of the senses tempted me no more: slowly the first valley fell from my consciousness as the skeleton of its prey falls from the eagle's talons.

Now that Ramakrishna had taken the best out of it, he left the first valley behind.

> I had entered the second valley. Here I was not obsessed with the clawing material beauty of what I saw. The light in which the world appeared now was more refined, more subtle, and soothing. I felt happy here. Fragments of beautiful colors, shapes, and sounds haunted and sweetened my hours in this valley. I thought of relaxing my meditation and staying here. Just then I was tempted to create life: "things of sex." For in the sublime light of the second valley, sex wears the appearance of beatitude and power. But no matter how it appears, the soul must resist its temptation. I set out to free my consciousness from the besetting beauty of sex. I heaped more fuel of devotion on the altar of God-quest. The fire of illumination burned very low at first, but gradually became brighter. And in a few more days, lo, it burned like daggers of light. And in those biting flames the second valley burned into cinders. Neither it nor its temptations fretted me further.
>
> Thus I reached the third stage. In this valley I found that the sense of power that I had experienced before, in the second, had increased a hundredfold. Now I felt that I could take the sun between the palms of my hands and crush it into a handful of burning dust. This sense of power must be resisted. It is nothing but a test of character. There is no temptation viler than the sense of power. The instant I had perceived the danger that beset me, I quickened my meditation to the utmost. It had to be more powerful than the power that I had to resist. I prayed—oh! how I prayed—to be free of my sense of power. Like the fangs of a viper it held me. But my soul would not yield to it. I rose on the wings of meditation higher and higher till height had no meaning for me. At that moment the serpent opened its mouth and fell from my side!

Now, like an elephant hurtling through a fence, I plunged into the valley of *hridaya jyoti*, the light of God's heart. As if my heart had become a torch lit by the flame from his, light fell from my soul over everything. Pebbles and stars—all sang with equal radiance a song of the ineffable. In this fourth valley I felt well-nigh secure from every temptation. Yet I kept a strict watch on myself. Though I was a chalice of light, yet I felt suspicious of temptation. That feeling served as a warning. I decided not to tarry here. Thus followed another long period of fasting, prayer, and meditation.

Fortunately this time I did not have to wait so very long. The light in my heart expanded. It flung a vast circle like a net of suns around and beyond. And lo, I had reached the next valley, the realm of utterance. My thoughts and feelings, every pulse and each cell of me was illumined! Through my throat and lips poured words of wonder and benediction. I praised the Lord all the time. Save, of him I could not bear to speak. And if anyone spoke of possessions and pleasures, their words smote me like rods. It got to be so that if any of my relatives came to consult me on family matters I would run away and hide myself in the woods of Panchavati. Relations or friends who sought to own me appeared to me as a deep well dragging me down—I feared to be suffocated in the water below in the dark earth. I felt as though I were drowning in their presence. Only by leaving them could I find peace. In other words, this valley is not full of tolerance and love for all. One must transcend it.

That is why I flung myself into deeper and steeper meditations yet. There was no peace or pleasure for me. "Either find him face to face or take my life," I counseled myself. As a tiger crouches in order to leap, so did I. I prayed; I waited; I watched. I would not linger in the valley of utterance; I must not give in to merely praising God. I must see him. So I sat couchant with prayers.

Suddenly I perceived something ahead. That instant, I leaped—in a trice I was in the sixth, the valley of Turiya. Here I was close to my beloved. I could see and feel him in the next chamber. Only a thin, transparent veil separated the soul from the self. At last I knew that I was in a room in the house of oneness.

From the sixth valley it is not difficult to pass on to the seventh. There, no word can enter, nor the chatter of human thought. Only your soul, clad in silence, can lift the veil that separates him from your embrace.

A long silence fell after Ramakrishna had finished speaking. But instead of meditating the rest of the day on what the Master had said, one of the young men questioned him, "People say that you are ignorant, my Lord, yet how do you know all that the sages of the past wrote? For what you have told us lies buried in tomes of metaphysics. I am told you are an ignorant man."

Ramakrishna answered in a way quite different from his usual answer, "I never studied profound books, but I have heard scholars discuss them. Having heard—and gathering what rang true for my own needs—I made a garland of them and put them around my neck. Then I flung every inch of it at the feet of God saying, 'Mother, take all your erudite tomes and laws. All I want is love of thee!'"

Just at that moment someone raised a very significant question: "My Lord, all that you have told us is pleasing to the soul and satisfying to the heart. But my wayward mind wishes to know this: he who starts his meditation with desire of oneness has to do so by saying, feeling, and realizing—'I am he. I am he!' But what about those who start the opposite way, saying, 'thou art not me, yet I seek thee!' What happens to them, my Lord? Do they too cross those valleys and become one with him, or do they remain separate from him forever?"

Ramakrishna answered without any pause or hesitation: "That is about ultimate matters. But there is no difference whether you call him 'thou' or call him 'I am he.' Men that realize him through 'thou' have a very lovely relation with him. It is very much like that of an old trusted servant with his master. As they both grow old, the master leans and depends on his friend the servant more and more. Toward the end of his life, the master consults his pearl of a servant regarding every serious matter that he wishes to undertake. One day, deeply pleased with his servitor's devotion, the master takes him by the hand and seats him on his own august seat. The servant is embarrassed, and in his excitement says, 'What are you doing, my Lord?' But the master holds him on the throne next to himself saying, 'You are the same as I, my beloved.' So, though we worship God as one apart, yet if we worship him with sincerity and consecration, he will someday very suddenly make us one with himself. That is samadhi."

There is a legend that at one time some friends of Ramakrishna urged him to explain samadhi. They said, "If you say something about it you prove everything. Give us a definition of samadhi, and that will give us a definition of God."

But the wary Holy One replied, "And if I give you a definition of God, what will you do with it? Oh, I know what you will eventually do; you will make a creed of it in order to found a new religion in my name. I did not come to earth to start another cult. Oh, no!"

However, it is reported that on another occasion Ramakrishna incidentally defined God. Some visitors asked him, "Will you please resolve what seems to us a contradiction? People say that you have attained identity: you are he. Yet you go about giving all the credit to the Divine Mother. You never say 'I'; you speak of God, Mother, she, thou. If you are 'I am he,' why do you call God 'thou?'"

The Master answered, "That is the ultimate matter of conduct. I have seen him and embraced him. I was infinite existence, absolute intelligence, and bliss. But I could not stay in that unconditioned state and yet be here in the conditioned. There, there is no limit: each and all are one infinite existence, unconditioned, indescribable. You cannot use words about it. Anything you say becomes finite. Naturally, you say 'thou, she, Mother.' Take the seven scales of music: Suppose you go on mounting—*do, re, mi*—till you reach the highest note; what will you do next? You will come to *do*. Each man, after he has reached silence, the highest pitch, utters *do* the moment he opens his mouth. And *do* is God."

11

A Recent Initiation

In order to afford the reader some knowledge of details, I shall describe the initiation of a friend of mine that took place recently. He and I had not met for the twelve years I was in America, and I had no knowledge that he had renounced the world and was doing certain spiritual exercises in order to attain illumination. Hence I was quite surprised when I saw him one day in the robe of a brahmachari, a novice, on the ferryboat crossing from Calcutta to the monastery. After the first pleasant shock of surprise at meeting him had passed, I looked at my friend's face. It was a sweet face in spite of his square jaw, narrow temples, pug nose, and piercing eyes. It was in the corners of his mouth, notwithstanding his thin, almost sharp, lips, that sweetness dwelt. I felt as surprised at that discovery as the man who found in the nest of a Himalayan eagle not that bird of prey, but a dove.

By now the ferryboat had reached the monastery landing. We got off and walked toward the sacred grounds. There was no time to ask him many questions, but I did ask one. He answered it, and many others, one morning about two months later.

It was about five o'clock in the morning—the day had just broken. He called me to go with him into a dilapidated garden. After meandering through abandoned groves of fruit trees and fragrant bushes, we reached a small enclosure where, under a banyan tree, lay a stone seat. My friend asked me to sit on it. Then he sat on the grass at my feet.

The buzzing of insects and the rising heat of the day were all that one perceived in that spot. There was nothing else to distract us.

My friend shut his eyes for about a quarter of an hour and meditated. I sat there, watching his face. His complexion was olive, his forehead was high. He wore his hair, as all brahmacharis do, cropped very closely. His nose and ears were utterly plebeian. They were a little too thick, it seemed to me, but when I looked at his hands lying open on his lap, I was struck by their length and flowerlike thinness. I noticed the strong and delicate lines in his palms sweeping up and across with a firmness, as if they had been ploughed therein. The tips of his fingers rose like mounts of sensitiveness.

Hardly had I finished reading the lines in his hand when he opened his eyes and shot a glance at me. Now, seeing me embarrassed, he began,

> It was when my father fell ill about eleven years ago that I came to the monastery to pray. I did not know why I was going there. You see, being the only son, and since my mother had died about half a year earlier, the entire care of my father had devolved upon me; it proved an extremely difficult task. But since circumstance rules life, I mustered all my courage and went to work. But every now and then a sense of fatigue would seize me. It was under one of those spells of fatigue that I went to the Ramakrishna Monastery to pray.
>
> There, after I had prayed and performed the arati [evensong], I felt renewed in strength and went home. In a week I exhausted all the joy and strength I had garnered into my soul, so I returned to pray there once more. Again the same joy and strength came into my heart.
>
> It was about my third or fourth visit there that I stumbled upon Swami B——, my guru. He happened to be a friend of my father's. Hence, finding me there, he asked about his health. Then, after I told him how badly my father had been feeling, the swami said to me, "Come

to see me when you feel like it." You know how deep his voice was; it was also resonant like a vast gong. His words smote me like a command. Well, a fortnight after that, my father grew better. He hoped to resume his work at the office soon. I hastened to the monastery and told the good news to the swami. He listened with quiet attention. When my recital was over, he asked me, "What are you going to do with yourself?"

"I do not know, my Lord. But my father wishes to see me married."

"And you, do you wish it?"

After weighing his words in my mind, I answered, "No, I do not wish it."

"Go, and meditate in the inner shrine; no one is likely to be there for the next two hours."

He dismissed me most summarily, I thought. But his command weighed on my mind. So I went into the shrine and meditated until dusk fell, when one of the monks came to prepare for arati. I got up and left. On my way home on the ferryboat I felt certain that I was going to become a monk.

The next day while massaging my father, I said to him that I did not wish to marry because I wanted to be a holy man in order to attain samadhi. I asked him to give me permission to renounce the world. He requested me to tell him my recent experiences. When I had done so my father said, "You can go to the swami tomorrow and tell him from me that you have my permission to renounce the world."

So I went to the monastery the next morning. But the swami was not there. I went every day for a whole week, but found him not. At last, on the tenth day, I camped there from sunrise to sunset. It was about eight o'clock in the evening that he returned from the law courts where he had been giving evidence in a civil suit.

He said to me, as he seated himself on the platform of the ghat: "I told the truth at the law courts but the lawyers believed me not. Like vultures they approach a dead body suspicious that it might be of a man feigning death. A beast becomes an expert of death yet suspects foul play from the dead. Lawyers are so used to extorting truth that when they hear it they dare not recognize it."

Then I told him what my father had desired me to say to the swami. He sat quietly. In the light of the half-moon he appeared very calm and reserved. His voice had no resonance—it hardly rose above a whisper. He ended a short speech with this sentence. "Very well, I will accept you as a brahmachari next month. Think the matter over carefully in the meantime." But, just as I rose to go, he remarked, "Now that your father has given you freedom, what are you going to give him?"

"Give him, my Lord?" I asked.

"Yes. If he is free from selfishness, that ought to bring out unselfishness from you, since like begets like in this world."

I answered not a syllable—I had nothing to say. Quietly I took the dust from his feet and walked out into the dark. Two days before I took the vow of a brahmachari, I went into the inner shrine and meditated for a whole afternoon. The truth suddenly came to me. I went to the swami and said, "My Lord, I cannot be anything but a brahmachari as long as my father lives, for I must serve him."

The swami said, "Good. I am glad to hear of your decision. I shall give you your first vow as I promised. After that you must study and meditate until you are ripe for the final initiation, which takes about ten years. Instead of living with us here these ten years, I give you permission to live with your father whom you love. And in the course of these years, if you decide to marry, do so."

At the end of ten years I returned to the swami and said, "My father is well again and urges me to renounce the world. He says that if I love him I should delay no longer." I will be initiated next week.

"What is this initial vow of a brahmachari under which you have been living?" I asked my friend.

He answered, "I will tell you next week."

About five days later he was initiated. He now wore his ocher-colored robe, and the light that shone on his face was indescribable.

It was during one of those days that he told me the rest of his story in the same dilapidated garden. We stayed there a whole day talking to each other.

My friend said,

> When the swami gave me brahmacharya, I vowed to lead a life of celibacy, truthfulness, and purity in thought, word, and deed. Then he taught me three meditations which are difficult to describe. Let me see … suppose you conceive all life as purity, and exhale purity out of yourself, not only through every one of your brain cells but also between the beats of your heart and through the pores of your body. In the case of great yogis, even the odor of their perspiration changes when they do this.
>
> The second meditation is similar. Suppose that you quicken your senses and emotions to feel that all life is *ahetuki daya sindhu*—causeless currents of love; that is, your life is a strong tide of love uncaused by any motive. After about two or three years, your heart becomes calm as a pool. Your mind grows clear like the eyes of a bird. All activities—even your breathing and eating—are characterized by a deep sanctity. Agitation and anxiety cannot come near you. Your breathing as well as your pulse never quickens, no matter what happens. Your deeds reiterate love that has no cause.
>
> After the second stage you begin to be sentient and possessed of great power. You can do your duties with perfect ease. You overcome all obstacles. You are sensitive to experiences which have been too subtle for you. You can read thoughts and hear silences.

Now you are taught the last meditation: "I renounce all power, even that of love." That was hard. It took me nearly five years. To renounce yourself is easy—but to renounce your unconscious thoughts and habits is difficult. Even your dreams must be purged of any sense of power and odor of miracles. Absolute surrender of yourself to the one Self. You cannot do it alone. The teacher must pray and meditate with you—though you be at home over there and he in the monastery here. You gradually find out that not only he, but others, strangers, are helping you. Who are they? They are the spiritual forces of life itself. As when you do evil, evil forces of life draw toward you, so, when you try to achieve self-less good, the good tendencies of life come to your aid. It is a supreme lesson in invisible cooperation.

Thus, through the help of others, and by your own efforts, you reach the threshold of reality. Your holy man sends for you, for you are ripe for initiation at last. It is absolutely necessary to raise your concentration to the highest power. Your master invites you to meditate with him, for he knows that you are ready. Many other holy men are invited to witness your last plunge. As all of them go on meditating on the same identical truth, you gradually feel the presence of Tat [That] precipitated in your midst. As if the Lord, unable to resist such devotion, had come down to reward it by uncovering his face. Just that instant your guru touches the middle of your spine with his forefinger. That rends the veil. Lo! With these mortal eyes you see the face of Immortality. The whole universe is bathed in light! Everything—from the dust of the road to the flight of a bird—throws away its vesture of appearance, and stands out like blades of bliss. Things are no more things, for they have become essences.

Here my friend stopped. He would speak no more. The silence that he had been alluding to seemed to rise between us. I waited for it to pass. After a long while when I felt that no sanctities were hovering about us, I asked my friend the question that seemed most important to me.

"Thank you," I said, "for what you have told me. But truly I do not want to know what you see or think. What I really want to know is how you feel."

"Feel?" asked my friend in bewilderment.

"Yes," I asked, "do you feel happy or unhappy? Do you feel one with the world, or apart from it? Are you hurt? Or—"

"I understand," he exclaimed with pleasure.

> Though I feel happy, I am acutely conscious of pain. I am aware of the pang that things and men and women inflict on one another. As an illustration of that, let me describe to you Ramakrishna's experience. In the early days of his illumination, when he had not quite mastered its force, he felt so one with the world that he bore marks of its pleasure and pain.
>
> One day, full of oneness, he was standing on the riverbank where a boat was moored. In a few minutes two of the boatmen started to quarrel. They struck each other. Ramakrishna, who was at least twenty yards away, yelled with pain. Then he ran into the Kali temple and prayed to the Mother: "Take away the sting of their quarrel from my body and soul. It hurts me so!" Hriday, his nephew, who had heard Ramakrishna's cry, hastened to find him. After looking about when he reached the temple, at last he found the Master crying and praying, "O Mother, remove the pain that is hurting the world. Free all of them from pain and hurt." Then, seeing Hriday, he stopped praying and showed him the bruises on his own body. Hriday says that he cannot obliterate from his memory the terrible red stripes and black bruises on the Master's body. He also says that Ramakrishna was full of pain and bliss at the same time. Can you understand the contradictory nature of that state? If you can understand the Master's large experience, you will understand the petty

one that is mine. How do I feel? I feel so blissful that all the pain of beings and things that I see and perceive is mine. I am so close that I am identical with them. Yet I am apart. While I feel the pangs of their being, I go on feeling the bliss that is beyond their reach.

Let me quote Sankara, who has a fine description of such an experience: "As the clouds pass and repass in the sky, so do all the experiences fall within the soul in oneness. And since all the black clouds cannot tarnish its emerald calm, so the pains and passions of the world cannot trouble the serenity of an illumined soul."

The pain of the world, a holy man masters, and is not mastered by it. The difference between a holy man and a common soul in pain is that the former transcends it by his own power of vision and insight, while the latter has to have it removed from without.

Though my friend had told me his story very simply, after he had left me, it raised some questions in my mind that needed answering. Fortunately a day or two later I came across an old holy man who helped me over my difficulties. Let me describe it as it happened in life.

It was on a summer night. The sky was clear. The stars hung low. Behind them there was an almost tangible haze like a veil of silver. Beyond it a shimmer of light like dust of gold that throbbed, then faded under the steep blue-black vault. The stars were so near and the heavens so far! Below about us hung a jet-black stillness which was broken by the occasional muttering noise of the palm fronds and the *ka-la, ka-la, ka-la,* a cry of the Ganges flowing at our feet.

The man who sat next to me was old. I had seen his gray hair and hollow cheeks in daylight. I had also heard him expounding the *Bhagavata* in a classroom that afternoon. What he had said impressed me. It was because of that that I had brought him to the riverbank. So I asked him my questions about initiations in general and his own initiation in particular. I asked him, "What did it do to you?"

"Let us begin at the beginning," he remarked. "First of all, you wanted to know about the final touch."

I said in agreement, "Yes, why does the master help his disciple to experience oneness? A man ought to win it by his own efforts."

After saying something to himself under his breath, the old man began: "The purpose of a holy man's life is to find God through his own efforts. But how can you find him without getting some glimpse of him ahead of time? Our form of initiation gives the initiate a brief look into the interior of his spirit's home. Once he has had that vision, no matter through whose assistance, he will always be homesick for it. And that nostalgia for another vision of God will enable him to look above this world the rest of his life. He will not be tempted by the tawdry world of time. That vision makes him safe from all except God, such is the power of it. That is why one has no right to take a disciple and train him if he cannot give his chela at least a temporary experience of oneness with the Beloved."

"Can anyone," I questioned him further, "be given that experience by the touch of a real holy man?"

"Oh, no. There are souls that are ripe, and souls that are not." The holy man explained, "Even Ramakrishna himself could not give it to some souls. One time there came to him a fellow called Kaviraj—a sharp apothecary and doctor. He used to come and pray for training. But Ramakrishna maintained a certain coolness toward him. One day Kaviraj said, 'Why don't you give me your touch?' He repeated the question. At last brought to bay, Ramakrishna yielded. He gave the fellow the last touch—it is given by the holy man at a certain moment by bringing his forefinger in contact with the middle part of the novice's spine. No sooner had Ramakrishna touched him than Kaviraj howled and danced with pain. It was ghastly. The pain of the body is a picture of joy compared with the sight of a man literally screaming with pain in his soul. Ramakrishna then seized him in his arms and rubbed the poor fellow back to his normal state. Then he added, 'Not this life, my son. The touch of bliss has become cobra's venom in you. You are not ripe yet. Go on praying and meditating until you are. And when you have ripened yourself, if there is no one here, God himself will come to earth to initiate you.'"

Now I asked the old holy man another question: "But this final touch, is it not a sort of hypnotism?" Apparently he was not ready for it. In order to answer me, he waited and thought the matter over in his mind.

At last, nearly a quarter of an hour later, he said, "Hypnotism is quite different from the touch of a master. Hypnotism is the impression of the will of one man upon another. In an initiation, the disciple's will is not overcome but increased by his own meditations. He meditates and prays with eyes and ears shut. He breathes very slowly and rhythmically. His mind and heart are not kindled from outside. He goes inward to his self. Hour after hour he pierces his way into the heart of silence. At last the teacher who has been sitting near him—with his eyes and ears shut—gives him the touch. That instant the initiate finds his own Self as the mother of all the realities of the world. In other words, the whole process, both for the master and the disciple, is not at all external. And the touch of the master does not cause the disciple to lose his consciousness. On the contrary, the latter becomes all the more keenly conscious of joys and sufferings of men, women, beasts, and plants around him. How different from a hypnotic state! When a man attains illumination he becomes the willpower and the consciousness of all that are. His will, instead of becoming quiescent, becomes the will of the whole universe. His discrimination grows ever sharp, his character ever moral, his taste infallible, and his vision limitless."

After the holy man had stopped, the palm fronds muttered a little more loudly, making the air overhead full of eerie sounds while the Ganges, like a sharp knife, went on cutting the roots of the embankment on which we sat. An owl hooted and flew over us. I thought out my final question with care, then asked, "My lord, now I understand what illumination does to a man. But what is the difference between illumination and samadhi?"

The holy man cast a glance at the distant stars. Then at the twinkling lights of the city far to the south. He said, "The word *illumination* is vague. You recall that there are three stages of spiritual realization. First of all, a soul sees itself as the adorer of the Infinite. Through that adoration, it finds fulfillment, claiming nothing for itself and investing him with all.

> Thou art the path,
> And the goal that paths never reach;
> Thou art the lawful Lord
> In whom laws are lost
> Like rivers in the sea.
>
> Thou feedest and sustainest
> All that one sees, or seems;
> Yet thou art ever hungry for love,
> And there is no end to thy thirst for peace.
>
> Though all time is as mail on thy nakedness;
> Though all space sandal thy feet,
> Yet they are torn by the thorns of my prayers,
> And thy body is pierced with bliss.
>
> All-healer, yet all wounds,
> All-life, yet ever-dying,
> All-praised, yet praiseless,
> All-ending, yet no end for thee!
>
> Thou art the agony of men,
> Thou art the cry of the wounded beast,
> Thou art the haughty mountain
> And the eagle swooping down its side.
>
> The unborn that sings under its mother's heart,
> The battle cry of the newborn child;

Temple of Sri Ramakrishna at Belur Math

The song in the throat of the lover
And the pang of joy that brims in the eye of a bride.

Thou art the curve-pattern that bird wings make in
    the sky,
Thou art the trembling grass
And the tiger that creeps under it.

Thou art the dark door of death,
Thou art the anguish of disease,
Thou the fear of the frightened,
And the secret shame of pride.

In the reed the song,
In the string the tune,
Of the drum its beat.

Thou art the taste in water,
Thou art the light in sun and moon,
The sounds fading into silence,
And the sanctity of sacred books.

Thou art the diadem of Beauty,
Thou art the crown of Truth,
Thou art the scepter of Reality,
Thou art good that destroys evil,
And holiness that vanquishes good.

"That," commented the holy man, "is the first stage of illumination. The second level of the experience is attained when the devotee no longer feels and adores God but thinks himself a part of him. With the exception of Ramakrishna, that is as far as the usual guru's touch can take any disciple. This is the farthest reach of what is called illumination. In that state you, as a part of God, are so highly conscious that all things live with you in God: you are aware of yourself as well as the selves of others with equal fullness. That is the furthest that illumination can take you. But when you attain samadhi, you go beyond. Words cannot describe how far beyond you go. You recall that line in the Upanishads,

'*Aham asmi prathamaja ritasya*—I am more ancient than the effulgent gods. For I am the firstborn of the essences. I am the artery of immortality, Amritsya Nabhai!'

"That is what happens to one when he attains samadhi: he becomes that artery of Immortality, which feeds and sustains all the other realities of experience. Though in that state your heart stops beating, and your mind seems extinguished, yet you are more alive and more conscious than ever before, because you have become the sap of Truth that nourishes all."

"Could Ramakrishna—could he not—give you an experience of samadhi?" I asked.

He answered, "He is the only master that could. Not any other holy man had the same abundance of spirituality as he. Others gave you illumination. But his touch lifted you on the highest plane of samadhi. Now you understand, my son," concluded the holy man, "that illumination is unity with all the realities, while samadhi is your identity with the *One* Reality in all."

He looked all round, at the river, the far-off city, and the heavens above. "The night has advanced far. It is time for sleep. Farewell, my son." He rose to go. "Samadhi should be experienced. It can't be explained." Now he lifted his face to the stars and chanted, "O Night, thou mirror of Silence … " Then, turning to me, he whispered, "Samadhi is your realization of that oneness that turns your Self into the matrix of the universe: *Nityo nityanam* …

> The eternal behind all eternal,
> The consciousness that crouches behind all
> consciousnesses,
> The One that is caught, then slips out of the many,
> The taller than the tallest,
> The minuter than the minutest,
> That cry of silence
> In the clamor of realities.
> The Truth of all truths,
> And the Godhood of God."

12

Holy Man or Incarnation of God

The best testimony that I have read of Ramakrishna's holiness is from the pen of the late Swami Premananda. He died before I reached the monastery, so the only way that I could touch the hem of his garment was through his writings. But I must say a word about the man, even secondhand, before I translate his epistles.

He was a very haughty brahmin before he met his Master. Though not so stately as Vivekananda and Turiyananda, he was a man of great charm. His Roman nose, strong mouth, and square chin betokened a man of action and decision. But that side of his features was fully balanced by his spacious brow and compassionate eyes. "Whenever he looked at people, he poured love into them," say those who knew him.

In his early youth, Premananda developed great independence of character. While he was studying at the university, he paid frequent visits to the Holy One of Dakshineswar despite all the advice of his parents and the ridicule of his friends. The very first time the Master saw him he asked Premananda, "My boy, have you thought out where you belong?" Premananda made no answer at the time.

One afternoon five months later Premananda brought his parents with him and said to the Master, "I know where I belong, I have brought my parents so that they can see with their own eyes what kind of a holy man I wish to serve." From that day, he was given lessons in meditation until he was initiated about six years later. After he had attained soul-illumination, his new name was revealed. He abandoned the homely name of Baburam that his parents had given him, and from then on he was called Premananda—bliss of love.

Though all-embracing, he showed his love in its fullness to the younger generation, in whom he took the most painstaking interest. Not only did he help them to solve their spiritual problems, but he also aided them in their athletic activities. If the young boys needed a football field, they went to him and he always secured one for them; if they needed boats to row on the Ganges, it was he who commandeered them from the monastery. Because of this, every young man of our generation who knew Premananda loved him. Though he was past fifty, and my contemporaries were only lads of sixteen or seventeen, his relation to them was that of a captain to his football team.

I did not know him personally, but what I heard of him all those years endeared him to me. So it was natural that I should be deeply elated when I came upon Premananda's written testimony about Ramakrishna. I hastened to translate it. It is necessary to mention that Premananda was no lukewarm believer. He believed Ramakrishna to be an incarnation of God and placed him on the same level with Jesus and Buddha. Yet he was fully aware of the difference between his Master and the other two. For he says:

> The present incarnation of God radiates renunciation in every shape and form. Each one of God's incarnations has its peculiarity. Think of feeding five thousand souls to repletion with five loaves of bread, walking on water, ascending to heaven, making trees bear fruit to feed multitudes.
>
> But such strange characteristics I fail to see in the new incarnation: Ramakrishna does no miracle.
>
> Then behold this: almost all previous incarnations

shed a glow of beauty that filled the world. But Rama-krishna lacks even that. When Girish asked the Master, "Why no glory of form this time?" The Blessed One answered, "In my days of prayer and penance I prayed:

> I want no physical beauty or glory, O Mother,
> Give me only illumination of the soul!"

He lacked beauty of form; also beauty of mind, for he was no scholar. Other incarnations before him con-founded the learned men of their time at a very early age. Buddha exhausted all the learning of his time only to despair of salvation, and that he milked the udders of the Upanishads there is no doubt. Lo! Our incarna-tion—by straining all his intellect and gasping with the last breath of his mind—all he could do was to read and write a little. Yet scholars used to crawl away from him to hide their scholarship. His effect on them was that of the sun on owls. Why did they crawl away like earth-worms into the darkness of the earth? Because he came from where their discussions could not reach. You can-not conceive all of the holy city, Benares, by looking at its map. Only he who is the citizen of the eternal—Benares the timeless—knows it. Ramakrishna knew how to unlock every door of the Timeless for he held the key of Immortality in his hands.

Ramakrishna had another peculiarity. Other incar-nations preached their respective beliefs. But he never preached a belief. One night, long past the middle of it, I heard him walk up and down the veranda, spitting. I went out to find what was happening to him. He was spitting, and praying thus: "O Mother, do not bring me honor by bringing me creed-believers. Propound no creed through me." Then he said to me, "Don't run after name and fame. Go across the dirty waters of all fame and all names—reach the shore of the Nameless. Let people come to get what they want from you; then they must go away. Be like a flower—blossom to your fullness. Let the bees rifle your heart. May the world be enchanted; but hold none captive by the beauty of your soul."

Other incarnations have insisted on their own light, and there have been some who held theirs to be the only light. But our Lord says, "As many lights as there are devoted pilgrims! If he is infinite, the roads to him must be infinite also." Ramakrishna lived so that he elicited the inner truth of every religion. And we are here not to quarrel about our differences, but to find God. If we lose him, we shall sink in a sea of torture, sin, and pain. Therefore find him by all means. Why bother about roads?

Enter the garden, eat its sweet mangoes, and depart. You did not enter the garden to count the leaves on the mango tree. Why waste time discussing whether worship of God should be through idols or without idols? Is he with form or without it? It does not matter whether the theory of reincarnation is all sound.

If you want to know of the eternal city, then ask those who have been to Benares. Having heard all they have to say, go forth, enter, and be its citizen. But if you stay at home and discourse, "The sacred city is thus. Oh! No, it is not thus," you may go on that way for a thousand times, yet it will bring you not even a hair's breadth nearer Benares. Whether I was born here before or not has no relation to the resolve that I will see him here and now in this life. Rigid belief in a creed is not helpful, but may do harm to your soul. If you know him you won't be bothered by religious doctrines! You may read and believe all the scriptures and revealed words of all the sons of God, yet you will not be able to find God. You must rise above books and teachers; and behold him whom they beheld. Then all the mysteries will suddenly unlock their secrets to you!

He, your Self, has the key. Beg for his compassion.

Consecrate your life to him. God is not to be trapped by the regimentation of rituals. He wants to be caught by your heart, by your longing, by your sincerity.

However, along with his peculiarity, each incarnation embodied for the world a certain ideal. Not that he lacked other ideals. But it was always one of them that dominated the rest. Buddha embodied the ideal of living without earthly desires and dreams. He was unattached through and through. He was so unattached that he did not even want salvation for himself. He wanted others to have it.

After Buddha came Sankara, the ideal of wisdom. When a mere stripling he was asked by his teacher, "Whence do you come; who are you; whither bound?" Sankara answered:

> I am not in the senses, nor in the mind.
> I am not in touch, nor am I taste;
> Breathing and beating of the heart
> Even they can hold me not;
> Eyes that see, see me not;
> Ears that hear, hear not my silence!
> For I am not the earth, nor in the air;
> The light that scorches, and the spaces of ether,
> Even they are tongue-tied when they seek to name
>   me;
> For I am infinite knowledge,
> I am life that is behind the living,
> I am the Absolute,
> Existence infinite …
> I am Bliss.

Sankara embodied wisdom. And to fulfill that wisdom later came the incarnation of love—Chaitanya. They, all the incarnations, imply each other. While the rabble think, they quarrel. To end all such quarreling came Ramakrishna. He has verified all the religions by his living and bound them together by their common aim: realization of God. It is because he was so full of love and compassion that Ramakrishna became the embodiment of tolerance and insight. His compassion was shown when he made a pilgrimage to Benares. Seeing the poor and the destitute, he said to the rich man who took him there, "I will not go hence to see the holy of holies until these are fed and clothed." Again, when he was dying of cancer of the throat, one day no one came to ask him for food, shelter, or spiritual light. It made him forget his pain: he wailed, "How I suffer because none have needed my help today."

He, who had to give up speaking and eating, yet cried aloud for others! Such was his compassion. I have seen, watched, and nursed him a year and a half. Each and every day he thought of someone to help.

He was never idle—always at work, gardening, or sweeping the rooms; petty little miscellaneous work of the monastery he did without losing the purpose of his life. He disliked disorder. He even taught me how best to fill a pan leaf with nuts and *chunam*. He was so practical.

He did not accept any religious teaching on hearsay. He proved its merits through practice. And that is why all religions led him to the same God.

Not only through all religions, but in all beings he saw the Lord. He had no preferences. He was intoxicated with the love of all creatures. He never succumbed to forming groups and denominations. He who sees God in all, and all things in God, needs no creed to fence himself in. The jewel of spirituality needs no casket. And the day we, the sons of Ramakrishna, go in for doctrines and creed-mongering will be our last hour before darkness and downfall. A river needs no fences. Only ponds are fenced in. No wonder they become poisoned in time. He has warned us against such sinister evils as saying about ourselves "We are Ramakrishnites. No soul can be saved without Ramakrishna, therefore all must embrace Ramakrishnaism." Beware of such quarrels! Beware!

Our scriptures say that holiness gives one power over one's entire self. Had you seen him you would have believed it. He had perfect dominion over each vein, each cell, and every blood corpuscle of his body. Though his throat pained him excruciatingly, when we wanted to wash it with medicine, yet were afraid to inflict further pain on him, he would say, "Wait ... now wash." Then he would remove his consciousness from that spot. Though we would do all that medical science ordered, he would feel no pain. It is because he controlled all of his body, heart, mind, and soul. Like all full-grown yogis, he could suspend the action of his heart and yet live. He could withdraw consciousness from any part of his self. I am not telling stories. I have witnessed with mine own eyes what I am setting down here.

Yet he lived in his body. How could he do it? He answered me once: "A fully realized soul, no matter who, lives as little in the body as does the meat inside a dried up fruit—just clinging slightly to one side of the skin."

He had no caste and said, "Devotees of God are beyond any caste." Sometimes I saw him unable to eat food offered by the high and mighty because the food was not offered by a pure heart. But sometimes he would eat from the plate of an outcast. One such outcast said, "Don't, sir, don't—I have eaten forbidden food." But Ramakrishna went on eating and said, "Your food is pure because your heart is sinless." If anybody offered him anything wishing for a boon, he never accepted it. Yet at the same time he could not abide those who were puritans, suffering from a perpetual fear of contamination. "Too much concentration on purity becomes a plague. People stricken with that fell disease find it hard to think of God."

One of our fellow disciples felt himself too weak to follow the spiritual path. He came to Ramakrishna and unburdened his heart's secret. The Master said, "Very well, *vakil-at-nama* [give me the power of attorney to represent you before God]." Now this is the severest thing to do, for it demands the strictest sincerity on the part of the giver. If he is sincere through and through, then his master can work for him. For the man who has such sincerity has so much power that he can command anything. That is what really happens. Ramakrishna said, "To give your master the task of realizing God for you is to renounce yourself so that you grow totally indifferent to the material world of good and evil!"

About books on philosophy and religion—he had a book with him entitled *Salvation—Its Realization*. We used to read it to him. He explained his love of books thus: "As long as you read about him, you are in his mood. You cannot meditate all the time, so fall back on the second-best thing—reading about him. Since the zephyr does not blow from the sea to cool you, you had better fan yourself with a fan."

About places of pilgrimage, he held that "he who has no God within will not find him in a holy city. He who has the Lord in his heart will find him there. Men bring sanctity with them to a place and make it holy. It is men's purity that makes a place of pilgrimage, otherwise how can a place purify a man?"

So with the blessings of Ramakrishna, sink yourselves in spirituality and do not stop sinking till you find the bottom—him. God is not to be found by discussion, but through realization. We must realize him in our present life and by every possible means. Without him there is no pathway to bliss. And nothing on earth can give you peace without him.

Premananda's paper ends here. He has perfect faith that Ramakrishna was an incarnation of God. But what about those who do not share that faith? Ramakrishna himself answers: "All pathways lead to the same God." And one of the laws the monastery lays down is this: "He who believes Ramakrishna to be a mere holy man is just as right as he who calls him an incarnation of God." And if I were to give any advice to the reader, I should say that it does not matter what anybody says; what really matters is the life that Ramakrishna lived. If the example of that life does not quicken our spirituality then no amount of words about him and from him can make any difference.

13

Ramakrishna and a Wayward Soul

Of Ramakrishna's many disciples, Girish Ghosh, the playwright, proved to be the most difficult. He was recognized as a man of genius before he was thirty. It was about that time that he lost his wife, and with her his faith in God. "How can God exist if he lets perish those who are young and beautiful?" He did not rest with such a question. He studied all the religions of the world for an answer to it. But they failed to satisfy him. Of course, in the meantime his companionship with the Bohemians of Calcutta theaters went on undermining his moral powers. It was about five years after his wife's death that, finding no solace in religion, Ghosh flung himself into unlimited dissipation. In a short time he became known as a drunkard. What looked strange to most people is that under the influence of liquor, he wrote two religious plays that ran for five years. Though he found little in any faith to sustain him, he found in the life of religious teachers abundant inspiration for his plays such as *Buddha*, *Chaitanya*, and *The Medieval Saint Vilwamangal* (based on the life of Tulsidas), which has been adapted into English and published under the title *Chintamani—The Quest of the Infinite*.

In all those plays Girish had a thesis to maintain, namely, "Religions are dreary and hard, but religious men are inspiring and compassionate." It was his study of the lives of the saints that made him all the more curious to find one in real life. Girish, whenever he was sober, searched for a holy man that measured up to his expectations. Though most of the holy men he met disappointed him, he kept an open mind on the matter.

At last one of his friends brought him the news that there was a holy man living at Dakshineswar who would satisfy his curiosity. There is a legend that Girish got gloriously drunk before he set out to meet Ramakrishna. No doubt he did that in order to annoy the man of God whom at their first meeting he insulted again and again. He said repeatedly, "I don't care for God, and what's more, though drinking is a sin, I drink just to show what I think of your God."

Ramakrishna answered, "But drink to God. Maybe he too drinks."

Girish demanded angrily, "How do you know?"

Ramakrishna answered, "If he did not drink, how could he have created this topsy-turvy world?" That took all the wind out of the sails of Girish.

Then he asked, "What is a guru?"

Ramakrishna answered, "A guru is a man who introduces another man to God. What's more, you have a guru of your own if you would consent to recognize him." This particular hint was utterly lost on the inebriated Girish.

Yet in order to give time for the thought to sink into the mind of Girish, Ramakrishna changed the subject by requesting, "Let me visit your theater, please."

Girish answered, "Very well, you are welcome any day you choose." After Girish had taken his departure, some critical soul said to the Master: "What a vile fellow! What do you find in him?"

"A great devotee of God," was the Blessed One's cryptic answer.

In a few days Ramakrishna went to see Girish act in one of his plays. At the end of the play, Girish took all the curtain calls, for he was a vain man. Later on, when the Holy One came to the green room to offer him his modicum of praise, Girish, full of audacity, said to him in a voice of studied modesty: "I am so glad that my acting has pleased you. Can you tell me what it lacks?"

Ramakrishna, without the slightest haste or hesitation, gave this opinion: "You are suffering from crookedness of soul."

Girish questioned eagerly, "How can I lose it, my Lord?"

The Master advised: "You need religion badly."

Those words annoyed Girish. He, who had never taken anyone's advice before, was so enraged by Ramakrishna that he lost his temper, and forthwith called the Master all the names with which his drunkard's mind was fertile. In a few moments it became quite apparent that the Blessed One had expected something of the sort, for there he stood, calm as a log, listening to Girish. When the latter had finished, Ramakrishna spoke a word of blessing, then left for Dakshineswar. Of course, the very next morning Girish sent one of his intimate friends to Ramakrishna to pray for forgiveness on his behalf. That emissary of his knew the Teacher too well to plead for forgiveness. Instead, he said, "Girish is too great a man to perish of drink, my Lord."

The Master answered, "But he uses such hard words."

"You must bear them," answered the friend.

That made the Master smile. He asked, with a twinkle of mischief in his eye, "Suppose he beats me to death?"

The friend answered, "That too you will bear, my Lord. He can't give you what he has not got. He gives abuse and violence as a snake gives out venom."

On hearing Girish's friend speak thus, Ramakrishna requested, "Get me a carriage at once, please. I must go and see him! Can you take me to his home?"

When he reached the house, he found Girish very tipsy. But Ramakrishna spoke to him with as much regard for his judgment as if he were talking to a sober man. That produced the desired effect on Girish.

Instead of losing his temper, he listened to the Holy One's speech. The latter stayed with him until he fell sound asleep.

From that day on, Girish became attached to Ramakrishna. But just the same, he could not give up drinking, nor could he eschew the company of his Bohemian friends.

The tactics that Ramakrishna used on him are worth recording. One day Girish came to Dakshineswar in his carriage. He was quite sober. Seeing him coming through the garden, Ramakrishna said to one of his chelas: "I see he is sober, but there is a flask of liquor in his carriage. You fetch it to me in secret." Girish came and seated himself in the Master's presence, who was discoursing on the Lord. The hours passed rapidly, and with their passage Girish grew thirstier and thirstier. At last, unable to bear it any longer, he rose to go to his carriage. But Ramakrishna stopped him: "You do not have to fetch it. I had it fetched. Here is the flask. Drink, my son."

From that day on, Girish drank less and less. And years later, when he drank no more, he is reported to have said, "You know why I gave up drinking. It is because my guru, Ramakrishna, never commanded me to. He not only gave us holiness, but also freedom. He asked us to do nothing for his sake."

But Girish's problem was more than drunkenness. His real difficulty lay in his horror of austerity. He longed to realize the Lord, yet he would not pray or meditate. People knew that he was impatient, and too fond of pleasure to perform any of the difficult rites prescribed in the scriptures.

As his intimacy with Ramakrishna increased, instead of finding peace of mind, he felt more and more troubled. Once he asked, "Suppose I give up the company of my Bohemian friends. Shall I do it for the sake of my religion?"

"No. That is not necessary. You must not give up the fallen," advised the Master. "God comes to earth for them. Are you purer than God?"

The very next time he came to see the Master, he asked, "Shall I give up drinking? Would not that bring me nearer God?"

"Your giving up anything will not get you far if you do not meditate and pray. You drink less and less every day; has that brought you nearer the Lord? You cannot hoodwink the Absolute by such theatrical acts."

"What am I to do? I can't pray. I can't meditate."

Ramakrishna suggested no other remedy that day, so Girish took his leave. The following fortnight he made every effort to pray and meditate on the Beloved. Alas! it did not succeed. At last he felt desperate. "This business of prayer must be settled one way or another." Saying so, he dressed himself in the height of style, as was his wont, and set out for Dakshineswar, for he wanted speech with his guru.

He found the latter in his room, surrounded by some disciples. Ramakrishna, who was talking to them, interrupted himself and spoke to Girish directly. It did not take him long to learn of Girish's trouble. He also gathered from the wretched fellow's lips that he had become desperate; he said that he preferred suicide to prayers and meditation.

"But, Girish, I am not asking you to do too much. Just think of the Lord a moment before eating your meals, and once before going to sleep. I think if you sincerely carry out those rites, that will be enough. Can you not do that?"

After a long pause, Girish answered with fearful finality: "I cannot do that, my Lord. I am an artist. I do not know when I eat, nor where I sleep." He pondered again awhile. After carefully weighing every word, he said, "I hate routine. I cannot stand hard and fast rules. I won't pray; I won't meditate. I cannot think of God even for one moment."

Those words made Ramakrishna think awhile. Then he said, "If you want to see the Lord, but will not take a single step forward to meet him, there is only one choice left. Can you give me *vakil-at-nama* [power of attorney]?"

"Power of attorney? What do you mean, my Lord?" questioned the bewildered Girish.

Ramakrishna explained, "I mean give me the right to pray for you. Do you want me to pray for you? From now on, be a true artist, eating what is given, sleeping where you can, asking nothing of anybody. You have no responsibility of any kind. Accept everything that happens, and ask for nothing for yourself. You must live by this rule: *Tvaya hrishikesha hridisthitena, yatha niyuktosmi tatha karomi* [as thou willest from within me, O subtle Master, so shall I do]. Promise to live absolutely at the mercy of the Lord."

Girish agreed and gave his guru the power of attorney then and there. He resolved to live "like a leaf, at the mercy of the sun and the wind; or, like a kitten, utterly dependent on the mother cat who might bring her charge up in a royal bed or in a garbage can. Complete resignation!"

Ramakrishna was a hard taskmaster. He now began to train Girish in his new attitude. It was difficult for Girish to demand nothing of anybody. Day after day, this Bohemian had to go without what he wanted until it was given to him. But he stuck to his promise to Ramakrishna. One day in his company the Master heard Girish say, "I will do this."

"What did you say, Girish?" questioned Ramakrishna. "You have no will to do the slightest act of selfishness. You are not to do anything, for I have the power of attorney. Remember, you live and move as the Lord within you wills. I am praying for you, but all my prayers will be set at naught if you do not renounce all initiative."

From that time on, a great change began to work in Girish. He saw that to surrender one's responsibility to another is to surrender one's self to the Self of the Universe, which forces one to live without any desire for personal happiness. But, headstrong as ever, he stuck to his promise, and by doing so he grew very religious. And in a short time he became one of the important spiritual forces of his time. He toiled at his art all the harder. No doubt because of that he became our greatest modern dramatist—in fact there is none between him and Kalidasa, Bhavabhuti, and Vyasa of the classical age.

Not only was he our greatest modern playwright, he was also a great actor and producer. It was he who revealed to the women of the underworld that they could change their lives for the better by taking up acting as a trade. He saved many wretched souls by training them to act. Not only that, he also lifted up and revealed to the eyes of the public at least half a dozen actresses of the highest rank, who had been hitherto condemned to a life of vice, while boys played the parts of women on the stage. Since Girish, all that has been changed.

One of his star actresses, now an old woman, called on my wife and myself and told us how "Father"—that is what she called Girish—worked. "He brought about a revolution in the life of womanhood in general. Women in terrible penury, instead of being forced down into the abyss of vice, were now rescued by the stage. But Father did not stop there. He brought us all in touch with the teachings of Ramakrishna. He wanted us to come to the monastery during the hours of worship and pray to God. Some of us were afraid, lest we soil the sacred grounds. Father answered: 'If Ramakrishna were living he would teach you and me himself. He loves us. Didn't he come to earth for the fallen like ourselves?'"

Our talks with many other old actors and actresses convinced us that Girish, by staying with his old Bohemian companions, did more spiritual good than if he had left them. After his soul's second birth, he did not act like a moral parvenu; he repudiated nothing of his past. Instead, he slowly permeated his friends and his writings with the spirit of Ramakrishna. And as for the power of attorney that he gave his Guru, Turiyananda and others testify that he never violated it. All of them affirm, "Girish was the most religious of us all: he lived, as he said he would, by the promptings of the Indweller." Even at death's door, he did not forget the power of attorney, for with his last breath he prayed: "This madness of matter is a terrible veil—remove it from mine eyes, O Ramakrishna!"

14

Mahaprasthan or Last Journey

I have already alluded to the fact that around 1885 it became quite clear that Ramakrishna was stricken with cancer of the throat. The Master reiterated to his disciples that the time was fast approaching when he would not be in their midst. No doubt that intimation saddened them all, and in order to rise to the occasion, all of them intensified their spiritual practices considerably. Vivekananda, the leading spirit of the band, urged them thus: "The Master is seriously ill. Who knows how long he will remain in the body? Let us strive hard to serve him by more prayers and meditation. If we do not work hard now, we shall repent after he is gone. Let us not waste our time in working out our petty human plans. Let not desire and worldliness fasten their tentacles upon us. Let us toil till we live divinity, breathe divinity, and act the will of God."

As soon as it was established that the Master was incurably sick, people began to come to him and urge him to cure himself miraculously. Each one of them said, "Master, if you are a saint, you can heal yourself."

Ramakrishna, whose throat hurt him every time he spoke, said to them, "Why make such silly proposals? This, here"—meaning himself—"was given up to God once and for all. How can I, or anyone, stoop to withdraw it?"

During this period of sickness, Ramakrishna concentrated almost all his attention on his own disciples. "This disease marks out the inner group from the outer. Those who have renounced all, live here. They belong to the inner mansion. They must strive together and create the Being that will inspire men and women for centuries to come."

Though the disease progressed rapidly during the ensuing year, he spared himself no pain: he instructed his band of chelas. He poured into their minds and souls all that he had within himself. Since no solid food could pass through his throat, he drank a little milk now and then. But milk could not sustain that tall frame of his, and the more his strength failed, the more he imposed hard spiritual practices on his disciples.

That was particularly so in the case of Vivekananda and the Holy Mother, for on them rested the leadership of the rest. The Master said to them, "I leave them in your care."

Within a year and a half, the terrible disease wrought ghastly ravages in the Master's body. At last, the end was in sight. Even then people came to urge him to do the miracle of curing himself. Not only outsiders, but also one or two of his disciples urged him to do so. But he answered them, "I cannot cure myself, for I have no will of my own. It is God's will now."

Every day it grew more and more difficult to make him lie in bed. He wished to sit up and speak to them—to unburden himself of all that he had realized. He sat in bed, propped up with pillows, and discoursed to each disciple on the problems that were before him.

On an afternoon in July it became quite evident that the end would come soon. The Master was in great pain, yet he insisted on sitting up in bed. He had his way. His beard had grown longer. The corners of his mouth were drawn in pain, but his dark, long slanting eyes blazed with light. That light, like the tide of a river, rose high and higher, then flooded his entire face. It was so beautiful and so powerful that no one could look at it long. The disciples had to look away until the Master withdrew the light. Sometimes he would stay thus for forty-five minutes. Then he would speak; though it hurt him like the sting of a hundred cobras, he answered the questions that rose in their minds. He did not wish to die without telling his disciples the last thing they wanted to know.

With a firmness not of this world he said:

> Why am I explaining all I know to you? Because I brought you with me. No teacher comes to earth without his own band of faithfuls. It is they who understand him first. Then they explain him to the world. I am telling you all, so that you will be able to explain without any obscurity and without any magic the simplicity of truth…. You and I came to earth as a band of minstrels. Minstrels sing at the door of every house, then depart—no one cares to know their name. We have sung at the doors of the earth! When we depart, they will not know our hidden names…. Pain is unavoidable so long as the spirit must speak through forms. It is the body— the form—that suffers…. One must renounce matter. If a man sits on a cushion and you want it, you must move him in order to find it. So must one remove materialism to find spirituality beneath. In course of time, every one of you will find the Spirit saturating all. But that comes later …

Here he pointed at a disciple and remarked, "He moves about like a naked sword, while the one yonder—Hirananda—is docile, but full of the sting of the Spirit; like a cobra under the charmer's flute—quite docile but the power to sting is there." He was silent for a while and then said quietly, as if making his own mind clear on the point: "Today I gave you all. I am taking nothing with me. I am a beggar now. Depend no more on me, nor on any other man. Depend on him. It is through his power that you will act. Through his power you will do great kindness to the world. After that is done, you, the minstrels, will return to the house of song whence you came."

Just then the dusk fell. Suddenly he passed into samadhi. His breathing ceased; his heart beat no more; and his pulse stopped. His body became stiff. By the light of the lamps the apostles watched him. At midnight he came out of samadhi and spoke for nearly an hour. About one in the morning he entered into samadhi again. His hair stood on end. His eyes were half-closed and brimmed with light. A smile that rose on his lips deepened and spread over his entire face. Then it began to ebb slowly from his brow and cheeks. It passed back to the corners of his mouth. There it flickered like a flame for several moments, then suddenly his lips hardened, and with it that ebbing smile froze into the rigidity of death.

15

Turiyananda's Conclusion

I have intimated in a previous chapter that I intended to deal at length with Swami Turiyananda's work. He was one of the disciples of Ramakrishna whom I knew. And since he is not living now, I think I may speak about him without any reserve.

I have already alluded to his great power and prestige among other holy persons. At his feet I learned more about the heart of the religious teachings of India than I can set forth in writing. It was because of his Himalayan spiritual stature that I returned to him to obtain a final measurement of the message of Ramakrishna.

Now the monastery in Benares, over which Turiyananda presided, was divided into two sections separated from each other by a high concrete wall. One of them was called *Gunatita* and the other *Saguna*.

In the former lived about a dozen monks who, through meditation and concentration, sought to realize the Gunatita—God without any name or form. They held no rites and rituals. Their days were spent in learning concentration and acquiring insight. They were the most devoted of scholars, as well. They studied all the Indian systems of philosophy and those of the West. Their dwelling, a two-story brick building, gave one the impression of unmitigated somberness. Every wall, every door, and every stick of furniture had no useless decoration. Beauty had been reduced to bare essentials in this home of silence and meditation. I do not know why Turiyananda, who was a yogi and holy man, never lived in the Gunatita section.

On the contrary, he dwelt in the Saguna part of the monastery. Saguna (through name and form) worship consists of realizing God through work, prayer, rituals, observances, and festivals. In fact the word *Saguna* covered a multitude of practices, such as feeding the hungry, succoring the needy, ministering to the sick, and giving instruction to those who asked for it. Owing to the range of the activities that the Saguna worshipers undertook, they had to own an estate full of buildings of all kinds and large gardens. In a remote corner of the latter, under some tall trees, stood the hut of Turiyananda. I have dwelled elsewhere in this book with Turiyananda's conception of salvation by good works, so I shall not go into the matter here. Let us learn from his lips the import of the message of Ramakrishna.

It was on a morning in June that I presented myself at the door of Turiyananda's hut. After entering, I found its interior filled, as usual, with cool shadows. There was not much sunlight within, but the atmosphere was clear enough to afford me a distinct vision of every person and object in the room. Turiyananda, clad in the ocher robe of sannyasins, sat on a couch in the middle of the room. One glance at his face made it more than vivid to me that he was all-holy. I took the dust from his feet, then crouched on the floor before him. Now I looked at him very carefully. This time that lionlike person was pouring upon me a sweetness and tenderness that was indescribable: his eyes, his mouth, even the slight forward inclination of his head, all showered on me the benediction of a lover and a seer. He gazed on me I know not how long, when those smiling lips opened and in a deep voice (deep as a bullfrog's, we say) he said, "You have certain questions for my ear, my son."

I answered, "Yes, my Lord, it is about your Master, and about this monastery."

"About him, all of you know my feeling. May he bless you with illumination," said Turiyananda.

"My lord," I began again, "if I understand Ramakrishna's stature at all, it is because I have beheld you."

"You mean, a dwarf like me conveys to you the Himalaya-humbling height of his soul?" Then Turiyananda laughed out loud. It was a very simple laugh: not a trace of malice in it, but plenty of mischief. He laughed so that tears stood in his eyes. It took him a little time to wipe his eyes dry with an end of his robe. "Please repeat your question to me," he said.

I said, "Please don't laugh at it. I want to know many things. But the question that I should like to ask first is about your work. Why do you live here in the Saguna section? Is Saguna worship really better than the Gunatita?"

Never in a hurry, Turiyananda pondered a little. He put his hands together, then looked at them. Now, fixing his gaze on me he began: "In the Gunatita—beyond name and form—the monks practice the arts of concentration and study Vedanta texts along with other metaphysics. They are in a hurry to find him, so they think of him all the time. When they cannot practice concentration they read the sacred books. Thus they keep themselves—mind and body—consecrated to one subject. The only times they interrupt their work are when they eat their solitary meals and sleep. They do not sleep much either. It is a hard life. But that is the price you pay for giving up the simpler path of name and form."

"But, my lord, you are one of the great holy men of our time. Why don't you go to the other side? Why do you stay and work here in this world?" I asked with impatience.

He laughed again. This time it was a gentle laughter. After the zephyr of mirth had subsided, he resumed: "It is well that I accept every epithet that comes my way. For a man who is a votary of God must accept whatever is hurled at him—a cow-dung cake or a lotus flower. As to why I do not go over to the other side, my son, your answer is in Ramakrishna. If he who became God stayed on this side after his realization, why not the smaller fry like myself? Then they who are working in and through Saguna name and form, are as sacred as those on the other, Gunatita, side. Those here are probably more sacred, for they are more numerous. God comes to earth for them. Then there is more fun to be had here. Think of the kinds of questions like yours that are asked to quicken our vanity. And after all, as our Master says, to earn salvation for one's own self is not amusing enough—I really mean amusement, since God is the most absorbing amusement. You must see the light in order to give sight to the blind, which is most amusing.

"The more numerous the ways of reaching him, all the more formidable grows the consensus of opinion that he exists. If you love God, and if you have seen him your way, it is in your own interest to urge others to see him through their unique methods. How else can you know that your way [of religion] has given you the ultimate God, if all the other religions do not reveal him every time a soul plunders the secret of Immortality? Ramakrishna taught us the ancient truth of India: *atmano mokshartha jagat jana hitayacha* [the blessings that will come to all and the salvation that will be yours]. Where else but in this part can one pursue both? Someone such as myself likes this Saguna worship. Each name and each form that is exists in order to articulate God. We must help all people to utter the thunder of Silence. Let the gem of salvation be set in the heart of every man and woman. For each one of them is here to give you verification of your God by finding him in his way."

"That explains why you who can easily cross over any time to the Gunatita, Absolute, stay here on this side of name and form?" I asked.

"I stay on this side," he said emphatically, "because it is the easier of the two. It is the path of the weak and the simple. Here is room for a man of action, for a pure mystic, and for a pure lover of God. The man of action, if he eschews all the material reward of his acts here or here-after, will find God in no time. A mystic who meditates and prays with-out any desire for acquiring power, he too will find the All-Powerful in a short time. And he who loves God's creatures finds him the instant his love is not caused by a motive, nor held by an earthly end. Here in the house of name and form there is room for all. It is the marketplace of the Infinite. I love to be here. Ramakrishna set us the example."

Turiyananda's face glowed with enthusiasm. His hands lay wide open and inert on his lap. If one could see the movement of his lips and the fire in his eyes while he was talking, one would at once feel the per-fect serenity and poise that characterized him. He embodied the phrase of the poet, "That man is fierce with tranquility."

Now I asked him the most vital of all my questions. I spoke with a studied slowness in order to make him receive my words without laugh-ing at them again.

"My Lord, what is the message that Ramakrishna has for the West?"

"The West must realize God more. Realization is what Ramakrishna symbolized. Religion is the record of our experience of God, not a the-ory of our own belief in God. To the West his message is the same as to the East: Find God. He said to Swami Vivekananda, in answer to the question, Can you see God?—'Yes, as I see you, only more intensely.' If Ramakrishna saw and became God, so can you and I. To be reli-gious is to experience and then to believe in God. Belief comes after experience. Belief that precedes experience is not important."

"Yet there is not one belief," I interrupted him. "Only one God, but so many religions and beliefs."

The holy man fell in line with my thought with perfect ease. He rejoined, "There is only one Truth, but there are so many ways of expe-riencing him. And there ought to be as many beliefs as there are expe-riences of God. Authentic and important beliefs are but statements of realization of our own inherent Godhood. Look how experiences and statements of them differ in such objective matters as the sun—our experiences differ exceedingly. An African's feeling about the sun is quite different from that of a Laplander. They have different stories to tell about the cycles of the sun; the former believes that it shines twelve hours a day, while the latter holds that it shines for six months in a year. Yet it is the same sun. Similarly with our experience of God.

"Though we all realize the one Beloved, our ways of stating him are quite different. Yet all of them verify and magnify his 'thousand-facedness.' Instead of seeing the same bleak, flat face all the time, we all see many different faces of the one Face of Silence. Does not that make the Lord all the more interesting? You cannot be bored by him, since by the time you have grown used to seeing one aspect of him, he has another to reveal to you. He is ever new, for he is forever the same. As to a growing child, its mother seems to display different sides of herself year after year, so does the Mother of the Universe to us. When we are spiritually young, God is our helper and sustainer. During our soul's adolescence we find in him our most intimate friend. In the growth of our spirit, he reveals himself as a symbol of our experience. And at the end we discover that all those faces that we have looked upon are but facets of our own immortal Self."

"How can we find that Self, my Lord?" I cried out. "So many religious teachers, so many Gurus, create but confusion!"

Turiyananda paused awhile. He looked at me, then through the small window at the garden without. Slowly he withdrew his gaze and fastened it upon me again. "There are gurus who have seen the Lord. Find one of those. He will take you into the very nuptial chamber where our souls are united with the Lord. Such a guru may come from any caste or religion. He may be a Hindu, a Muslim, or a Christian, but he alone has the power and the right to take on a disciple. If you have come across one such, go to that guru, and he will give you the key to the chamber of the bridegroom."

Here someone interrupted us, and the rest of my questions had to remain unasked until the morrow. The next day, about four o'clock in the afternoon, Turiyananda discoursed to me as we walked up and down on the green turf of the monastery gardens. He appeared quite different, as if he were another man—alert, athletic, noticing things quickly and clearly. He shouted to a passing white-robed brahmachari and asked him about the health of certain patients in the hospital. He stopped and chatted with the gardener working at a small bush about the diseases of certain trees and plants, yet all that time—nearly two hours—he kept the thread of our conversation uninterrupted. It was during one of the pauses in his chat with the gardener that he asked me, "You have another inquiry to make. What is it, my son?"

So I put forth another question: "If all people can find God in their own way, then why not through Yoga practices?"

"Yoga practices are singular," he said.

> Have you dived deep into Shivananda's pamphlet on that? It is a deep work—that is why it is so short. You must not be deluded by what the Yoga teachers say. For Shivananda is right. If you learn to control your breath, if you increase your powers of concentration, all those things tend to make you strong. Even physical health is affected by them. *Na tasya roga na jara na mrityu praptasya yogagnimayam shariram*—he has no age, disease, nor decay, who has put on the flame garb of Yoga. That is true, but perpetual youth is no good to you if you cannot find him, the Ageless, who does not have to be even young.
>
> Here is another important thing that people intent on Yoga practices overlook. Suppose you concentrate hard on a thought, such as: *God is infinite beauty.* In the course of your thinking, you will pass over many phases of your own experiences to which you have not paid any attention before. You will pass from your experiences

into those of others. Gradually, after a year or two, you will be able to think so hard that your concentration will rise to its highest power. Then your body will begin to behave strangely. Your breathing will cease for many minutes. Your pulse will slacken, and your consciousness of the external world will be reduced nearly to nothing. If you repeat that process a few times more, your concentration will be so intense that occasionally your heart will stop beating for a short while. At last, when your object is attained and you have fathomed the full magnitude of God's infinite beauty, lo, incidentally, you have acquired the so-called occult powers of Yoga.

There is no doubt that while concentrating on the Divine, the rishis, sages of ancient India, stumbled upon the science of Yoga. It was just an incident of their spiritual life. Alas, unfortunately, later came a race of bastard holy men who did not care much for God. They wanted fireworks, so they prostituted Yoga into a science for acquiring occult power. Ramakrishna warned us against any and every form of spiritual prostitution. If you want power, why don't you become a general, a robber baron, or a highwayman? Why turn Yoga into an end in itself? I have known Yoga teachers who can do many strange things, but they cannot find God. These prestidigitators—for that they are, and no more—think that they can do something that no one else can, but that is not true. Ramakrishna, who was no Yogi, could beat any Yogi at his own game. For in the process of finding God, his heart, breathing, and nervous system suspended work automatically. He acquired this entire bag of Yogi tricks without ever bothering about it.

Beware, my son! If you search for and find God, all the occult powers will be won unto you. And, what is more astonishing is that once the beatific vision has been vouchsafed unto you, you will never be tempted to abuse your powers. Like those great men, who, given the freedom of a city never use it, so does one with the privileges of the house of Immortality. The children of Immortality never stoop to magic or display of power.

Besides, we are living in an age when we have neither time nor patience for the thaumaturgy of occultism and Yoga. Men and women nowadays are in a great hurry. Hence they will take shortcuts to the Infinite. In the Kaliyuga, this age, the only thing they have to do is to go on wanting the Lord sincerely. If they want him long, he will reveal himself to their mortal eyes. There is no doubt of it. He is like the mother cat who cannot resist the crying call of her kitten very long. Look at Rama- krishna. He found the Mother by simply crying and pleading with her. Do so yourself and she will at once take down the mask of the sun from her face and reveal to you her face of compassion that is within you. Oh! it is so easy to find God in our time! Look, my child, the sun is setting. It is time to commune with her. Come into my dwelling and meditate with me. *Hari Om, Hari Om.*

16
Last Impression

Now that I had gathered together as many legends and stories of Ramakrishna as the time at my disposal permitted, I went to pay my last visit to Dakshineswar, the scene of his spiritual struggles and triumphs. I was urged to make a final pilgrimage there by one of the old women who knew the Master and who had told me some interesting tales about him.

Early one morning, just when the first flake of sun-gold had fallen on the Ganges, we entered Dakshineswar. The all-too-familiar picture of age and decay that characterized the place was before us once more. The many-domed temples and their decaying gray walls looked uninviting. The gardens that surrounded them were full of weeds. None of the glow and glamour of the old days was discernible anywhere. Instead, a steadily augmenting ruin greeted us on every side. Even the trees under which Ramakrishna meditated were decaying. Unable to bear the sight of so much desolation, I asked my aged mentor to take me within the temple. There too I found no relief. The long corridors and the majestic ceilings of the shrine were one vast horror. Plaster and paint were peeling; spiders had woven their webs everywhere, and numberless black pigeons had made their nests in every crevice and corner of the ceiling. And far away from the dim inner shrine rose the chant of the ministrant *purohit* (priest) like the croon of a hungry ghost.

I started to walk away while I complained bitterly to my ancient guide: "Where has all the joy, Ananda, and glory, jyoti, vanished? Why wears this place such an expression of loneliness?" Her face, as full of wrinkles as an old barn with spider webs, slowly lit up. Between the innumerable lines of her visage ran a current of expression as clear as crystal waters flowing between the cracks of a black rock.

"Oh, thou dream-seeker," she ejaculated. "His glory was not of this earth. As the music is not in the pipe but in the soul of the player, so was his holiness: It was in him. This place, where I have seen hundreds of pilgrims brought on barges like fortresses of color, is now deserted. Why? Because he is not here. No one else—even the queen and her bejeweled women drawing their veils of cerise, amber, and pigeon-throated silk against those hard walls, white as the shining moon—could bring this place to life. It died the moment Ramakrishna went. Priests, scholars, and rajahs, they cannot create life. It was his being that made this place. Even the trees are dying because their roots do not feel his feet treading the ground above them."

"Why did they allow everything—the relics, the simple souvenirs— to die out?" I complained again. "If this were Europe, they would have preserved everything because it has made history."

The old crone laughed at me, then unburdened her mind. "Renunciation is what Ramakrishna lived and preached. How can you make history out of renunciation? Oh, I heard him. I also saw his face. Sometimes he used to go by our cottage after his meditations in Panchavati. Had you seen that face of scorching ecstasy then, you would understand: He renounced even his body. He was free. He left nothing bound to himself. He even liberated the room where he lived from the bonds of remembering him. He did not wish to trap souls or places: he was not a fowler of the Infinite. He came to free the world."

"If he leaves nothing behind, how are we to know of him?" I asked dialectically.

"But he has made Being," answered the old prophetess. "Wherever men and women meditate and live selflessness, there he incarnates. If you wish to make him live again, renounce all and seek God."

"That is all fine talk, Mother," I fretted. "I grant you that a teacher comes to earth to free us. But there are certain symbols, certain memories, that he must leave behind to guide later generations."

"They are not here," she explained. "They are in the monastery across the river. There, men and women meditate as he did—that is his symbol—there they try to live as he did to make God become man. Is not that the right way to remember him?"

"I suppose I can't make it clear to you," I announced frankly. "I have never seen such a disregard of time and place as in this God-mad country of ours. I am afraid you find me a slave of such illusions as history and geography. I suppose, according to you, even writing and talking about him is useless. They will not bring him to life, will they?"

"What good are words when you are to tap the silence of infinite compassion?" rang her paradoxical question. "Ramakrishna used to tell a story about himself: Once he went to call on a great initiate, Tailanga. Tailanga lived in Benares. But he observed a strict vow of silence. No one ever heard him speak. Ramakrishna came back from his visit to that silent initiate and told us all about it. He said, 'Wonderful talks he and I had. Nearly a week we sat beside each other and meditated. A great talker is Tailanga; he unburdens his thoughts with such clear words.' We said to Ramakrishna, 'But he never speaks.' Ramakrishna answered, 'What has that got to do with it?'

"Now you see, my son, how crippled your written and spoken words are. They cannot limp to any place. God fools us with little brains. But Ramakrishna could not be fooled. So he became God."

"Well, Mother, so be it. I shall leave this place of decay and death now, and go across to the monastery whose youth and vigor are more to my taste." And I turned to go.

But she would not let me depart. She said, "Let me bless you, my child. But promise to dine with me today."

I promised readily. Pleased with my words, she blessed me. She said, "You loiter here awhile. I will go home and cook. At midday, dine in my cottage. Then go across to the monastery. May Ramakrishna load your heart with an agony for God."

Though the conversation of my wise old hostess was most interesting, I had to take leave of her. I had an appointment—in fact my last interview—with the Pundit at the monastery. That chronicler of Ramakrishna's conversations was coming all the way from the city of Calcutta to see me that afternoon.

As we rowed across the river, the gray temple towers and the decaying trees of Dakshineswar sank out of sight. Like a banner, on the other shore rose the white turret of the monastery temple. The palms spread their fans in the air through which the afternoon sun shone fiercely. Now we saw ocher-robed figures moving about through green gardens. Turret by turret, roof by roof, the yellow-walled monastery came into full view and slowly vanished again as we made our boat fast under the stone embankment. Leaping over, I ran up the steps of the ghat like a happy squirrel. The life and vigor of the place possessed me at once.

I ran along the wall of the first building, and suddenly beheld the Pundit sitting on the red-tiled terrace waiting for me. After I had seated myself near him, I looked at his bearded face, then said, "My lord, I leave tomorrow."

He put his fingers through his white beard a few times, then remarked, "Are the Ramakrishna legends that you have gathered tall enough? The legends ought to measure up to his sky-humbling stature."

I said, "No, they are not tall. They seem to me quite natural and normal. They are mostly based on reality."

"I do not mean that," he rejoined, bringing his lion-head of a face close to mine. "I mean, whatever legend grows up about him will become true."

"I do not understand you." I was puzzled.

"It is simple enough," the Pundit ejaculated with a backward movement of his head. "Look at Christ: even his birth without any earthly father became a reality. Why? Because his being was so living and so tall that in order to explain him they had to invent immaculate conception. The same was the case with Buddha. He was so divine that they had to invent the same origin for him, an immaculate conception, in order to grasp his essence. All legends become history when their central character is spiritual enough to sustain and give life to them."

"The story of the immaculate conception came after Buddha and Christ had become God," I repeated to myself.

The Pundit said, "Yes. The same thing is happening to Ramakrishna. He was so spiritual that in order to explain him, people have to resort to many supernatural explanations. It has been my lot to chronicle only his discourses."

"I wish it were my lot to chronicle the legends," I remarked. "Unfortunately, what people tell me is more or less embedded in facts. Someday I will find those who will tell me of the supernatural legends. But, not to change the subject, I should like to ask you, sir, is there any reason why all of you allow the property at Dakshineswar to fall into ruin while you take good care of this place, which was built years after Ramakrishna's death?"

"There is no reason," he answered without the slightest delay. "You see how strong the trees look here, how fine the turf, and how healthy the cows, not to speak of the holy men. But this is where Ramakrishna lives. Wherever a few of the servants of Truth dwell, Being precipitates itself. And where there is Being, life grows. All that you see here is a reflection of Being."

"Then that is true of all the disciples and followers of Ramakrishna," I commented.

"Who can deny it?" he expatiated, "When the Master died, we had no place to go to. Now Benares, Kankhal, Bombay, Bangalore, Madras, and dozens of other cities in India, and those that are abroad, have their Ramakrishna ashrama where men and women gather, irrespective of religion and race, to live so that a deathless Being is precipitated. It has come faster than I dreamt. But such is the power of the inner life that the Holy One lives! We who lived with him know that his light is steeper than all darkness and will be shed upon the world as long as we can create it through living. It can grow wherever men choose to dwell in purity, holiness, and infinite tolerance."

"Why have they not chosen to live in Dakshineswar?" I asked again.

He looked at me with those topaz eyes of his. It was uncomfortable to be gazed at so. Apparently he felt my discomfort, so he averted his gaze and said, "I cannot perceive the reason why you should identify the inner Dakshineswar with the outer? Ramakrishna lives in the inner, which is in every soul. Wherever that soul goes, it goes with him. It is homeless in time as it is houseless in space."

"Then a hundred years from now no pilgrims will flock to that place across which he toiled and triumphed?" I demanded.

"But men must make pilgrimage to the sanctities within them. Why should they go to a place without? I hope no one will cheapen and exploit that place, Dakshineswar. Ramakrishna has left nothing there that can, in the slightest, serve as a pretext for starting a new cult with its horrors of priestcraft and terrors of commercialism."

"Then you too are against history?" I criticized him.

The Pundit said, "Ramakrishna was a galloping torch that came to earth to light other torches—souls of men and women—so that each one of them would become God. He wanted every one of us not to find a religion, but to *be* religion. He set us that example."

"No priest, no rabbi, no padre—it is very difficult for an average man to give up all that to find God within himself," I said.

To that remark of mine he answered, "But those mendicants,

priests, do not make religion. It is men and women who long for God and who make him. Ramakrishna said so. And it is true of our time. This is a new age. It is the high noon of freedom and equality. Men are not surrendering their uniqueness of soul and intelligence to other men. On the contrary they are asserting with tumultuous pride that each one of them is a son of God. If that is so in the outer life of man, how much more so must it be in the inner realm. Men do not wish to bend the knee any more to *avatars* and masters. They themselves would be the avatars. Every soul is golden-wombed. It must give birth to God, the timeless. That you cannot bring about by preserving Dak-shineswar, Kapilavastu, and Bethlehem. What do places or creeds have to do with the purity of that Being that men pour into this world through the realization of their inner life? Wherever men and women flock to kindle and quicken their souls, there incarnates the truth of Ramakrishna."

A strange light came into the Pundit's eyes. It was like tears—so full and so tangible.

By now the afternoon was far spent. The opposite shore—Dak-shineswar—sank into deepening purple dusk. The boats loosed their sails that had been gleaming like sunset clouds of amber, amethyst, and rose. They slowly drifted shoreward, and in a few minutes about a dozen of them were moored at the monastery ghat. Then their half-naked boat-men, like brown Tritons, trooped up the steps with baskets of fruits, flowers, and rice to offer to the monks as *dakshina*, presents. They left their offerings at the door of a hut, then walked toward the inner shrine in order to attend arati.

Swiftly the day was passing into the night. Silence like a black panther began to prowl about us. We felt beset with sanctities. The Pundit said to me, "Do you meditate, or do you go hence now?"

"I go, my lord," I answered, "to begin my story. This evening I do not meditate." He blessed me, then added, "I must go and pray. May your soul pour compassion upon all. Farewell!"

In a minute he was gone. As I slowly went down the steps of the ghat, the sound of a gong smote the air. I listened as I sat still in my boat. Soon came the chant of many voices. I knew what they were saying, so I chanted!

> O thou river of miracles that is within me, pour the heal-
> ing waters of compassion on the wounded body of man
> and make him whole.

Now that I had hymned silence we rowed our boat toward Calcutta. As we drifted down the tide, my imagination wandered back to the inner shrine of the monastery. I imagined myself sitting within, still attend-ing arati. With my mind's eyes I saw those innumerable lamps lift their fragrant flames toward the image of Ramakrishna on the altar. The yellow-robed monk waved lit candles before it, while I sat outside and sang again and again "O river of miracles … "

By the time we had reached the Calcutta side of the Ganges, it was starry night. The blue-black sky vaulted above, haughty with aloof-ness, and the stars hung so low that they seemed intimate. Far off in the west, the lamps of the various monastery buildings and of the boats below were being lighted one by one.

What did it all mean? Shall I ever be able to tell even a fraction of the joy and peace that was vouchsafed me by those ocher-robed monks? Is it possible that men and women can live such a vivid life that it becomes a galloping torch of Truth that the material darkness of our time cannot obscure? What had I witnessed? Did I dream those days in the monastery? Or did I truly live as I had never lived before?

Cogitating these questions I reached home. Can words translate for the reader Tat (That) which burns in the eyes of those monks across the river? Can anything in any language render the militant peace of the soul that men and women have won for themselves and for the world they live in? And is there one single metaphor or symbol anywhere or in any age that adequately conveys the meaning of Tat (That)? Holiness alone can explain holiness. And only insofar as we ourselves become children of Immortality shall we be able to understand those children of God who have sought to help humankind.

Sri Ramakrishna

by Swami Nikhilananda

Kamarpukur, the birthplace of Sri Ramakrishna

1
The Early Years

Sri Ramakrishna, the God-man of modern India, was born at Kamarpukur. This village in the Hooghly District preserved during the nineteenth century the idyllic simplicity of the rural areas of Bengal. Situated far from the railway, it was untouched by the glamor of the city. It contained rice fields, tall palms, royal banyans, a few lakes, and two cremation grounds. South of the village a stream took its leisurely course. A mango orchard, dedicated by a neighboring *zemindar* to the public use, was frequented by the boys for their noonday sports. A highway passed through the village to the great temple of Jagannath at Puri, and the villagers, most of whom were farmers and craftsmen, entertained many passing holy men and pilgrims. The dull round of rural life was broken by lively festivals, the observance of sacred days, religious singing, and other innocent pleasures.

About his parents, Sri Ramakrishna once said, "My mother was the personification of rectitude and gentleness. She did not know much about the ways of the world; innocent of the art of concealment, she would say what was on her mind. People loved her for her openheartedness. My father, an orthodox brahmin, never accepted gifts from the *sudras.* He spent much of his time in worship and meditation, and in repeating God's name and chanting his glories. Whenever in his daily prayers he invoked the Goddess Gayatri, his chest flushed and tears rolled down his cheeks. He spent his leisure hours making garlands for the family deity, Raghuvir."

Khudiram Chattopadhyaya and Chandra Devi, the parents of Sri Ramakrishna, were married in 1799. At that time Khudiram was living in his ancestral village of Dereypore, not far from Kamarpukur. Their first son, Ramkumar, was born in 1805, and their first daughter, Katyayani, in 1810. In 1814 Khudiram was ordered by his landlord to bear false witness in court against a neighbor. When he refused to do so, the landlord brought a false case against him and deprived him of his ancestral property. Thus dispossessed, he arrived, at the invitation of another landlord, in the quiet village of Kamarpukur, where he was given a dwelling and about an acre of fertile land. The crops from this little property were enough to meet his family's simple needs. Here he lived in simplicity, dignity, and contentment.

Ten years after his coming to Kamarpukur, Khudiram made a pilgrimage on foot to Rameswar, at the southern extremity of India. Two years later was born his second son, whom he named Rameswar. Again in 1835, at the age of sixty, he made a pilgrimage, this time to Gaya. Here, from ancient times, Hindus have come from the four corners of India to discharge their duties to their departed ancestors by offering them food and drink at the sacred footprint of the Lord Vishnu. At this holy place Khudiram had a dream in which the Lord Vishnu promised to be born as his son. And Chandra Devi, too, in front of the Siva temple at Kamarpukur, had a vision indicating the birth of a divine child. Upon his return, the husband found that she had conceived.

It was on February 18, 1836, that the child, to be known afterward as Ramakrishna, was born. In memory of the dream at Gaya he was given the name of Gadadhar, the "Bearer of the Mace," an epithet of Vishnu. Three years later a little sister was born.

Boyhood

Gadadhar grew up into a healthy and restless boy, full of fun and sweet mischief. He was intelligent and precocious and endowed with a prodigious memory. On his father's lap he learned by heart the names of his ancestors and the hymns to the gods and goddesses, and at the village school he was taught to read and write. But his greatest delight was to listen to recitations of stories from Hindu mythology and the epics. These he would afterward recount from memory, to the great joy of the villagers. Painting he enjoyed; the art of molding images of the gods and goddesses he learned from the potters. But arithmetic was his great aversion.

At the age of six or seven Gadadhar had his first experience of spiritual ecstasy. One day in June or July, when he was walking along a narrow path between paddy fields, eating the puffed rice that he carried in a basket, he looked up at the sky and saw a beautiful, dark thunder cloud. As it spread, rapidly enveloping the whole sky, a flight of snow-white cranes passed in front of it. The beauty of the contrast overwhelmed the boy. He fell to the ground, unconscious, and the puffed rice went in all directions. Some villagers found him and carried him home in their arms. Gadadhar said later that, in that state, he had experienced an indescribable joy.

Gadadhar was seven years old when his father died. This incident profoundly affected him. For the first time, the boy realized that life on earth was impermanent. Unobserved by others, he began to slip into the mango orchard or into one of the cremation grounds, and he spent hours absorbed in his own thoughts. He also became more helpful to his mother in the discharge of her household duties. He gave more attention to reading and hearing the religious stories recorded in the Puranas. And he became interested in the wandering monks and pious pilgrims who would stop at Kamarpukur on their way to Puri. These holy persons, the custodians of India's spiritual heritage and the living witnesses of the ideal of renunciation of the world and all-absorbing love of God, entertained the little boy with stories from the Hindu epics, stories of saints and prophets, and also stories of their own adventures. He, for his part, fetched their water and fuel and served them in various ways. Meanwhile, he was observing their meditation and worship.

At the age of nine Gadadhar was invested with the sacred thread. This ceremony conferred upon him the privileges of his brahmin lineage, including the worship of the family deity, Raghuvir, and imposed upon him the many strict disciplines of a brahmin's life. During the ceremony of investiture, he shocked his relatives by accepting a meal cooked by his nurse, a sudra woman. His father would never have dreamed of doing such a thing. But, in a playful mood, Gadadhar had once promised this woman that he would eat her food, and now he fulfilled his plighted word. The woman had piety and religious sincerity, and these were more important to the boy than the conventions of society.

Gadadhar was now permitted to worship Raghuvir. Thus began his first training in meditation. He so gave his heart and soul to the worship that the stone image very soon appeared to him as the living Lord of the Universe. His tendency to lose himself in contemplation was first noticed at this time. Behind his boyish lightheartedness was seen a deepening of his spiritual nature.

About this time, on the Sivaratri night, consecrated to the worship of Siva, a dramatic performance was arranged. The principal actor, who was to play the part of Siva, suddenly fell ill, and Gadadhar was persuaded to act in his place. While friends were dressing him for the role of Siva—smearing his body with ashes, matting his locks, placing a trident in his hand and a string of *rudraksha* beads around his neck— the boy appeared to become absentminded. He approached the stage with slow and measured step, supported by his friends. He looked the living image of Siva. The audience loudly applauded what it took to be his skill as an actor, but it was soon discovered that he was really lost in meditation. His countenance was radiant and tears flowed from his eyes. He was lost to the outer world. The effect of this scene on the audience was tremendous. The people felt blessed as by a vision of Siva himself. The performance had to be stopped, and the boy's mood lasted till the following morning.

Gadadhar himself now organized a dramatic company with his young friends. The stage was set in the mango orchard. The themes were selected from the stories of the *Ramayana* and the *Mahabharata*. Gadadhar knew by heart almost all the roles, having heard them from professional actors. His favorite theme was the Vrindavan episode of Krishna's life, depicting those exquisite love stories of Krishna and the milkmaids and the cowherd boys. Gadadhar would play the parts of Radha or Krishna and would often lose himself in the character he was portraying. His natural feminine grace heightened the dramatic effect. The mango orchard would ring with the loud *kirtan* of the boys. Lost in song and merrymaking, Gadadhar became indifferent to the routine of school.

In 1849 Ramkumar, the eldest son, went to Calcutta to improve the financial condition of the family.

Gadadhar was on the threshold of youth. He had become the pet of the women of the village. They loved to hear him talk, sing, or recite from the holy books. They enjoyed his knack of imitating voices. Their woman's instinct recognized the innate purity and guilelessness of this boy of clear skin, flowing hair, beaming eyes, smiling face, and inexhaustible fun. The pious elderly women looked upon him as Gopala, the Baby Krishna, and the younger ones saw in him the youthful Krishna of Vrindavan. He himself so idealized the love of the *gopis* for Krishna that he sometimes yearned to be born as a woman, if he must be born again, in order to be able to love Sri Krishna with all his heart and soul.

Coming to Calcutta

At the age of sixteen Gadadhar was summoned to Calcutta by his elder brother Ramkumar, who wished assistance in his priestly duties. Ramkumar had opened a Sanskrit academy to supplement his income, and it was his intention gradually to turn his younger brother's mind to education. Gadadhar applied himself heart and soul to his new duty as family priest to a number of Calcutta families. His worship was very different from that of the professional priests. He spent hours decorating the images and singing hymns and devotional songs; he performed with love the other duties of his office. People were impressed with his ardor. But to his studies he paid scant attention.

Ramkumar did not at first oppose the ways of his temperamental brother. He wanted Gadadhar to become used to the conditions of city life. But one day he decided to warn the boy about his indifference to the world. After all, in the near future Gadadhar must, as a householder, earn his livelihood through the performance of his brahminical duties; and these required a thorough knowledge of Hindu law, astrology, and kindred subjects. He gently admonished Gadadhar and asked him to pay more attention to his studies. But the boy replied spiritedly, "Brother, what shall I do with a mere breadwinning education? I would rather acquire that wisdom which will illumine my heart and give me satisfaction for ever."

Breadwinning Education

The anguish of the inner soul of India found expression through these passionate words of the young Gadadhar. For what did his unsophisticated eyes see around him in Calcutta, at that time the metropolis of India and the center of modern culture and learning? Greed and lust held sway in the higher levels of society, and the occasional religious practices were merely outer forms from which the soul had long ago departed. Gadadhar had never seen anything like this at Kamarpukur among the simple and pious villagers. The sadhus and wandering monks whom he had served in his boyhood had revealed to him an altogether different India. He had been impressed by their devotion and purity, their self-control and renunciation. He had learned from them and from his own intuition that the ideal of life as taught by the ancient sages of India was the realization of God.

When Ramkumar reprimanded Gadadhar for neglecting a "bread-winning education," the inner voice of the boy reminded him that the legacy of his ancestors—the legacy of Rama, Krishna, Buddha, Sankara, Ramanuja, Chaitanya—was not worldly security but the knowledge of God, and that these noble sages were the true representatives of Hindu society. Each of them was seated, as it were, on the crest of the wave that followed each successive trough in the tumultuous course of Indian national life. All demonstrated that the life current of India is spirituality. This truth was revealed to Gadadhar through that inner vision that scans past and future in one sweep, unobstructed by the barriers of time and space. But he was unaware of the history of the profound change that had taken place in the land of his birth during the previous one hundred years.

Hindu society during the eighteenth century had been passing through a period of decadence. It was the twilight of Muslim rule, and there was anarchy and confusion in all spheres. Superstitious practices dominated the religious life of the people. Rites and rituals passed for the essence of spirituality. Greedy priests became the custodians of heaven. True philosophy was supplanted by dogmatic opinions. The pundits took delight in vain polemics.

In 1757 English traders laid the foundation of British rule in India. Gradually the government was systematized and lawlessness suppressed.

The Hindus were much impressed by the military power and political acumen of the new rulers. In the wake of the merchants came the English educators, social reformers, and Christian missionaries—all bearing a culture completely alien to the Hindu mind. In different parts of the country, educational institutions were set up and Christian churches established. Young Hindu men were offered the heady wine of Western culture of the late eighteenth and early nineteenth centuries, and they drank it to the very dregs.

The first effect of the draught was a complete effacement from the minds of educated Hindus of the time-honored beliefs and traditions of Hindu society. They came to believe that there was no transcendental Truth. The world perceived by the senses was all that existed. God and religion were illusions of the untutored mind. True knowledge could be derived only from the analysis of nature. So atheism and agnosticism became the fashion of the day. The youth of India, taught in English schools, took malicious delight in openly breaking the customs and traditions of their society. They would do away with the caste system and remove the discriminatory laws about food. Social reform, the spread of secular education, widow remarriage, abolition of early marriage—they considered these the panacea for the degenerate condition of Hindu society.

The Christian missionaries gave the finishing touch to the process of transformation. They ridiculed as relics of a barbarous age the images and rituals of the Hindu religion. They tried to persuade India that the teachings of her saints and seers were the cause of her downfall, that her Vedas, Puranas, and other scriptures were filled with superstition. Christianity, they maintained, had given the white races position and power in this world and assurance of happiness in the next; therefore Christianity was the best of all religions. Many intelligent young Hindus became converted. The man in the street was confused. The majority of the educated grew materialistic in their mental outlook. Everyone living near Calcutta or the other strongholds of Western culture, even those who attempted to cling to the orthodox traditions of Hindu society, became infected by the new uncertainties and the new beliefs.

But the soul of India was to be resuscitated through a spiritual awakening. We hear the first call of this renaissance in the spirited retort of the young Gadadhar: "Brother, what shall I do with a mere breadwinning education?"

Ramkumar could hardly understand the import of his young brother's reply. He described in bright colors the happy and easy life of scholars in Calcutta society. But Gadadhar intuitively felt that the scholars, to use one of his own vivid illustrations, were like so many vultures, soaring high on the wings of their uninspired intellect, with their eyes fixed on the charnel pit of greed and lust. So he stood firm and Ramkumar had to give way.

2

Dakshineswar

Kali Temple at Dakshineswar

At that time there lived in Calcutta a rich widow named Rani Rasmani, belonging to the sudra caste, and known far and wide not only for her business ability, courage, and intelligence, but also for her largeness of heart, piety, and devotion to God. She was assisted in the management of her vast property by her son-in-law Mathur Mohan.

In 1847 the rani purchased twenty acres of land at Dakshineswar, a village about four miles north of Calcutta. Here she created a temple garden and constructed several temples. Her Ishta, or Chosen Ideal, was the Divine Mother, Kali.

The temple garden stands directly on the east bank of the Ganges. The northern section of the land and a portion to the east contain an orchard, flower gardens, and two small reservoirs. The southern section is paved with brick and mortar. The visitor arriving by boat ascends the steps of an imposing bathing ghat that leads to the *chandni,* a roofed terrace, on either side of which stand, in a row, six temples of Siva. East of the terrace and the Siva temples is a large court, paved, rectangular in shape, and running north and south. Two temples stand in the center of this court: the larger one, to the south and facing south, is dedicated to Kali, and the smaller one, facing the Ganges, is dedicated to Radhakanta, that is, Krishna, the consort of Radha. Nine domes with spires surmount the temple of Kali, and before it stands the spacious *natmandir,* or music hall, the terrace of which is supported by stately pillars. At the northwest and southwest corners of the temple compound are two *nahabats,* or music towers, from which music flows at different times of day, especially at sunup, noon, and sundown, when the worship is performed in the temples. Three sides of the paved courtyard— all except the west—are lined with rooms set apart for kitchens, storerooms, dining rooms, and quarters for the temple staff and guests. The chamber in the northwest angle, just beyond the last of the Siva temples, is of special interest to us; for here Sri Ramakrishna was to spend a considerable part of his life. To the west of this chamber is a semicircular porch overlooking the river. In front of the porch runs a footpath, north and south, and beyond the path is a large garden, and below the garden the Ganges. The orchard to the north of the buildings contains the Panchavati, the banyan, and the bel tree, associated with Sri Ramakrishna's spiritual practices. Outside and to the north of the temple compound proper is the *kuthi,* or bungalow, used by members of Rani Rasmani's family visiting the garden. And north of the temple garden, separated from it by a high wall, is a powder magazine belonging to the British government.

Siva

In the twelve Siva temples are installed the emblems of the great God of renunciation in his various aspects, worshiped daily with proper rites. Siva requires few articles of worship. White flowers and bel leaves and a little Ganges water offered with devotion are enough to satisfy the benign deity and win from him the boon of liberation.

Radhakanta

The temple of Radhakanta, also known as the temple of Vishnu, contains the images of Radha and Krishna, the symbol of union with God through ecstatic love. The two images stand on a pedestal facing west.

The floor is paved with marble. From the ceiling of the porch hang chandeliers protected from dust by coverings of red cloth. Canvas screens shield the images from the rays of the setting sun. Close to the threshold of the inner shrine is a small brass cup containing holy water. Devoted visitors reverently drink a few drops from the vessel.

Kali

The main temple is dedicated to Kali, the Divine Mother, here worshiped as Bhavatarini, the savior of the universe. The floor of this temple also is paved with marble. The basalt image of the Mother, dressed in gorgeous gold brocade, stands on a white marble image of the prostrate body of her divine consort, Siva, the symbol of the Absolute. On the feet of the goddess are, among other ornaments, anklets of gold. Her arms are decked with jeweled ornaments of gold. She wears necklaces of gold and pearls, a golden garland of human heads, and a girdle of human arms. She wears a golden crown, golden earrings, and a golden nose ring with a pearl drop. She has four arms. The lower left hand holds a severed human head and the upper grips a bloodstained saber. One right hand offers boons to her children; the other allays their fear. The majesty of her posture can hardly be described. It combines the terror of destruction with the reassurance of motherly tenderness. For she is the cosmic power, the totality of the universe, a glorious harmony of the pairs of opposites. She deals out death as she creates and preserves. She has three eyes, the third being the symbol of divine wisdom; they strike dismay into the wicked, yet pour out affection for her devotees.

The whole symbolic world is represented in the temple garden— the trinity of the Nature Mother (Kali), the Absolute (Siva), and Love (Radhakanta), and the arch spanning heaven and earth. The terrific goddess of the Tantra, the soul-enthralling flute player of the *Bhagavata*, and the Self-absorbed Absolute of the Vedas live together, creating the greatest synthesis of religions. All aspects of Reality are represented there. But of this divine household, Kali is the pivot, the sovereign mistress.

Kali, the Divine Mother
(Sri Ramakrishna worshiped this image in the Dakshineswar temple)

She is Prakriti, the Procreatrix, Nature, the Destroyer, the Creator. Nay, she is something greater and deeper still for those who have eyes to see. She is the universal Mother, "my Mother" as Ramakrishna would say, the all-powerful, who reveals herself to her children under different aspects and divine incarnations, the visible God, who leads the elect to the invisible Reality; and, if it so pleases her, she takes away the last trace of ego from created beings and merges it with the consciousness of the Absolute, the undifferentiated God. Through her grace, "the finite ego loses itself in the illimitable Ego—Atman—Brahman."[1]

Rani Rasmani spent a fortune for the construction of the temple garden and another fortune for its dedication ceremony, which took place on May 31, 1855.

Sri Ramakrishna—henceforth we shall call Gadadhar by this familiar name[2]—came to the temple garden with his elder brother Ramkumar, who was appointed priest of the Kali temple. Sri Ramakrishna did not at first approve of Ramkumar's working for the sudra Rasmani. The example of their orthodox father was still fresh in Sri Ramakrishna's mind. He objected also to the eating of the cooked offerings of the temple, since, according to orthodox Hindu custom, such food can be offered to the deity only in the house of a brahmin. But the holy atmosphere of the temple grounds, the solitude of the surrounding wood, the loving care of his brother, the respect shown him by Rani Rasmani and Mathur Babu, the living presence of the Goddess Kali in the temple, and, above all, the proximity of the sacred Ganges, which Sri Ramakrishna always held in the highest respect, gradually overcame his disapproval, and he began to feel at home.

Within a very short time, Sri Ramakrishna attracted the notice of Mathur Babu, who was impressed by the young man's religious fervor and wanted him to participate in the worship in the Kali temple. But Sri Ramakrishna loved his freedom and was indifferent to any worldly career. The profession of the priesthood in a temple founded by a rich woman did not appeal to his mind. Further, he hesitated to take upon himself the responsibility for the ornaments and jewelry of the temple. Mathur had to wait for a suitable occasion.

At this time, there came to Dakshineswar a youth of sixteen, destined to play an important role in Sri Ramakrishna's life. Hriday, a distant nephew[3] of Sri Ramakrishna, hailed from Sihore, a village not far from Kamarpukur, and had been his boyhood friend. Clever, exceptionally energetic, and endowed with great presence of mind, he moved, as will be seen later, like a shadow about his uncle and was always ready to help him, even at the sacrifice of his personal comfort. He was destined to be a mute witness of many of the spiritual experiences of Sri Ramakrishna and the caretaker of his body during the stormy days of his spiritual practice. Hriday came to Dakshineswar in search of a job, and Sri Ramakrishna was glad to see him.

Unable to resist the persuasion of Mathur Babu, Sri Ramakrishna at last entered the temple service, on condition that Hriday should be asked to assist him. His first duty was to dress and decorate the image of Kali.

One day the priest of the Radhakanta temple accidentally dropped the image of Krishna on the floor, breaking one of its legs. The pundits advised the rani to install a new image, since the worship of an image with a broken limb was against the scriptural injunctions. But the rani was fond of the image, and she asked Sri Ramakrishna's opinion. In an abstracted mood, he said, "This solution is ridiculous. If a son-in-law of the rani broke his leg, would she discard him and put another in his place? Wouldn't she rather arrange for his treatment? Why should she not do the same thing in this case, too? Let the image be repaired and worshiped as before." It was a simple, straightforward solution and was accepted by the rani. Sri Ramakrishna himself mended the break. The priest was dismissed for his carelessness, and at Mathur Babu's earnest request, Sri Ramakrishna accepted the office of priest in the Radhakanta temple.

3

Spiritual Longing and God-Vision

Sri Ramakrishna as a Priest

Born in an orthodox brahmin family, Sri Ramakrishna knew the formalities of worship, its rites and rituals. The innumerable gods and goddesses of the Hindu religion are the human aspects of the indescribable and incomprehensible Spirit, as conceived by the finite human mind. They understand and appreciate human love and emotion, help us to realize our secular and spiritual ideals, and ultimately enable us to attain liberation from the miseries of phenomenal life. The source of light, intelligence, wisdom, and strength is the one alone from whom comes the fulfillment of desire. Yet, as long as we are bound by human limitations, we cannot but worship God through human forms. We must use human symbols. Therefore Hinduism asks the devotees to look on God as the ideal father, the ideal mother, the ideal husband, the ideal son, or the ideal friend. But the name ultimately leads to the Nameless, the form to the Formless, the word to the Silence, the emotion to the serene realization of peace in Existence-Knowledge-Bliss Absolute. The gods gradually merge in the one God.

But until that realization is achieved, the devotee cannot dissociate human factors from his worship. Therefore the deity is bathed and clothed and decked with ornaments. He is fed and put to sleep. He is propitiated with hymns, songs, and prayers. And there are appropriate rites connected with all these functions. For instance, to secure for himself external purity, the priest bathes himself in holy water and puts on a holy cloth. He purifies the mind and the sense organs by appropriate meditations. He fortifies the place of worship against evil forces by drawing around it circles of fire and water. He awakens the different spiritual centers of the body and invokes the Supreme Spirit in his heart. Then he transfers the Supreme Spirit to the image before him and worships the image, regarding it no longer as clay or stone, but as the embodiment of Spirit, throbbing with life and consciousness. After the worship, the Supreme Spirit is recalled from the image to its true sanctuary, the heart of the priest. The real devotee knows the absurdity of worshiping the transcendental Reality with material articles—clothing that which pervades the whole universe and the beyond, putting on a pedestal that which cannot be limited by space, feeding that which is disembodied and incorporeal, singing before that whose glory the music of the spheres tries vainly to proclaim. But, through these rites, the devotee aspires to go ultimately beyond rites and rituals, forms and names, words and praise, and to realize God as the all-pervading consciousness.

Hindu priests are thoroughly acquainted with the rites of worship, but few of them are aware of their underlying significance. They move their hands and limbs mechanically, in obedience to the letter of the scriptures, and repeat the holy mantras like parrots. But from the very beginning, the inner meaning of these rites was revealed to Sri Ramakrishna. As he sat facing the image, a strange transformation came over his mind. While going through the prescribed ceremonies, he would actually find himself encircled by a wall of fire protecting him and the place of worship from unspiritual vibrations, or he would feel the rising of the mystic kundalini through the different centers of the body. The glow on his face, his deep absorption, and the intense atmosphere of the temple impressed everyone who saw him worship the deity.

Ramkumar wanted Sri Ramakrishna to learn the intricate rituals of the worship of Kali. To become a priest of Kali, one must undergo a special form of initiation from a qualified guru, and for Sri Ramakrishna a suitable brahmin was found. But no sooner did the brahmin speak the holy word in his ear than Sri Ramakrishna, overwhelmed with emotion, uttered a loud cry and plunged into deep concentration.

Mathur begged Sri Ramakrishna to take charge of the worship in the Kali temple. The young priest pleaded his incompetence and his ignorance of the scriptures. Mathur insisted that devotion and sincerity would more than compensate for any lack of formal knowledge and make the Divine Mother manifest herself through the image. In the end, Sri Ramakrishna had to yield to Mathur's request. He became the priest of Kali.

In 1856 Ramkumar breathed his last. Sri Ramakrishna had already witnessed more than one death in the family. He had come to realize how impermanent is life on earth. The more he was convinced of the transitory nature of worldly things, the more eager he became to realize God, the Fountain of Immortality.

The First Vision of Kali

Indeed, he soon discovered what a strange goddess he had chosen to serve. He became gradually enmeshed in the web of her all-pervading presence. To the ignorant she is, to be sure, the image of destruction; but he found in her the benign, all-loving Mother. Her neck is encircled with a garland of heads, her waist with a girdle of human arms, two of her hands hold weapons of death, and her eyes dart a glance of fire, but strangely enough, Ramakrishna felt in her breath the soothing touch of tender love and saw in her the seed of Immortality. She stands on the bosom of her consort, Siva, because she is the Sakti, the power, inseparable from the Absolute. She is surrounded by jackals and other unholy creatures, the denizens of the cremation ground. But is not the Ultimate

Reality above holiness and unholiness? She appears to be reeling under the spell of wine. But who would create this mad world unless under the influence of a divine drunkenness? She is the highest symbol of all the forces of nature, the synthesis of their antinomies, the Ultimate Divine in the form of woman. She now became to Sri Ramakrishna the only reality, and the world became an unsubstantial shadow. Into her worship he poured his soul. Before him, she stood as the transparent portal to the shrine of ineffable Reality.

The worship in the temple intensified Sri Ramakrishna's yearning for a living vision of the Mother of the Universe. He began to spend in meditation the time not actually employed in the temple service, and for this purpose he selected an extremely solitary place. A deep jungle, thick with underbrush and prickly plants, lay to the north of the temples. Used at one time as a burial ground, it was shunned by people even during the daytime for fear of ghosts. There, Sri Ramakrishna began to spend the whole night in meditation, returning to his room in the morning with eyes swollen as though from much weeping. While meditating, he would lay aside his cloth and his brahminical thread. Explaining this strange conduct, he once said to Hriday, "Don't you know that when one thinks of God, one should be freed from all ties? From our very birth we have the eight fetters of hatred, shame, lineage, pride of good conduct, fear, secretiveness, caste, and grief. The sacred thread reminds me that I am a brahmin and therefore superior to all. When calling on the Mother, one has to set aside all such ideas." Hriday thought his uncle was becoming insane.

As his love for God deepened, Sri Ramakrishna began either to forget or to drop the formalities of worship. Sitting before the image, he would spend hours singing the devotional songs of great devotees of the Mother, such as Kamalakanta and Ramprasad. Those rhapsodical songs, describing the direct vision of God, only intensified Sri Ramakrishna's longing. He felt the pangs of a child separated from its mother. Sometimes, in agony, he would rub his face against the ground and weep so bitterly that people, thinking he had lost his earthly mother, would sympathize with him in his grief. Sometimes, in moments of skepticism, he would cry, "Art thou true, Mother, or is it all fiction— mere poetry without any reality? If thou dost exist, why do I not see thee? Is religion a mere fantasy and art thou only a figment of man's imagination?" Sometimes he would sit on the prayer carpet for two hours like an inert object. He began to behave in an abnormal manner, most of the time unconscious of the world. He almost gave up food; and sleep left him altogether.

But he did not have to wait very long. He has thus described his first vision of the Mother:

> I felt as if my heart was being squeezed like a wet towel. I was overpowered with a great restlessness and a fear that it might not be my lot to realize her in this life. I could not bear the separation from her any longer. Life seemed to be not worth living. Suddenly my glance fell on the sword that was kept in the Mother's temple. I determined to put an end to my life. When I jumped up like a mad-man and seized it, suddenly the blessed Mother revealed herself. The buildings with their different parts, the temple, and everything else vanished from my sight, leaving no trace whatsoever, and in their stead I saw a limitless, infinite, effulgent ocean of consciousness. As far as the eye could see, the shining billows were madly rushing at me from all sides with a terrific noise to swallow me up! I was panting for breath. I was caught in the rush and collapsed, unconscious. What was happening in the outside world I did not know; but within me there was a steady flow of undiluted bliss, altogether new, and I felt the presence of the Divine Mother.

On his lips when he regained consciousness of the world was the word *Mother*.

God-Intoxicated State

Yet this was only a foretaste of the intense experiences to come. The first glimpse of the Divine Mother made him the more eager for her uninterrupted vision. He wanted to see her both in meditation and with eyes open. But the Mother began to play a teasing game of hide-and-seek with him, intensifying both his joy and his suffering. Weeping bitterly during the moments of separation from her, he would pass into a trance and then find her standing before him, smiling, talking, consoling, bidding him be of good cheer, and instructing him.

During this period of spiritual practice he had many uncommon experiences. When he sat to meditate, he would hear strange clicking sounds in the joints of his legs, as if someone were locking them up, one after the other, to keep him motionless; and at the conclusion of his meditation he would again hear the same sounds, this time unlocking them and leaving him free to move about. He would see flashes like a swarm of fireflies floating before his eyes, or a sea of deep mist around him, with luminous waves of molten silver. Again, from a sea of translucent mist he would behold the Mother rising, first her feet, then her waist, body, face, and head, and finally her whole person; he would feel her breath and hear her voice. Worshiping in the temple, sometimes he would become exalted, sometimes he would remain motionless as stone, sometimes he would almost collapse from excessive emotion.

Many of his actions, contrary to all tradition, seemed sacrilegious to the people. He would take a flower and touch it to his own head, body, and feet, and then offer it to the goddess. Or, like a drunkard, he would reel to the throne of the Mother, touch her chin by way of showing his affection for her, and sing, talk, joke, laugh, and dance. Or he would take a morsel of food from the plate and hold it to her mouth, begging her to eat it, and would not be satisfied till he was convinced that she had really eaten. After the Mother had been put to sleep at night, from his own room he would hear her ascending to the upper story of the temple with the light steps of a happy girl, her anklets jingling. Then he would discover her standing with flowing hair, her black form silhouetted against the night sky, looking at the Ganges or at the distant lights of Calcutta.

Naturally the temple officials took him for an insane person. His worldly well-wishers brought him to skilled physicians, but no medicine could cure his malady. Many a time he doubted his sanity himself. For he had been sailing across an uncharted sea, with no earthly guide to direct him. His only haven of security was the Divine Mother herself. To her he would pray, "I do not know what these things are. I am ignorant of mantras and the scriptures. Teach me, Mother, how to realize thee. Who else can help me? Art thou not my only refuge and guide?" And the sustaining presence of the Mother never failed him in his distress or doubt. Even those who criticized his conduct were greatly impressed with his purity, guilelessness, truthfulness, integrity, and holiness. They felt an uplifting influence in his presence.

It is said that samadhi, or trance, no more than opens the portal of the spiritual realm. Sri Ramakrishna felt an unquenchable desire to enjoy God in various ways. For his meditation he built a place in the northern wooded section of the temple garden. With Hriday's help he planted there five sacred trees. The spot, known as the Panchavati, became the scene of many of his visions.

As his spiritual mood deepened he more and more felt himself to be a child of the Divine Mother. He learned to surrender himself completely to her will and let her direct him.

"O Mother," he would constantly pray, "I have taken refuge in thee. Teach me what to do and what to say. Thy will is paramount everywhere and is for the good of thy children. Merge my will in thy will and make me thy instrument."

His visions became deeper and more intimate. He no longer had to meditate to behold the Divine Mother. Even while retaining consciousness of the outer world, he would see her as tangibly as the temples, the trees, the river, and the persons around him.

On a certain occasion Mathur Babu stealthily entered the temple to watch the worship. He was profoundly moved by the young priest's devotion and sincerity. He realized that Sri Ramakrishna had transformed the stone image into the living goddess.

Sri Ramakrishna one day fed a cat with the food that was to be offered to Kali. This was too much for the manager of the temple garden, who considered himself responsible for the proper conduct of the worship. He reported Sri Ramakrishna's insane behavior to Mathur Babu.

Sri Ramakrishna has described the incident: "The Divine Mother revealed to me in the Kali temple that it was she who had become everything. She showed me that everything was full of Consciousness. The image was Consciousness, the altar was Consciousness, the water vessels were Consciousness, the door sill was Consciousness, the marble floor was Consciousness—all was Consciousness. I found everything inside the room soaked, as it were, in bliss—the bliss of God. I saw a wicked man in front of the Kali temple, but in him also I saw the power of the Divine Mother vibrating. That was why I fed a cat with the food that was to be offered to the Divine Mother. I clearly perceived that all this was the Divine Mother—even the cat. The manager of the temple garden wrote to Mathur Babu saying that I was feeding the cat with the offering intended for the Divine Mother. But Mathur Babu had insight into the state of my mind. He wrote back to the manager, 'Let him do whatever he likes. You must not say anything to him.'"

One of the painful ailments from which Sri Ramakrishna suffered at this time was a burning sensation in his body, and he was cured by a strange vision. During worship in the temple, following the scriptural injunctions, he would imagine the presence of the "sinner" in himself and the destruction of this "sinner." One day he was meditating in the Panchavati, when he saw come out of him a red-eyed man of black complexion, reeling like a drunkard. Soon there emerged from him another person, of serene countenance, wearing the ocher cloth of a sannyasi and carrying in his hand a trident. The second person attacked the first and killed him with the trident. Thereafter Sri Ramakrishna was free of his pain.

About this time he began to worship God by assuming the attitude of a servant toward his master. He imitated the mood of Hanuman, the monkey chieftain of the Ramayana, the ideal servant of Rama and traditional model for this self-effacing form of devotion. When he meditated on Hanuman, his movements and his way of life began to resemble those of a monkey. His eyes became restless. He lived on fruits and roots. With his cloth tied around his waist, a portion of it hanging in the form of a tail, he jumped from place to place instead of walking. And after a short while he was blessed with a vision of Sita, the divine consort of Rama, who entered his body and disappeared there with the words, "I bequeath to you my smile."

Mathur had faith in the sincerity of Sri Ramakrishna's spiritual zeal, but began now to doubt his sanity. He had watched him jumping about like a monkey. One day, when Rani Rasmani was listening to Sri Ramakrishna's singing in the temple, the young priest abruptly turned and slapped her. While apparently listening to his song, she had actually been thinking of a lawsuit. She accepted the punishment as though the Divine Mother herself had imposed it, but Mathur was distressed. He begged Sri Ramakrishna to keep his feelings under control and to heed the conventions of society. God himself, he argued, follows laws. God never permitted, for instance, flowers of two colors to grow on the same stalk. The following day Sri Ramakrishna presented Mathur Babu with two hibiscus flowers growing on the same stalk, one red and one white.

Mathur and Rani Rasmani began to ascribe the mental ailment of Sri Ramakrishna in part, at least, to his observance of rigid continence. Thinking that a natural life would relax the tension of his nerves, they engineered a plan with two women of ill fame. But as soon as the women entered his room, Sri Ramakrishna beheld in them the manifestation of the Divine Mother of the Universe and went into samadhi uttering her name.

Haladhari

In 1858 there came to Dakshineswar a cousin of Sri Ramakrishna, Haladhari by name, who was to remain there about eight years. On account of Sri Ramakrishna's indifferent health, Mathur appointed this man to the office of priest in the Kali temple. He was a complex character, versed in the letter of the scriptures, but hardly aware of their spirit. He loved to participate in hair-splitting theological discussions, and by the measure of his own erudition, he proceeded to gauge Sri Ramakrishna. An orthodox brahmin, he thoroughly disapproved of his cousin's unorthodox actions, but he was not unimpressed by Sri Ramakrishna's purity of life, ecstatic love of God, and yearning for realization.

One day Haladhari upset Sri Ramakrishna with the statement that God is incomprehensible to the human mind. Sri Ramakrishna has described the great moment of doubt when he wondered whether his visions had really misled him: "With sobs I prayed to the Mother, 'Canst thou have the heart to deceive me like this because I am a fool?' A stream of tears flowed from my eyes. Shortly afterward I saw a volume of mist rising from the floor and filling the space before me. In the midst of it there appeared a face with flowing beard, calm, highly expressive, and fair. Fixing its gaze steadily upon me, it said solemnly, 'Remain in *bhava-mukha*, on the threshold of relative consciousness.' This it repeated three times and then it gently disappeared in the mist, which itself dissolved. This vision reassured me."

A garbled report of Sri Ramakrishna's failing health, indifference to worldly life, and various abnormal activities reached Kamarpukur and filled the heart of his poor mother with anguish. At her repeated request he returned to his village for a change of air. But his boyhood friends did not interest him anymore. A divine fever was consuming him. He spent a great part of the day and night in one of the cremation grounds, in meditation. The place reminded him of the impermanence of the human body, of human hopes and achievements. It also reminded him of Kali, the goddess of destruction.

Marriage and After

In a few months his health showed improvement, and he recovered to some extent his natural buoyancy of spirit. His happy mother was encouraged to think it might be a good time to arrange his marriage. The boy was now twenty-three years old. A wife would bring him back to earth, and she was delighted when her son welcomed her suggestion. Perhaps he saw in it the finger of God.

Saradamani, a little girl of five, lived in the neighboring village of Jayrambati. Even at this age, she had been praying to God to make her character as stainless and fragrant as the white tuberose. Looking at the full moon, she would say, "O God, there are dark spots even on the moon. But make my character spotless." It was she who was selected as the bride for Sri Ramakrishna.

The marriage ceremony was duly performed. Such early marriage in India is in the nature of a betrothal, the marriage being consummated when the girl attains puberty. But in this case the marriage remained forever unconsummated. Sri Ramakrishna lived at Kamarpukur about a year and a half and then returned to Dakshineswar.

Hardly had he crossed the threshold of the Kali temple when he found himself again in the whirlwind. His madness reappeared tenfold. The same meditation and prayer, the same ecstatic moods, the same burning sensation, the same weeping, the same sleeplessness, the same indifference to the body and the outside world, the same divine delirium. He subjected himself to fresh disciplines in order to eradicate greed and lust, the two great impediments to spiritual progress. With a rupee in one hand and some earth in the other, he would reflect on the comparative value of these two for the realization of God, and finding them equally worthless, he would toss them, with equal indifference, into the Ganges. Women he regarded as the manifestations of the Divine Mother. Never, even in a dream, did he feel the impulses of lust. And, to root out of his mind the idea of caste superiority, he cleaned a pariah's house with his long and neglected hair. When he sat in meditation, birds would perch on his head and peck in his hair for grains of food. Snakes would crawl over his body, and neither would be aware of the other. Sleep left him altogether. Day and night, visions flitted before him. He saw the sannyasi who had previously killed the "sinner" in him again coming out of his body, threatening him with the trident, and ordering him to concentrate on God. Or the same sannyasi would visit distant places, following a luminous path, and bring him reports of what was happening there. Sri Ramakrishna said later that in the case of an advanced devotee, the mind itself becomes the guru, living and moving like an embodied being.

Rani Rasmani, the founder of the temple garden, passed away in 1861. After her death, her son-in-law Mathur became the sole executor of the estate. He placed himself and his resources at the disposal of Sri Ramakrishna and began to look after his physical comfort. Sri Ramakrishna later spoke of him as one of his five "suppliers of stores" appointed by the Divine Mother. Whenever a desire arose in his mind, Mathur fulfilled it without hesitation.

The Brahmani

There came to Dakshineswar at this time a brahmin woman who was to play an important part in Sri Ramakrishna's spiritual unfolding. Born in East Bengal, she was adept in the Tantrik and Vaishnava methods of worship. She was slightly over fifty years of age, handsome, and garbed in the orange robe of a nun. Her sole possessions were a few books and two pieces of wearing cloth.

Sri Ramakrishna welcomed the visitor with great respect, described to her his experiences and visions, and told her of people's belief that these were symptoms of madness. She listened to him attentively and said, "My son, everyone in this world is mad. Some are mad for money, some for creature comforts, some for name and fame, and you are mad for God." She assured him that he was passing through the almost unknown spiritual experience described in the scriptures as *mahabhava*, the most exalted rapture of divine love. She told him that this extreme exaltation had been described as manifesting itself through nineteen physical symptoms, including the shedding of tears, a tremor of the body, horripilation, perspiration, and a burning sensation. The bhakti scriptures, she declared, had recorded only two instances of the experience, namely, those of Sri Radha and Sri Chaitanya.

Very soon a tender relationship sprang up between Sri Ramakrishna and the Brahmani, she looking upon him as the Baby Krishna, and he upon her as mother. Day after day she watched his ecstasy during the kirtan and meditation, his samadhi, his mad yearning; and she recognized in him a power to transmit spirituality to others. She came to the conclusion that such things were not possible for an ordinary devotee, not even for a highly developed soul. Only an incarnation of God was capable of such spiritual manifestations. She proclaimed openly that Sri Ramakrishna, like Sri Chaitanya, was an incarnation of God.

When Sri Ramakrishna told Mathur what the Brahmani had said about him, Mathur shook his head in doubt. He was reluctant to accept him as an incarnation of God, an avatar comparable to Rama, Krishna, Buddha, and Chaitanya, though he admitted Sri Ramakrishna's extraordinary spirituality. Whereupon the Brahmani asked Mathur to arrange a conference of scholars who should discuss the matter with her. He agreed to the proposal and the meeting was arranged. It was to be held in the natmandir in front of the Kali temple.

Two famous pundits of the time were invited: Vaishnavcharan, the leader of the Vaishnava society, and Gauri. The first to arrive was Vaishnavcharan, with a distinguished company of scholars and devotees. The Brahmani, like a proud mother, proclaimed her view before him and supported it with quotations from the scriptures. As the pundits discussed the deep theological question, Sri Ramakrishna, perfectly indifferent to everything happening around him, sat in their midst like a child, immersed in his own thoughts, sometimes smiling, sometimes chewing a pinch of spices from a pouch, or saying to Vaishnavcharan with a nudge, "Look here. Sometimes I feel like this, too." Presently Vaishnavcharan arose to declare himself in total agreement with the view of the Brahmani. He declared that Sri Ramakrishna had undoubtedly experienced mahabhava and that this was the certain sign of the rare manifestation of God in a man. The people assembled there, especially the officers of the temple garden, were struck dumb. Sri Ramakrishna said to Mathur, like a boy, "Just fancy, he too says so! Well, I am glad to learn that after all it is not a disease."

When, a few days later, Pundit Gauri arrived, another meeting was held, and he agreed with the view of the Brahmani and Vaishnavcharan. To Sri Ramakrishna's remark that Vaishnavcharan had declared him to be an avatar, Gauri replied, "Is that all he has to say about you? Then he has said very little. I am fully convinced that you are that mine of spiritual power, only a small fraction of which descends on earth, from time to time, in the form of an incarnation."

"Ah!" said Sri Ramakrishna with a smile, "You seem to have quite outbid Vaishnavcharan in this matter. What have you found in me that makes you entertain such an idea?"

Gauri said, "I feel it in my heart and I have the scriptures on my side. I am ready to prove it to anyone who challenges me."

"Well," Sri Ramakrishna said, "it is you who say so; but, believe me, I know nothing about it."

Thus the insane priest was, by verdict of the great scholars of the day, proclaimed a divine incarnation. His visions were not the result of an overheated brain; they had precedent in spiritual history. And how did the proclamation affect Sri Ramakrishna himself? He remained the simple child of the Mother that he had been since the first day of his life. Years later, when two of his householder disciples openly spoke of him as a divine incarnation and the matter was reported to him, he said with a touch of sarcasm, "Do they think they will enhance my glory that way? One of them is an actor on the stage and the other a physician. What do they know about incarnations? Why, years ago pundits like Gauri and Vaishnavcharan declared me to be an avatar. They were great scholars and knew what they said. But that did not make any change in my mind."

Sri Ramakrishna was a learner all his life. He would often quote a proverb to his disciples: "Friend, the more I live, the more I learn." When the excitement created by the Brahmani's declaration was over, he set himself to the task of practicing spiritual disciplines according to the traditional methods laid down in the Tantra and Vaishnava scriptures. Hitherto he had pursued his spiritual ideal according to the promptings of his own mind and heart. Now he accepted the Brahmani as his guru and set foot on the traditional highways.

4

Sadhanas or Spiritual Disciplines

Tantra

According to the Tantra, the Ultimate Reality is *Chit*, or Consciousness, which is identical with *Sat*, or Being, and with *Ananda*, or Bliss. This Ultimate Reality, Satchidananda, Existence-Knowledge-Bliss Absolute, is identical with the Reality preached in the Vedas. And the human individual is identical with this Reality; but under the influence of *maya*, or illusion, we have forgotten our true nature. We take to be real a merely apparent world of subject and object, and this error is the cause of bondage and suffering. The goal of spiritual discipline is the rediscovery of our true identity with the divine Reality.

For the achievement of this goal, the Vedanta prescribes an austere negative method of discrimination and renunciation, which can be followed by only a few individuals endowed with sharp intelligence and unshakable willpower. But Tantra takes into consideration the natural weakness of human beings, their lower appetites, and their love for the concrete. It combines philosophy with rituals, meditation with ceremonies, renunciation with enjoyment. The underlying purpose is gradually to train the aspirant to meditate on his identity with the Ultimate.

The average person wishes to enjoy the material objects of the world. Tantra bids him enjoy these, but, at the same time, discover in them the presence of God. Mystical rites are prescribed by which, slowly, the sense objects become spiritualized and sense attraction is transformed into a love of God. So the very "bonds" of man are turned into "releasers." The very poison that kills is transmuted into the elixir of life. Outward renunciation is not necessary. Thus, the aim of Tantra is to sublimate *bhoga*, or enjoyment, into yoga, or union with Consciousness. For, according to this philosophy, the world with all its manifestations is nothing but the sport of Siva and Sakti, the Absolute and its inscrutable power.

The disciplines of Tantra are graded to suit aspirants of all degrees. Exercises are prescribed for people with "animal," "heroic," and "divine" outlooks. Certain of the rites require the presence of members of the opposite sex. Here the aspirant learns to look on woman as the embodiment of the Goddess Kali, the Mother of the Universe. The very basis of Tantra is the motherhood of God and the glorification of woman. Every part of a woman's body is to be regarded as incarnate divinity. But the rites are extremely dangerous. The help of a qualified guru is absolutely necessary. An unwary devotee may lose his foothold and fall into a pit of depravity.

According to the Tantra, Sakti is the active creative force in the universe. Siva, the Absolute, is a more or less passive principle. Further, Sakti is as inseparable from Siva as fire's power to burn is from fire itself. Sakti, the creative power, contains in its womb the universe, and therefore is the Divine Mother. All women are her symbols. Kali is one of her several forms. The meditation on Kali, the creative power, is the central discipline of the Tantra. While meditating, the aspirant at first regards himself as one with the Absolute and then thinks that out of that impersonal Consciousness emerge two entities, namely, his own self and the living form of the goddess. He then projects the goddess into the tangible image before him and worships it as the Divine Mother.

Sri Ramakrishna set himself to the task of practicing the disciplines of Tantra; and at the bidding of the Divine Mother herself he accepted the Brahmani as his guru. He performed profound and delicate ceremonies in the Panchavati and under the bel tree at the northern extremity of the temple compound. He practiced all the disciplines of the sixty-four principal Tantra books, and it took him never more than three days to achieve the result promised in any one of them. After the observance of a few preliminary rites, he would be overwhelmed with a strange divine fervor and would go into samadhi, where his mind would dwell in exaltation. Evil ceased to exist for him. The word *carnal* lost its meaning. The whole world and everything in it appeared as the *lila*, the sport, of Siva and Sakti. He beheld everywhere manifest the power and beauty of the Mother; the whole world, animate and inanimate, appeared to him as pervaded with Chit, Consciousness, and with Ananda, Bliss.

He saw in a vision the ultimate cause of the universe as a huge luminous triangle giving birth every moment to an infinite number of worlds. He heard the Anahata Sabda, the great sound Om, of which the innumerable sounds of the universe are only so many echoes. He acquired the eight supernatural powers of yoga, which make a man almost omnipotent, and these he spurned as of no value whatsoever to the Spirit. He had a vision of the divine maya, the inscrutable power of God, by which the universe is created and sustained, and into which it is finally absorbed. In this vision he saw a woman of exquisite beauty, about to become a mother, emerging from the Ganges and slowly approaching the Panchavati. Presently she gave birth to a child and began to nurse it tenderly. A moment later, she assumed a terrible aspect, seized the child with her grim jaws, and crushed it. Swallowing it, she reentered the waters of the Ganges.

But the most remarkable experience during this period was the awakening of the kundalini Sakti, the "serpent power." He actually saw the power, at first lying asleep at the bottom of the spinal column, then waking up and ascending along the mystic *sushumna* canal and through its six centers, or lotuses, to the *sahasrara*, the thousand-petalled lotus in the top of the head. He further saw that as the kundalini went upward, the different lotuses bloomed. And this phenomenon was accompanied by visions and trances. Later on, he described to his disciples and devotees the various movements of the kundalini: the fishlike, birdlike, monkeylike, and so on. The awakening of the kundalini is the beginning of spiritual consciousness, and its union with Siva in the sahasrara, ending in samadhi, is the consummation of the Tantrik disciplines.

About this time it was revealed to him that in a short while many devotees would seek his guidance.

Vaishnava Disciples

After completing the Tantrik sadhana, Sri Ramakrishna followed the Brahmani in the disciplines of Vaishnavism. The Vaishnavas are worshipers of Vishnu, the "all-pervading," the supreme God, who is also known as Hari and Narayana. Of Vishnu's various incarnations the two with the largest number of followers are Rama and Krishna.

Vaishnavism is exclusively a religion of bhakti. Bhakti is intense love of God, attachment to him alone; it is of the nature of bliss and bestows upon the lover immortality and liberation. God, according to Vaishnavism, cannot be realized through logic or reason; and, without bhakti, all penances, austerities, and rites are futile. Man cannot realize God by self-exertion alone. For the vision of God, God's grace is absolutely necessary, and this grace is felt by the pure of heart. The mind is to be purified through bhakti. The pure mind then remains forever immersed in the ecstasy of God-vision. It is the cultivation of this divine love that is the chief concern of the Vaishnava religion.

There are three kinds of formal devotion: *tamasic, rajasic,* and *sattvic.* If a person, while showing devotion to God, is actuated by malevolence, arrogance, jealousy, or anger, then his devotion is tamasic, since it is influenced by *tamas,* the quality of inertia. If he worships God from a desire for fame or wealth, or from any otherworldly ambition, then his devotion is rajasic, since it is influenced by *rajas,* the quality of activity. But if a person loves God without any thought of material gain, if he performs his duties to please God alone and maintains toward all created beings the attitude of friendship, then his devotion is called sattvic, since it is influenced by *sattva,* the quality of harmony. But the highest devotion transcends the three *gunas,* or qualities, and is a spontaneous, uninterrupted inclination of the mind toward God, the Inner Soul of all beings; it wells up in the heart of a true devotee as soon as he hears the name of God or mention of God's attributes. A devotee possessed of this love would not accept the happiness of heaven if it were offered him. His one desire is to love God under all conditions—in pleasure and pain, life and death, honor and dishonor, prosperity and adversity.

There are two stages of bhakti. The first is known as *vaidhi-bhakti,* or love of God qualified by scriptural injunctions. The devotees of this stage are prescribed regular and methodical worship, hymns, prayers, the repetition of God's name, and the chanting of his glories. This lower bhakti, in course of time, matures into *para-bhakti,* or supreme devotion, known also as *prema,* the most intense form of divine love. Divine love is an end in itself. It exists potentially in all human hearts, but in the case of bound creatures it is misdirected to earthly objects.

To develop the devotee's love for God, Vaishnavism humanizes God. God is to be regarded as the devotee's parent, master, friend, child, husband, or sweetheart, each succeeding relationship representing an intensification of love. These *bhavas,* or attitudes toward God, are known as *santa, dasya, sakhya, vatsalya,* and *madhur.* The rishis of the Vedas; Hanuman; the cowherd boys of Vrindavan; Rama's mother, Kausalya; and Radhika, Krishna's sweetheart, exhibited, respectively, the most perfect examples of these forms. In the ascending scale, the glories of God are gradually forgotten, and the devotee realizes more and more the intimacy of divine communion. Finally, he regards himself as the mistress of his Beloved, and no artificial barrier remains to separate him from his Ideal. No social or moral obligation can bind to the earth his soaring spirit. He experiences perfect union with the Godhead. Unlike the Vedantist, who strives to transcend all varieties of the subject-object relationship, a devotee of the Vaishnava path wishes to retain both his own individuality and the personality of God. To him God is not an intangible Absolute, but the Purushottama, the Supreme Person.

While practicing the discipline of the *madhur bhava,* the male devotee often regards himself as a woman in order to develop the most intense form of love for Sri Krishna, the only purusha, or man, in the universe. This assumption of the attitude of the opposite sex has a deep psychological significance. It is a matter of common experience that an idea may be cultivated to such an intense degree that every idea alien to it is driven from the mind. This peculiarity of the mind may be utilized for the subjugation of the lower desires and the development of the spiritual nature. Now, the idea that is the basis of all desires and passions in a man is the conviction of his indissoluble association with a male body. If he can inoculate himself thoroughly with the idea that he is a woman, he can get rid of the desires peculiar to his male body. Again, the idea that he is a woman may, in turn, be made to give way to another higher idea, namely, that he is neither man nor woman, but the impersonal Spirit. The impersonal Spirit alone can enjoy real communion with the impersonal God. Hence the highest realization of the Vaishnava draws close to the transcendental experience of the Vedantist.

A beautiful expression of the Vaishnava worship of God through love is to be found in the Vrindavan episode of the *Bhagavata*. The gopis, or milkmaids, of Vrindavan regarded the six-year-old Krishna as their Beloved. They sought no personal gain or happiness from this love. They surrendered to Krishna their bodies, minds, and souls. Of all the gopis, Radhika, or Radha, because of her intense love for him, was the closest to Krishna. She manifested mahabhava and was united with her Beloved. This union represents, through sensuous language, a super-sensuous experience.

Sri Chaitanya, also known as Gauranga, Gora, or Nimai, born in Bengal in 1485 and regarded as an incarnation of God, is a great prophet of the Vaishnava religion. Chaitanya declared the chanting of God's name to be the most efficacious spiritual discipline for the Kaliyuga.

Sri Ramakrishna, as the monkey Hanuman, had already worshiped God as his Master. Through his devotion to Kali he had worshiped God as his Mother. He was now to take up the other relationships prescribed by the Vaishnava scriptures.

Ramlala

About the year 1864 there came to Dakshineswar a wandering Vaish-nava monk, Jatadhari, whose ideal deity was Rama. He always carried with him a small metal image of the deity, which he called by the endearing name of Ramlala, the Boy Rama. Toward this little image he displayed the tender affection of Kausalya for her divine son, Rama. As a result of lifelong spiritual practice he had actually found in the metal image the presence of his Ideal. For him, Ramlala was no longer a metal image, but the living God. He devoted himself to nursing Rama, feeding Rama, playing with Rama, taking Rama for a walk, and bathing Rama. And he found that the image responded to his love.

Sri Ramakrishna, much impressed with his devotion, requested Jatadhari to spend a few days at Dakshineswar. Soon Ramlala became the favorite companion of Sri Ramakrishna, too. Later on he described to the devotees how the little image would dance gracefully before him, jump on his back, insist on being taken in his arms, run to the fields in the sun, pluck flowers from the bushes, and play pranks like a naughty boy. A very sweet relationship sprang up between him and Ramlala, for whom he felt the love of a mother.

One day Jatadhari requested Sri Ramakrishna to keep the image and bade him adieu with tearful eyes. He declared that Ramlala had fulfilled his innermost prayer and that he now had no more need of formal worship. A few days later Sri Ramakrishna was blessed through Ramlala with a vision of Ramachandra, whereby he realized that the Rama of the *Ramayana*, the son of Dasaratha, pervades the whole universe as Spirit and Consciousness; that he is its creator, sustainer, and destroyer; that, in still another aspect, he is the transcendental Brahman, without form, attribute, or name.

While worshiping Ramlala as the divine child, Sri Ramakrishna's heart became filled with motherly tenderness, and he began to regard himself as a woman. His speech and gestures changed. He began to move freely with the ladies of Mathur's family, who now looked upon him as one of their own sex. During this time he worshiped the Divine Mother as her companion or handmaid.

In Communion with the Divine Beloved

Sri Ramakrishna now devoted himself to scaling the most inaccessible and dizzy heights of dualistic worship, namely, the complete union with Sri Krishna as the Beloved of the heart. He regarded himself as one of the gopis of Vrindavan, mad with longing for her divine sweetheart. At his request Mathur provided him with woman's dress and jewelry. In this love-pursuit, food and drink were forgotten. Day and night he wept bitterly. The yearning turned into a mad frenzy; for the divine Krishna began to play with him the old tricks he had played with the gopis. He would tease and taunt, now and then revealing himself, but always keeping at a distance. Sri Ramakrishna's anguish brought on a return of the old physical symptoms: the burning sensation, an oozing of blood through the pores, a loosening of the joints, and the stopping of physiological functions.

The Vaishnava scriptures advise one to propitiate Radha and obtain her grace in order to realize Sri Krishna. So the tortured devotee now turned his prayer to her. Within a short time he enjoyed her blessed vision. He saw and felt the figure of Radha disappearing into his own body.

He said later on, "It is impossible to describe the heavenly beauty and sweetness of Radha. Her very appearance showed that she had completely forgotten herself in her passionate attachment to Krishna. Her complexion was a light yellow."

Now one with Radha, he manifested the great ecstatic love, the mahabhava, which had found in her its fullest expression. Later Sri Ramakrishna said, "The manifestation in the same individual of the nineteen different kinds of emotion for God is called, in the books on bhakti, mahabhava. An ordinary man takes a whole lifetime to express even a single one of these. But in this body [meaning himself] there has been a complete manifestation of all nineteen."

The love of Radha is the precursor of the resplendent vision of Sri Krishna, and Sri Ramakrishna soon experienced that vision. The enchanting form of Krishna appeared to him and merged in his person. He became Krishna; he totally forgot his own individuality and the world; he saw Krishna in himself and in the universe. Thus he attained the fulfillment of the worship of the personal God. He drank from the fountain of immortal bliss. The agony of his heart vanished forever. He realized *amrita*, immortality, beyond the shadow of death.

One day, listening to a recitation of the *Bhagavata* on the veranda of the Radhakanta temple, he fell into a divine mood and saw the enchanting form of Krishna. He perceived the luminous rays issuing from Krishna's lotus feet in the form of a stout rope, which touched first the *Bhagavata* and then his own chest, connecting all three—God, the scripture, and the devotee. "After this vision," he used to say, "I came to realize that Bhagavan, bhakta, and *Bhagavata*—God, devotee, and scripture—are in reality one and the same."

Vedanta

The Brahmani was the enthusiastic teacher and astonished beholder of Sri Ramakrishna in his spiritual progress. She became proud of the achievements of her unique pupil. But the pupil himself was not permitted to rest; his destiny beckoned him forward. His Divine Mother would allow him no respite till he had left behind the entire realm of duality with its visions, experiences, and ecstatic dreams. But for the new ascent, the old tender guides would not suffice. The Brahmani, on whom he had depended for three years, saw her son escape from her to follow the command of a teacher with masculine strength, a sterner mien, a gnarled physique, and a virile voice. The new guru was a wandering monk, the sturdy Totapuri, whom Sri Ramakrishna learned to address affectionately as Nangta, the "Naked One," because of his total renunciation of all earthly objects and attachments, including even a piece of wearing cloth.

Totapuri was the bearer of a philosophy new to Sri Ramakrishna, the nondualistic Vedanta philosophy, whose conclusions Totapuri had experienced in his own life. This ancient Hindu system designates the Ultimate Reality as Brahman, also described as Satchidananda, Existence-Knowledge-Bliss Absolute. Brahman is the only real existence. In it there is no time, no space, no causality, no multiplicity. But through maya, its inscrutable power, time, space, and causality are created and the One appears to break into the many. The eternal Spirit appears as a manifold of individuals endowed with form and subject to the conditions of time. The Immortal becomes a victim of birth and death. The Changeless undergoes change. The sinless Pure Soul, hypnotized by its own maya, experiences the joys of heaven and the pains of hell. But these experiences based on the duality of the subject-object relationship are unreal. Even the vision of a personal God is, ultimately speaking, as illusory as the experience of any other object. Man attains his liberation, therefore, by piercing the veil of maya and rediscovering his total identity with Brahman. Knowing himself to be one with the Universal Spirit, he realizes ineffable peace. Only then does he go beyond the fiction of birth and death; only then does he become immortal. And this is the ultimate goal of all religions—to dehypnotize the soul now hypnotized by its own ignorance.

The path of the Vedantic discipline is the path of *neti*, or negation, in which, by stern determination, all that is unreal is both negated and renounced. It is the path of jnana, knowledge, the direct method of realizing the Absolute. After the negation of everything relative, including the discriminating ego itself, the aspirant merges in the One without a second, in the bliss of *nirvikalpa* samadhi, where subject and object are alike dissolved. The soul goes beyond the realm of thought. The domain of duality is transcended. Maya is left behind with all its changes and modifications. The Real Man towers above the delusions of creation, preservation, and destruction. An avalanche of indescribable Bliss sweeps away all relative ideas of pain and pleasure, good and evil. There shines in the heart the glory of the Eternal Brahman, Existence-Knowledge-Bliss Absolute: knower, knowledge, and known are dissolved in the ocean of one eternal Consciousness; love, lover, and beloved merge in the unbounded sea of supreme Felicity; birth, growth, and death vanish in infinite Existence. All doubts and misgivings are quelled forever;

the oscillations of the mind are stopped; the momentum of past actions is exhausted. Breaking down the ridgepole of the tabernacle in which the soul has made its abode for untold ages, stilling the body, calming the mind, drowning the ego, the sweet joy of Brahman wells up in that superconscious state. Space disappears into nothingness, time is swallowed in eternity, and causation becomes a dream of the past. Only Existence is. Ah! Who can describe what the soul then feels in its communion with the Self?

Even when man descends from this dizzy height, he is devoid of ideas of "I" and "mine"; he looks on the body as a mere shadow, an outer sheath encasing the soul. He does not dwell on the past, takes no thought for the future, and looks with indifference on the present. He surveys everything in the world with an eye of equality; he is no longer touched by the infinite variety of phenomena; he no longer reacts to pleasure and pain. He remains unmoved whether he—that is to say, his body—is worshiped by the good or tormented by the wicked, for he realizes that it is the one Brahman that manifests itself through everything. The impact of such an experience devastates the body and mind. Consciousness becomes blasted, as it were, with an excess of light. In the Vedanta books, it is said that after the experience of nirvikalpa samadhi, the body drops off like a dry leaf. Only those who are born with a special mission for the world can return from this height to the valleys of normal life. They live and move in the world for the welfare of humankind. They are invested with a supreme spiritual power. A divine glory shines through them.

Totapuri

Totapuri arrived at the Dakshineswar temple garden toward the end of 1864. Perhaps born in the Punjab, he was the head of a monastery in that province of India and claimed leadership of seven hundred sannyasis. Trained from early youth in the disciplines of the Advaita Vedanta, he looked upon the world as an illusion. The gods and goddesses of the dualistic worship were to him mere fantasies of the deluded mind. Prayers, ceremonies, rites, and rituals had nothing to do with true religion, and about these he was utterly indifferent. Exercising self-exertion and unshakable willpower, he had liberated himself from attachment to the sense objects of the relative universe. For forty years he had practiced austere discipline on the bank of the sacred Narmada and had finally realized his identity with the Absolute. Thenceforward he roamed in the world as an unfettered soul, a lion free from the cage. Clad in a loincloth, he spent his days under the canopy of the sky both in storm and sunshine, feeding his body on the slender pittance of alms. He had been visiting the estuary of the Ganges. On his return journey along the bank of the sacred river, led by the inscrutable divine will, he stopped at Dakshineswar.

Totapuri, discovering at once that Sri Ramakrishna was prepared to be a student of Vedanta, asked to initiate him into its mysteries. With the permission of the Divine Mother, Sri Ramakrishna agreed to the proposal. But Totapuri explained that only a sannyasi could receive the teaching of Vedanta. Sri Ramakrishna agreed to renounce the world, but with the stipulation that the ceremony of his initiation into the monastic order be performed in secret, to spare the feelings of his old mother, who had been living with him at Dakshineswar.

On the appointed day, in the small hours of the morning, a fire was lighted in the Panchavati. Totapuri and Sri Ramakrishna sat before it. The flame played on their faces. "Ramakrishna was a small brown man with a short beard and beautiful eyes, long dark eyes, full of light, obliquely set and slightly veiled, never very wide open, but seeing half-closed a great distance both outwardly and inwardly. His mouth was open over his white teeth in a bewitching smile, at once affectionate and mischievous. Of medium height, he was thin to emaciation and extremely delicate. His temperament was high-strung, for he was super-sensitive to all the winds of joy and sorrow, both moral and physical. He was indeed a living reflection of all that happened before the mirror of his eyes, a two-sided mirror, turned both out and in."[1] Facing him, the other rose like a rock. He was very tall and robust, a sturdy and tough oak. His constitution and mind were of iron. He was the strong leader of men.

In the burning flame before him Sri Ramakrishna performed the rituals of destroying his attachment to relatives, friends, body, mind, sense organs, ego, and the world. The leaping flame swallowed it all, making the initiate free and pure. The sacred thread and the tuft of hair were consigned to the fire, completing his severance from caste, sex, and society. Last of all, he burned in that fire, with all that is holy as his witness, his desire for enjoyment here and hereafter. He uttered the sacred mantras giving assurance of safety and fearlessness to all beings, who were only manifestations of his own Self. The rites completed, the disciple received from the guru the loincloth and ocher robe, the emblems of his new life.

The teacher and the disciple repaired to the meditation room nearby. Totapuri began to impart to Sri Ramakrishna the great truths of Vedanta.

"Brahman," he said, "is the only reality, ever pure, ever illumined, ever free, beyond the limits of time, space, and causation. Though apparently divided by names and forms through the inscrutable power of maya, that enchantress who makes the impossible possible, Brahman is really one and undivided. When a seeker merges in the beatitude of samadhi, he does not perceive time and space or name and form, the offspring of maya. Whatever is within the domain of maya is unreal. Give it up. Destroy the prison house of name and form and rush out of it with the strength of a lion. Dive deep in search of the Self and realize it through samadhi. You will find the world of name and form vanishing into void, and the puny ego dissolving in Brahman-consciousness. You will realize your identity with Brahman, Existence-Knowledge-Bliss Absolute."

Quoting the Upanishad, Totapuri said, "That knowledge is shallow by which one sees or hears or knows another. What is shallow is worthless and can never give real felicity. But the knowledge by which one does not see another or hear another or know another, which is beyond duality, is great, and through such knowledge one attains the infinite Bliss. How can the mind and senses grasp that which shines in the heart of all as the Eternal Subject?"

Totapuri asked the disciple to withdraw his mind from all objects of the relative world, including the gods and goddesses, and to concentrate on the Absolute. But the task was not easy even for Sri Ramakrishna. He found it impossible to take his mind beyond Kali, the Divine Mother of the Universe. "After the initiation," Sri Ramakrishna once said, describing the event,

> Nangta began to teach me the various conclusions of the Advaita Vedanta and asked me to withdraw the mind completely from all objects and dive deep into the Atman. But in spite of all my attempts I could not altogether cross the realm of name and form and bring my mind to the unconditioned state. I had no difficulty in taking the mind from all the objects of the world. But the radiant and too familiar figure of the blissful Mother, the embodiment of the essence of Pure Consciousness, appeared before me as a living reality. Her bewitching smile prevented me from passing into the great beyond. Again and again I tried, but she stood in my way every time.
>
> In despair I said to Nangta, "It is hopeless. I cannot raise my mind to the unconditioned state and come face to face with Atman."
>
> He grew excited and sharply said, "What? You can't do it? But you have to."
>
> He cast his eyes around. Finding a piece of glass he

took it up and stuck it between my eyebrows. "Concentrate the mind on this point!" he thundered.

Then with stern determination I again sat to meditate. As soon as the gracious form of the Divine Mother
appeared before me, I used my discrimination as a
sword and with it clove her in two. The last barrier fell.
My spirit at once soared beyond the relative plane and
I lost myself in samadhi.

Sri Ramakrishna remained completely absorbed in samadhi for
three days. "Is it really true?" Totapuri cried out in astonishment. "Is it
possible that he has attained in a single day what it took me forty years
of strenuous practice to achieve? Great God! It is nothing short of a miracle!" With the help of Totapuri, Sri Ramakrishna's mind finally came
down to the relative plane.

Totapuri, a monk of the most orthodox type, never stayed at a place
more than three days. But he remained at Dakshineswar eleven months.
He too had something to learn.

Totapuri had no idea of the struggles of ordinary persons in the toils
of passion and desire. Having maintained all through life the guilelessness of a child, he laughed at the idea of being led astray by the
senses. He was convinced that the world was maya and had only to be
denounced to vanish forever. A born nondualist, he had no faith in a
personal God. He did not believe in the terrible aspect of Kali, much
less in her benign aspect. Music and the chanting of God's holy name
were to him only so much nonsense. He ridiculed the spending of emotion on the worship of a personal God.

Kali and Maya

Sri Ramakrishna, on the other hand, though fully aware, like his guru,
that the world is illusory, instead of slighting maya, like an orthodox
monist, acknowledged its power in the relative life. He was all love and

reverence for maya, perceiving in it a mysterious and majestic expression of divinity. To him maya itself was God, for everything was God. It was one of the faces of Brahman. What he had realized on the heights of the transcendental plane, he also found here below, everywhere about him, under the mysterious garb of names and forms. And this garb was a perfectly transparent sheath, through which he recognized the glory of the divine Immanence. Maya, the mighty weaver of the garb, is none other than Kali, the Divine Mother. She is the primordial divine energy, Sakti, and she can no more be distinguished from the supreme Brahman than can the power of burning be distinguished from fire. She projects the world and again withdraws it. She spins it as the spider spins its web. She is the Mother of the Universe, identical with the Brahman of Vedanta, and with the Atman of Yoga. As eternal lawgiver, she makes and unmakes laws; it is by her imperious will that karma yields its fruit. She ensnares men and women with illusion and again releases them from bondage with a look of her benign eyes. She is the supreme mistress of the cosmic play, and all objects, animate and inanimate, dance by her will. Even those who realize the Absolute in nirvikalpa samadhi are under her jurisdiction as long as they still live on the relative plane.

Thus, after nirvikalpa samadhi, Sri Ramakrishna realized maya in an altogether new role. The binding aspect of Kali vanished from before his vision. She no longer obscured his understanding. The world became the glorious manifestation of the Divine Mother. Maya became Brahman. The transcendental itself broke through the immanent. Sri Ramakrishna discovered that maya operates in the relative world in two ways, and he termed these *avidyamaya* and *vidyamaya*. Avidyamaya represents the dark forces of creation: sensuous desires, evil passions, greed, lust, cruelty, and so on. It sustains the world system on the lower planes. It is responsible for the round of man's birth and death. It must be fought and vanquished. But vidyamaya is the higher force of creation: the spiritual virtues, the enlightening qualities, kindness, purity, love, devotion.

Vidyamaya elevates man to the higher planes of consciousness. With the help of vidyamaya the devotee rids himself of avidyamaya; he then becomes *mayatita*, free of maya. The two aspects of maya are the two forces of creation, the two powers of Kali; and she stands beyond them both. She is like the effulgent sun, bringing into existence and shining through and standing behind the clouds of different colors and shapes, conjuring up wonderful forms in the blue autumn heaven.

The Divine Mother asked Sri Ramakrishna not to be lost in the featureless Absolute but to remain in bhavamukha, on the threshold of relative consciousness, the borderline between the Absolute and the Relative. He was to keep himself at the sixth center of Tantra, from which he could see not only the glory of the seventh, but also the divine manifestations of the kundalini in the lower centers. He gently oscillated back and forth across the dividing line. Ecstatic devotion to the Divine Mother alternated with serene absorption in the ocean of absolute unity. He thus bridged the gulf between the personal and the impersonal, the immanent and the transcendent aspects of Reality. This is a unique experience in the recorded spiritual history of the world.

Totapuri's Lesson

From Sri Ramakrishna, Totapuri had to learn the significance of Kali, the great fact of the relative world, and of maya, her indescribable power.

One day, when guru and disciple were engaged in an animated discussion about Vedanta, a servant of the temple garden came there and took a coal from the sacred fire that had been lighted by the great ascetic. He wanted it to light his tobacco. Totapuri flew into a rage and was about to beat the man. Sri Ramakrishna rocked with laughter. "What a shame!" he cried. "You are explaining to me the reality of Brahman and the illusoriness of the world; yet now you have so far forgotten yourself as to be about to beat a man in a fit of passion. The power of maya is indeed inscrutable!" Totapuri was embarrassed.

About this time Totapuri was suddenly laid up with a severe attack of dysentery. On account of this miserable illness, he found it impossible to meditate. One night the pain became excruciating. He could no longer concentrate on Brahman. The body stood in the way. He became incensed with its demands. A free soul, he did not at all care for the body. So he determined to drown it in the Ganges. Thereupon he walked into the river. But, lo! He walks to the other bank.[2] Is there not enough water in the Ganges? Standing dumbfounded on the other bank he looks back across the water. The trees, the temples, the houses, are silhouetted against the sky. Suddenly, in one dazzling moment, he sees on all sides the presence of the Divine Mother. She is in everything; she is everything. She is in the water; she is on land. She is the body; she is the mind. She is pain; she is comfort. She is knowledge; she is ignorance. She is life; she is death. She is everything that one sees, hears, or imagines. She turns "yea" into "nay," and "nay" into "yea." Without her grace no embodied being can go beyond her realm. Man has no free will. He is not even free to die. Yet, again, beyond the body and mind she resides in her transcendental, absolute aspect. She is the Brahman that Totapuri had been worshiping all his life.

Totapuri returned to Dakshineswar and spent the remaining hours of the night meditating on the Divine Mother. In the morning he went to the Kali temple with Sri Ramakrishna and prostrated himself before the image of the Mother. He now realized why he had spent eleven months at Dakshineswar. Bidding farewell to the disciple, he continued on his way, enlightened.

Sri Ramakrishna later described the significance of Totapuri's lessons: "When I think of the Supreme Being as inactive—neither creating nor preserving nor destroying—I call him Brahman or Purusha, the impersonal God. When I think of him as active—creating, preserving, and destroying—I call him Sakti or Maya or Prakriti, the personal God. But the distinction between them does not mean a difference. The personal and the impersonal are the same thing, like milk and its whiteness, the diamond and its luster, the snake and its wriggling motion. It is impossible to conceive of the one without the other. The Divine Mother and Brahman are one."

After the departure of Totapuri, Sri Ramakrishna remained for six months in a state of absolute identity with Brahman. "For six months at a stretch," he said, "I remained in that state from which ordinary men can never return; generally the body falls off, after three weeks, like a sere leaf. I was not conscious of day and night. Flies would enter my mouth and nostrils just as they do a dead body's, but I did not feel them. My hair became matted with dust."

His body would not have survived but for the kindly attention of a monk who happened to be at Dakshineswar at that time and who somehow realized that for the good of humanity Sri Ramakrishna's body must be preserved. He tried various means, even physical violence, to recall the fleeing soul to the prison house of the body, and during the resultant fleeting moments of consciousness he would push a few morsels of food down Sri Ramakrishna's throat. Presently Sri Ramakrishna received the command of the Divine Mother to remain on the threshold of relative consciousness. Soon thereafter he was afflicted with a serious attack of dysentery. Day and night the pain tortured him, and his mind gradually came down to the physical plane.

Company of Holy Persons and Devotees

From now on Sri Ramakrishna began to seek the company of devotees and holy persons. He had gone through the storm and stress of spiritual disciplines and visions. Now he realized an inner calmness and appeared to others as a normal person. But he could not bear the company of worldly people or listen to their talk. Fortunately the holy atmosphere of Dakshineswar and the liberality of Mathur attracted monks and holy persons from all parts of the country. Sadhus of all denominations—monists and dualists, Vaishnavas and Vedantists, Saktas and worshipers of Rama—flocked there in ever-increasing numbers. Ascetics and visionaries came to seek Sri Ramakrishna's advice. Vaishnavas had come during the period of his Vaishnava sadhana, and Tantriks when he practiced the disciplines of Tantra. Vedantists began to arrive after the departure of Totapuri. In the room of Sri Ramakrishna, who was then in bed with dysentery, the Vedantists engaged in scriptural discussions, and, forgetting his own physical suffering, he solved their doubts by referring directly to his own experiences. Many of the visitors were genuine spiritual souls, the unseen pillars of Hinduism, and their spiritual lives were quickened in no small measure by the sage of Dakshineswar. Sri Ramakrishna in turn learned from them anecdotes concerning the ways and the conduct of holy persons, which he subsequently narrated to his devotees and disciples. At his request Mathur provided him with large stores of foodstuffs, clothes, and so forth, for distribution among the wandering monks.

Sri Ramakrishna had not read books, yet he possessed an encyclopedic knowledge of religions and religious philosophies. This he acquired from his contacts with innumerable holy persons and scholars. He had a unique power of assimilation; through meditation he made this knowledge a part of his being. Once, when he was asked by a disciple about the source of his seemingly inexhaustible knowledge, he replied, "I have not read; but I have heard the learned. I have made a garland of their knowledge, wearing it round my neck, and I have given it as an offering at the feet of the Mother."

Sri Ramakrishna used to say that when the flower blooms, the bees come to it for honey of their own accord. Now many souls began to visit Dakshineswar to satisfy their spiritual hunger. He, the devotee and aspirant, became the Master. Gauri, the great scholar who had been one of the first to proclaim Sri Ramakrishna an incarnation of God, paid the Master a visit in 1870 and with the Master's blessings renounced the world. Narayan Shastri, another great pundit, who had mastered the six systems of Hindu philosophy and had been offered a lucrative post by the maharaja of Jaipur, met the Master and recognized in him one who had realized in life those ideals that he himself had encountered merely in books. Sri Ramakrishna initiated Narayan Shastri, at his earnest request, into the life of sannyas. Pundit Padmalochan, the court pundit of the maharaja of Burdwan, well known for his scholarship in both the Vedanta and the Nyaya systems of philosophy, accepted the Master as an incarnation of God. Krishnakishore, a Vedantist scholar, became devoted to the Master. And there arrived Viswanath Upadhyaya, who was to become a favorite devotee; Sri Ramakrishna always addressed him as "captain." He was a high officer of the king of Nepal and had received the title of colonel in recognition of his merit. A scholar of the Gita, the *Bhagavata*, and the Vedanta philosophy, he daily performed the worship of his chosen deity with great devotion. "I have read the Vedas and the other scriptures," he said. "I have also met a good many monks and devotees in different places. But it is in Sri Ramakrishna's presence that my spiritual yearnings have been fulfilled. To me he seems to be the embodiment of the truths of the scriptures."

The knowledge of Brahman in nirvikalpa samadhi had convinced Sri Ramakrishna that the gods of the different religions are but so many readings of the Absolute, and that the Ultimate Reality could never be expressed by human tongue. He understood that all religions lead their devotees by differing paths to one and the same goal. Now he became eager to explore some of the alien religions; for to him, understanding meant actual experience.

Islam

Toward the end of 1866 he began to practice the disciplines of Islam. Under the direction of his Muslim guru, he abandoned himself to his new sadhana. He dressed as a Muslim and repeated the name of Allah. His prayers took the form of the Islamic devotions. He forgot the Hindu gods and goddesses—even Kali—and gave up visiting the temples. He took up residence outside the temple precincts. After three days he saw the vision of a radiant figure, perhaps Mohammed. This figure gently approached him and finally lost himself in Sri Ramakrishna. Thus he realized the Muslim God. Thence he passed into communion with Brahman. The mighty river of Islam also led him back to the ocean of the Absolute.

Christianity

Eight years later, some time in November 1874, Sri Ramakrishna was seized with an irresistible desire to learn the truth of the Christian religion. He began to listen to readings from the Bible by Sambhu Charan Mallick, a gentleman of Calcutta and a devotee of the Master. Sri Ramakrishna became fascinated by the life and teachings of Jesus. One day he was seated in the parlor of Jadu Mallick's garden house[3] at Dakshineswar, when his eyes became fixed on a painting of the Madonna and Child. Intently watching it, he became gradually overwhelmed with divine emotion. The figures in the picture took on life, and the rays of light emanating from them entered his soul. The effect of this experience was stronger than that of the vision of Mohammed. In dismay he cried out, "O Mother! What are you doing to me?" And, breaking through the barriers of creed and religion, he entered a new realm of ecstasy. Christ possessed his soul. For three days he did not set foot in the Kali temple. On the fourth day, in the afternoon, as he was walking in the Panchavati, he saw coming toward him a person with beautiful large eyes, serene countenance, and fair skin. As the two faced each other, a voice rang out in the depths of Sri Ramakrishna's soul: "Behold the Christ, who shed his heart's blood for the redemption of the world, who suffered a sea of anguish for love of men. It is he, the Master Yogi, who is in eternal union with God. It is Jesus, Love Incarnate." The Son of Man embraced the Son of the Divine Mother and merged in him. Sri Ramakrishna realized his identity with Christ, as he had already realized his identity with Kali, Rama, Hanuman, Radha, Krishna, Brahman, and Mohammed. The Master went into samadhi and communed with the Brahman with attributes. Thus he experienced the truth that Christianity, too, was a path leading to God-consciousness. Till the last moment of his life he believed that Christ was an incarnation of God. But Christ, for him, was not the only incarnation; there were others—Buddha, for instance, and Krishna.

Attitude toward Different Religions

Sri Ramakrishna accepted the divinity of Buddha and used to point out the similarity of his teachings to those of the Upanishads. He also showed great respect for the Tirthankaras, who founded Jainism, and for the ten gurus of Sikhism. But he did not speak of them as divine incarnations. He was heard to say that the gurus of Sikhism were the reincarnations of King Janaka of ancient India. He kept in his room at Dakshineswar a small statue of Tirthankara Mahavira and a picture of Christ, before which incense was burned morning and evening.

Without being formally initiated into their doctrines, Sri Ramakrishna thus realized the ideals of religions other than Hinduism. He did not need to follow any doctrine. All barriers were removed by his overwhelming love of God. So he became a master who could speak with authority regarding the ideas and ideals of the various religions of the world. "I have practiced," said he, "all religions—Hinduism, Islam, Christianity—and I have also followed the paths of the different Hindu sects. I have found that it is the same God toward whom all are directing their steps, though along different paths. You must try all beliefs and traverse all the different ways once. Wherever I look, I see men quarrelling in the name of religion—Hindus, Muslims, Brahmos, Vaishnavas, and the rest. But they never reflect that he who is called Krishna is also called Siva and bears the name of the Primal Energy, Jesus, and Allah as well—the same Rama with a thousand names. A lake has several ghats. At one, the Hindus take water in pitchers and call it *jal;* at another, the Muslims take water in leather bags and call it *pani;* at a third, the Christians call it *water.* Can we imagine that it is not jal, but only pani or water? How ridiculous! The substance is one under different names, and everyone is seeking the same substance; only climate, temperament, and name create differences. Let each man follow his own path. If he sincerely and ardently wishes to know God, peace be unto him! He will surely realize him."

In 1867 Sri Ramakrishna returned to Kamarpukur to recuperate from the effect of his austerities. The peaceful countryside, the simple and artless companions of his boyhood, and the pure air did him much good. The villagers were happy to get back their playful, frank, witty, kindhearted, and truthful Gadadhar, though they did not fail to notice the great change that had come over him during his years in Calcutta. His wife, Sarada Devi, now fourteen years old, soon arrived at Kamarpukur. Her spiritual development was much beyond her age, and she was able to understand immediately her husband's state of mind. She became eager to learn from him about God and to live with him as his attendant. The Master accepted her cheerfully both as his disciple and as his spiritual companion. Referring to the experiences of these few days, she once said, "I used to feel always as if a pitcher full of bliss were placed in my heart. The joy was indescribable."

Pilgrimage

On January 27, 1868, Mathur Babu with a party of some one hundred and twenty-five persons set out on a pilgrimage to the sacred places of northern India. At Vaidyanath in Behar, when the Master saw the inhabitants of a village reduced by poverty and starvation to mere skeletons, he requested his rich patron to feed the people and give each a piece of cloth. Mathur demurred at the added expense. The Master declared bitterly that he would not go on to Benares, but would live with the poor and share their miseries. He actually left Mathur and sat down with the villagers. Whereupon Mathur had to yield.

On another occasion, two years later, Sri Ramakrishna showed a similar sentiment for the poor and needy. He accompanied Mathur on a tour to one of the latter's estates at the time of the collection of rents. For two years, the harvests had failed and the tenants were in a state of extreme poverty. The Master asked Mathur to remit their rents, distribute help to them, and, in addition, give the hungry people a sumptuous feast. When Mathur grumbled, the Master said, "You are only the steward of the Divine Mother. They are the Mother's tenants. You must spend the Mother's money. When they are suffering, how can you refuse to help them? You must help them." Again Mathur had to give in. Sri Ramakrishna's sympathy for the poor sprang from his perception of God in all created beings. His sentiment was not that of the humanist or philanthropist. To him the service of man was the same as the worship of God.

The party entered holy Benares by boat along the Ganges. When Sri Ramakrishna's eyes fell on this city of Siva, where had accumulated for ages the devotion and piety of countless worshipers, he saw it to be made of gold, as the scriptures declare. He was visibly moved. During his stay in the city he treated every particle of its earth with utmost respect. At the Manikarnika Ghat, the great cremation ground of the city, he actually saw Siva, with ash-covered body and tawny matted hair, serenely approaching each funeral pyre and breathing into the ears of the corpses the mantra of liberation; and then the Divine Mother removing from the dead their bonds. Thus he realized the significance of the scriptural statement that anyone dying in Benares attains salvation through the grace of Siva. He paid a visit to Trailanga Swami, the celebrated monk, whom he later declared to be a real paramahamsa, a veritable image of Siva.

Sri Ramakrishna visited Allahabad, at the confluence of the Ganges and the Jamuna, and then proceeded to Vrindavan and Mathura, hallowed by the legends, songs, and dramas about Krishna and the gopis. Here he had numerous visions and his heart overflowed with divine emotion. He wept and said, "O Krishna! Everything here is as it was in the olden days. You alone are absent." He visited the great woman saint, Gangamayi, regarded by Vaishnava devotees as the reincarnation of an intimate attendant of Radha. She was sixty years old and had frequent trances. She spoke of Sri Ramakrishna as an incarnation of Radha. With great difficulty he was persuaded to leave her.

On the return journey Mathur wanted to visit Gaya, but Sri Ramakrishna declined to go. He recalled his father's vision at Gaya before his own birth and felt that in the temple of Vishnu he would become permanently absorbed in God. Mathur, honoring the Master's wish, returned with his party to Calcutta.

From Vrindavan the Master had brought a handful of dust. Part of this he scattered in the Panchavati; the rest he buried in the little hut where he had practiced meditation. "Now this place," he said, "is as sacred as Vrindavan."

In 1870 the Master went on a pilgrimage to Nadia, the birthplace of Sri Chaitanya. As the boat by which he traveled approached the bank close to Nadia, Sri Ramakrishna had a vision of the "two brothers," Sri

Chaitanya and his companion Nityananda, "bright as molten gold" and with haloes, rushing to greet him with uplifted hands. "There they come! There they come!" he cried. They entered his body and he went into a deep trance.

Relation with His Wife

In 1872 Sarada Devi paid her first visit to her husband at Dakshineswar. Four years earlier she had seen him at Kamarpukur and had tasted the bliss of his divine company. Since then she had become even more gentle, tender, introspective, serious, and unselfish. She had heard many rumors about her husband's insanity. People had shown her pity in her misfortune. The more she thought, the more she felt that her duty was to be with him, giving him, in whatever measure she could, a wife's devoted service. She was now eighteen years old. Accompanied by her father, she arrived at Dakshineswar, having come on foot the distance of eighty miles. She had had an attack of fever on the way. When she arrived at the temple garden the Master said sorrowfully, "Ah! You have come too late. My Mathur is no longer here to look after you." Mathur had passed away the previous year.

The Master took up the duty of instructing his young wife, and this included everything from housekeeping to the knowledge of Brahman. He taught her how to trim a lamp, how to behave toward people according to their differing temperaments, and how to conduct herself before visitors. He instructed her in the mysteries of spiritual life—prayer, meditation, *japa*, deep contemplation, and samadhi. The first lesson that Sarada Devi received was, "God is everybody's beloved, just as the moon is dear to every child. Everyone has the same right to pray to him. Out of his grace he reveals himself to all who call upon him. You too will see him if you but pray to him."

Totapuri, coming to know of the Master's marriage, had once remarked, "What does it matter? He alone is firmly established in the knowledge of Brahman who can adhere to his spirit of discrimination and renunciation even while living with his wife. He alone has attained the supreme illumination who can look on man and woman alike as Brahman. A man with the idea of sex may be a good aspirant, but he is still far from the goal." Sri Ramakrishna and his wife lived together at Dakshineswar, but their minds always soared above the worldly plane.

A few months after Sarada Devi's arrival, Sri Ramakrishna arranged, on an auspicious day, a special worship of Kali, the Divine Mother. Instead of an image of the deity, he placed on the seat the living image, Sarada Devi herself. The worshiper and the worshiped went into deep samadhi, and in the transcendental plane their souls were united. After several hours Sri Ramakrishna came down again to the relative plane, sang a hymn to the Great Goddess, and surrendered, at the feet of the living image, himself, his rosary, and the fruit of his lifelong sadhana. This is known in Tantra as the *Shorasi Puja*, the "adoration of woman." Sri Ramakrishna realized the significance of the great statement of the Upanishad: "O Lord, thou art the woman, thou art the man; thou art the boy, thou art the girl; thou art the old, tottering on their crutches. Thou pervadest the universe in its multiple forms."

By his marriage Sri Ramakrishna admitted the great value of marriage in man's spiritual evolution, and by adhering to his monastic vows he demonstrated the imperative necessity of self-control, purity, and continence in the realization of God. By his unique spiritual relationship with his wife, he proved that husband and wife can live together as spiritual companions. Thus his life is a synthesis of the ways of life of the householder and the monk.

The "Ego" of the Master

In the nirvikalpa samadhi Sri Ramakrishna had realized that Brahman alone is real and the world illusory. By keeping his mind six months on the plane of the nondual Brahman, he had attained the state of the *vijnani*, the knower of Truth in a special and very rich sense, who sees Brahman not only in himself and in the transcendental Absolute, but in everything of the world. In this state of vijnana, sometimes, bereft of body-consciousness, he would regard himself as one with Brahman; sometimes, conscious of the dual world, he would regard himself as God's devotee, servant, or child. In order to enable the Master to work for the welfare of humanity, the Divine Mother had kept in him a trace of ego, which he described—according to his mood—as the "ego of knowledge," the "ego of devotion," the "ego of a child," or the "ego of a servant." In any case, this ego of the Master, consumed by the fire of the knowledge of Brahman, was an appearance only, like a burned string. He often referred to this ego as the "ripe ego" in contrast with the ego of the bound soul, which he described as the "unripe" or "green" ego. The ego of the bound soul identifies itself with the body, relatives, possessions, and the world; but the "ripe ego," illumined by divine knowledge, knows the body, relatives, possessions, and the world to be unreal and establishes a relationship of love with God alone. Through this "ripe ego," Sri Ramakrishna dealt with the world and his wife. One day, while stroking his feet, Sarada Devi asked the Master, "What do you think of me?" Quick came the answer: "The Mother who is worshiped in the temple is the mother who has given birth to my body and is now living in the nahabat, and it is she again who is stroking my feet at this moment. Indeed, I always look on you as the personification of the blissful Mother Kali."

Sarada Devi, in the company of her husband, had rare spiritual experiences. She said, "I have no words to describe my wonderful exaltation of spirit as I watched him in his different moods. Under the influence of divine emotion he would sometimes talk on abstruse subjects, sometimes laugh, sometimes weep, and sometimes become perfectly motionless in samadhi. This would continue throughout the night. There was such an extraordinary divine presence in him that now and then I would shake with fear and wonder how the night would pass. Months went by in this way. Then one day he discovered that I had to keep awake the whole night lest, during my sleep, he should go into samadhi—for it might happen at any moment—and so he asked me to sleep in the nahabat."

Summary of the Master's Spiritual Experiences

We have now come to the end of Sri Ramakrishna's sadhana, the period of his spiritual discipline. As a result of his supersensuous experiences he reached certain conclusions regarding himself and spirituality in general. His conclusions about himself may be summarized as follows:

First, he was an incarnation of God, a specially commissioned person whose spiritual experiences were for the benefit of humanity. Whereas it takes an ordinary man a whole life's struggle to realize one or two phases of God, he had in a few years realized God in all his phases.

Second, he knew that he had always been a free soul, that the various disciplines through which he had passed were really not necessary for his own liberation but were solely for the benefit of others. Thus the terms *liberation* and *bondage* were not applicable to him. As long as there are beings who consider themselves bound, God must come down to earth as an incarnation to free them from bondage, just as a magistrate must visit any part of his district in which there is trouble.

Third, he came to foresee the time of his death. His words with respect to this matter were literally fulfilled.

About spirituality in general the following were his conclusions:

First, he was firmly convinced that all religions are true, that every doctrinal system represents a path to God. He had followed all the main paths and all had led him to the same goal. He was the first religious prophet recorded in history to preach the harmony of religions.

Second, the three great systems of thought known as dualism, qualified nondualism, and absolute nondualism—Dvaita, Visishtadvaita, and Advaita—he perceived to represent three stages in man's progress toward the Ultimate Reality. They were not contradictory but complementary and suited to different temperaments. For the ordinary man with strong attachment to the senses, a dualistic form of religion, prescribing a certain amount of material support, such as music and other symbols, is useful. A man of God-realization transcends the idea of worldly duties, but the ordinary mortal must perform his duties, striving to be unattached and to surrender the results to God. The mind can comprehend and describe the range of thought and experience up to the Visishtadvaita, and no further. The Advaita, the last word in spiritual experience, is something to be felt in samadhi, for it transcends mind and speech. From the highest standpoint, the Absolute and its manifestation are equally real—the lord's name, his abode, and the Lord himself are of the same spiritual essence. Everything is Spirit, the difference being only in form.

Third, Sri Ramakrishna realized the wish of the Divine Mother that through him she should found a new order, consisting of those who would uphold the universal doctrines illustrated in his life.

Fourth, his spiritual insight told him that those who were having their last birth on the mortal plane of existence and those who had sincerely called on the Lord even once in their lives must come to him.

During this period Sri Ramakrishna suffered several bereavements. The first was the death of a nephew named Akshay. After the young man's death Sri Ramakrishna said, "Akshay died before my very eyes. But it did not affect me in the least. I stood by and watched a man die. It was like a sword being drawn from its scabbard. I enjoyed the scene, and laughed and sang and danced over it. They removed the body and cremated it. But the next day as I stood there [pointing to the southeast verandah of his room], I felt a racking pain for the loss of Akshay, as if somebody were squeezing my heart like a wet towel. I wondered at it and thought that the Mother was teaching me a lesson. I was not much concerned even with my own body—much less with a relative. But if such was my pain at the loss of a nephew, how much more must be the grief of the householders at the loss of their near and dear ones!"

In 1871 Mathur died, and some five years later Sambhu Mallick— who, after Mathur's passing away, had taken care of the Master's comfort. In 1873 his elder brother Rameswar died, and in 1876, his beloved mother. These bereavements left their imprint on the tender human heart of Sri Ramakrishna, albeit he had realized the immortality of the soul and the illusoriness of birth and death.

In March 1875, about a year before the death of his mother, the Master met Keshab Chandra Sen. The meeting was a momentous event for both Sri Ramakrishna and Keshab. Here the Master for the first time came into actual contact with a worthy representative of modern India.

5

Contemporaries

Brahmo Samaj

Keshab was the leader of the Brahmo Samaj, one of the two great movements that, during the latter part of the nineteenth century, played an important part in shaping the course of the renaissance of India. The founder of the Brahmo movement had been the great Raja Rammohan Roy (1774–1833). Though born in an orthodox brahmin family, Rammohan Roy had shown great sympathy for Islam and Christianity. He had gone to Tibet in search of the Buddhist mysteries. He had extracted from Christianity its ethical system, but had rejected the divinity of Christ as he had denied the Hindu incarnations. The religion of Islam influenced him, to a great extent, in the formulation of his monotheistic doctrines. But he always went back to the Vedas for his spiritual inspiration. The Brahmo Samaj, which he founded in 1828, was dedicated to the "worship and adoration of the Eternal, the Unsearchable, the Immutable Being, who is the author and preserver of the universe." The Samaj was open to all without distinction of color, creed, caste, nation, or religion.

The real organizer of the Samaj was Devendranath Tagore (1817–1905), often called Devendra. He was the father of the poet Rabindranath. His physical and spiritual beauty, aristocratic aloofness, penetrating intellect, and poetic sensibility made him the foremost leader of the educated Bengalis. These addressed him by the respectful epithet of maharshi, the "great seer." The maharshi was a Sanskrit scholar and, unlike Raja Rammohan Roy, drew his inspiration entirely from the Upanishads. He was an implacable enemy of image worship and also fought to stop the infiltration of Christian ideas into the Samaj. He gave the movement its faith and ritual. Under his influence, the Brahmo Samaj professed one self-existent Supreme Being who had created the universe out of nothing, the God of truth, infinite wisdom, goodness, and power, the eternal and omnipotent, the One without a second. Man should love him and do his will, believe in him and worship him, and thus merit salvation in the world to come.

By far the ablest leader of the Brahmo movement was Keshab Chandra Sen (1838–1884). Unlike Raja Rammohan Roy and Devendranath Tagore, Keshab was born of a middle-class Bengali family and had been brought up in an English school. He did not know Sanskrit and very soon broke away from the popular Hindu religion. Even at an early age he came under the spell of Christ and professed to have experienced the special favor of John the Baptist, Christ, and St. Paul. When he strove to introduce Christ to the Brahmo Samaj, a rupture became inevitable with Devendranath. In 1868 Keshab broke with the older leader and founded the Brahmo Samaj of India, Devendra retaining leadership of the first Brahmo Samaj, now called the Adi Samaj.

Keshab possessed a complex nature. When passing through a great moral crisis, he spent much of his time in solitude and felt that he heard the voice of God. When a devotional form of worship was introduced into the Brahmo Samaj, he spent hours in singing kirtan with his followers. He visited England in 1870 and impressed the English people with his musical voice, his simple English, and his spiritual fervor. He was entertained by Queen Victoria. Returning to India, he founded centers of the Brahmo Samaj in various parts of the country. Not unlike a professor of comparative religion in a European university, he began to discover, about the time of his first contact with Sri Ramakrishna, the harmony of religions. He became sympathetic toward the Hindu gods and goddesses, explaining them in a liberal fashion. Further, he believed that he was called by God to dictate to the world God's newly revealed law, the new dispensation, the Navavidhan.

In 1878 a schism divided Keshab's Samaj. Some of his influential followers accused him of violating the Brahmo principles by marrying his daughter to a wealthy man before she had attained the marriageable age approved by the Samaj. This group seceded and established the Sadharan Brahmo Samaj, Keshab remaining the leader of the Navavidhan. Keshab now began to be drawn more and more toward the Christ ideal, though under the influence of Sri Ramakrishna his devotion to the Divine Mother also deepened. His mental oscillation between Christ and the Divine Mother of Hinduism found no position of rest.

In Bengal and some other parts of India, the Brahmo movement took the form of unitarian Christianity, scoffed at Hindu rituals, and preached a crusade against image worship. Influenced by Western culture, it declared the supremacy of reason, advocated the ideals of the French Revolution, abolished the caste system among its own members, stood for the emancipation of women, agitated for the abolition of early marriage, sanctioned the remarriage of widows, and encouraged various educational and social reform movements.

The immediate effect of the Brahmo movement in Bengal was the checking of the proselytizing activities of the Christian missionaries. It also raised Indian culture in the estimation of its English masters. But it was an intellectual and eclectic religious ferment born of the necessity of the time. Unlike Hinduism, it was not founded on the deep inner experiences of sages and prophets. Its influence was confined to a comparatively few educated men and women of the country, and the vast masses of the Hindus remained outside it. It monotonously sounded only one of the notes in the rich gamut of the eternal religion of the Hindus.

Arya Samaj

The other movement playing an important part in the nineteenth-century religious revival of India was the Arya Samaj. The Brahmo Samaj, essentially a movement of compromise with European culture, tacitly admitted the superiority of the West. But the founder of the Arya Samaj was a pugnacious Hindu sannyasi who accepted the challenge of Islam and Christianity and was resolved to combat all foreign influence in India. Swami Dayananda (1824–1883) launched this movement in Bombay in 1875, and soon its influence was felt throughout western India. The Swami was a great scholar of the Vedas, which he explained as being strictly monotheistic. He preached against the worship of images and reestablished the ancient Vedic sacrificial rites. According to him, the Vedas were the ultimate authority on religion, and he accepted every word of them as literally true. The Arya Samaj became a bulwark against the encroachments of Islam and Christianity, and its orthodox flavor appealed to many Hindu minds.

It also assumed leadership in many social reform movements. The caste system became a target of its attack. It liberated women from many of their social disabilities. The cause of education received from it a great impetus. It started agitation against early marriage and advocated the remarriage of Hindu widows. Its influence was strongest in the Punjab, the battleground of Hindu and Islamic cultures. A new fighting attitude was introduced into the slumbering Hindu society. Unlike the Brahmo Samaj, the influence of the Arya Samaj was not confined to intellectuals. It was a force that spread to the masses. It was a dogmatic movement intolerant of those who disagreed with its views, and it emphasized only one way, the Arya Samaj way, to the realization of Truth. Sri Ramakrishna met Swami Dayananda when the latter visited Bengal.

Keshab Chandra Sen

Keshab Chandra Sen and Sri Ramakrishna met for the first time in the garden house of Jaygopal Sen at Belgharia, a few miles from Dakshineswar, where the great Brahmo leader was staying with some of his disciples. In many respects the two were poles apart, though an irresistible inner attraction was to make them intimate friends. The Master had realized God as pure Spirit and Consciousness, but he believed in the various forms of God as well. Keshab, on the other hand, regarded image worship as idolatry and gave allegorical explanations of the Hindu deities. Keshab was an orator and a writer of books and magazine articles; Sri Ramakrishna had a horror of lecturing and hardly knew how to write his own name. Keshab's fame spread far and wide, even reaching the distant shores of England; the Master still led a secluded life in the village of Dakshineswar. Keshab emphasized social reforms for India's regeneration; to Sri Ramakrishna God-realization was the only goal of life. Keshab considered himself a disciple of Christ and accepted, in a diluted form, the Christian sacraments and Trinity; Sri Ramakrishna was the simple child of Kali, the Divine Mother, though he too, in a different way, acknowledged Christ's divinity. Keshab was a householder and took a real interest in the welfare of his children, whereas Sri Ramakrishna was a paramahamsa and completely indifferent to the life of the world. Yet, as their acquaintance ripened into friendship, Sri Ramakrishna and Keshab held each other in great love and respect. Years later, at the news of Keshab's death, the Master felt as if half his body had become paralyzed. Keshab's concepts of the harmony of religions and the motherhood of God were deepened and enriched by his contact with Sri Ramakrishna.

Sri Ramakrishna, dressed in a red-bordered dhoti, one end of which was carelessly thrown over his left shoulder, came to Jaygopal's garden house accompanied by Hriday. No one took notice of the unostentatious visitor. Finally the Master said to Keshab, "People tell me you have seen God; so I have come to hear from you about God." A magnificent conversation followed. The Master sang a thrilling song about Kali and forthwith went into samadhi. When Hriday uttered the sacred Om in his ears, he gradually came back to consciousness of the world, his face still radiating a divine brilliance. Keshab and his followers were amazed. The contrast between Sri Ramakrishna and the Brahmo devotees was very interesting. There sat this small man, thin and extremely delicate. His eyes were illumined with an inner light. Good humor gleamed in his eyes and lurked in the corners of his mouth. His speech was Bengali of a homely kind with a slight, delightful stammer, and his words held all enthralled by their wealth of spiritual experience, their inexhaustible store of simile and metaphor, their power of observation, their bright and subtle humor, their wonderful catholicity, their ceaseless flow of wisdom. And around him now were the sophisticated persons of Bengal, the best products of Western education, with Keshab, the idol of young Bengal, as their leader.

Keshab's sincerity was enough for Sri Ramakrishna. Henceforth the two saw each other frequently, either at Dakshineswar or at the temple of the Brahmo Samaj. Whenever the Master was in the temple at the time of divine service, Keshab would request him to speak to the congregation. And Keshab would visit the saint, in his turn, with offerings of flowers and fruits.

Other Brahmo Leaders

Gradually other Brahmo leaders began to feel Sri Ramakrishna's influence. But they were by no means uncritical admirers of the Master. They particularly disapproved of his ascetic renunciation and condemnation of "woman and gold."* They measured him according to their own ideals of the householder's life. Some could not understand his samadhi and described it as a nervous malady. Yet they could not resist his magnetic personality.

Among the Brahmo leaders who knew the Master closely were Pratap Chandra Mazumdar, Vijaykrishna Goswami, Trailokyanath Sannyal, and Shivanath Shastri.

Shivanath was greatly impressed by the Master's utter simplicity and abhorrence of praise. One day, he was seated with Sri Ramakrishna in the latter's room when several rich men of Calcutta arrived. The Master left the room for a few minutes. In the meantime Hriday, his nephew, began to describe his samadhi to the visitors. The last few words caught the Master's ear as he entered the room. He said to Hriday: "What a mean-spirited fellow you must be to extol me thus before these rich men! You have seen their costly apparel and their gold watches and chains, and your object is to get from them as much money as you can. What do I care about what they think of me? [Turning to the gentlemen] No, my friends, what he has told you about me is not true. It

---

* The term *woman and gold* occurs in the teachings of Sri Ramakrishna to designate the chief impediments to spiritual progress. This favorite expression of the Master, *kaminikanchan*, has often been misconstrued. By it he meant only "lust and greed," the baneful influence of which retards the aspirant's spiritual growth. He used the word *kamini*, or "woman," as a concrete term for the sex instinct when addressing his male devotees. He advised women, on the other hand, to shun "man." *Kanchan*, or "gold," symbolizes greed, which is the other obstacle to spiritual life.

Sri Ramakrishna never taught his disciples to hate any woman, or womankind in general. This can be seen clearly by going through all his teachings under this head and judging them collectively. The Master looked on all women as so many images of the Divine Mother of the Universe. He paid the highest homage to womankind by accepting a woman as his guide while practicing the very profound spiritual disciplines of Tantra. His wife, known and revered as the Holy Mother, was his constant companion and first disciple. At the end of his spiritual practice he literally worshiped his wife as the embodiment of the Goddess Kali, the Divine Mother. After his passing away the Holy Mother became the spiritual guide not only of a large number of householders, but also of many monastic members of the Ramakrishna Order.

was not love of God that made me absorbed in God and indifferent to external life. I became positively insane for some time. The sadhus who frequented this temple told me to practice many things. I tried to follow them, and the consequence was that my austerities drove me to insanity." This is a quotation from one of Shivanath's books. He took the Master's words literally and failed to see their real import.

Shivanath vehemently criticized the Master for his otherworldly attitude toward his wife. He writes,

> Ramakrishna was practically separated from his wife, who lived in her village home. One day when I was complaining to some friends about the virtual widowhood of his wife, he drew me to one side and whispered in my ear: "Why do you complain? It is no longer possible; it is all dead and gone." Another day as I was inveighing against this part of his teaching, and also declaring that our program of work in the Brahmo Samaj includes women, that ours is a social and domestic religion, and that we want to give education and social liberty to women, the saint became very much excited, as was his way when anything against his settled conviction was asserted—a trait we so much liked in him—and exclaimed, "Go, thou fool, go and perish in the pit that your women will dig for you." Then he glared at me and said: "What does a gardener do with a young plant? Does he not surround it with a fence, to protect it from goats and cattle? And when the young plant has grown up into a tree and it can no longer be injured by cattle, does he not remove the fence and let the tree grow freely?" I replied, "Yes, that is the custom with gardeners." Then he remarked, "Do the same in your spiritual life; become strong, be full-grown; then you may seek them." To which I replied, "I don't agree with you in thinking that women's work is like that of cattle, destructive; they are our associates and helpers in our spiritual struggles and social progress"—a view with

which he could not agree, and he marked his dissent by shaking his head. Then referring to the lateness of the hour he jocularly remarked, "It is time for you to depart; take care, do not be late; otherwise *your woman* will not admit you into her room." This evoked hearty laughter.

Pratap Chandra Mazumdar, the right-hand man of Keshab and an accomplished Brahmo preacher in Europe and America, bitterly criticized Sri Ramakrishna's use of uncultured language and also his austere attitude toward his wife. But he could not escape the spell of the Master's personality. In the course of an article about Sri Ramakrishna, Pratap wrote in the *Theistic Quarterly Review:*

> What is there in common between him and me? I, a Europeanized, civilized, self-centered, semi-skeptical, so-called educated reasoner, and he, a poor, illiterate, unpolished, half-idolatrous, friendless Hindu devotee? Why should I sit long hours to attend to him, I, who have listened to Disraeli and Fawcett, Stanley and Max Müller, and a whole host of European scholars and divines? … And it is not I only, but dozens like me, who do the same…. He worships Siva, he worships Kali, he worships Rama, he worships Krishna, and is a confirmed advocate of Vedantic doctrines…. He is an idolater, yet is a faithful and most devoted meditator on the perfections of the One Formless, Absolute, Infinite Deity…. His religion is ecstasy, his worship means transcendental insight, his whole nature burns day and night with a permanent fire and fever of a strange faith and feeling…. So long as he is spared to us, gladly shall we sit at his feet to learn from him the sublime precepts of purity, unworldliness, spirituality, and inebriation in the love of God…. He, by his childlike bhakti, by his strong conceptions of an ever-ready Motherhood, helped to unfold it [God as our Mother] in our minds wonderfully…. By associating with him we learned to realize better the divine attributes as scattered over the three

hundred and thirty millions of deities of mythological
India, the gods of the Puranas.

The Brahmo leaders received much inspiration from their contact
with Sri Ramakrishna. It broadened their religious views and kindled in
their hearts the yearning for God-realization; it made them understand
and appreciate the rituals and symbols of Hindu religion, convinced
them of the manifestation of God in diverse forms, and deepened their
thoughts about the harmony of religions. The Master, too, was impressed
by the sincerity of many of the Brahmo devotees. He told them about
his own realizations and explained to them the essence of his teachings,
such as the necessity of renunciation, sincerity in the pursuit of one's
own course of discipline, faith in God, the performance of one's duties
without thought of results, and discrimination between the real and the
unreal.

This contact with the educated and progressive Bengalis opened Sri
Ramakrishna's eyes to a new realm of thought. Born and brought up in
a simple village, without any formal education, and taught by the orthodox holy persons of India in religious life, he had had no opportunity
to study the influence of modernism on the thoughts and lives of the
Hindus. He could not properly estimate the result of the impact of Western education on Indian culture. He was a Hindu of the Hindus, renunciation being to him the only means to the realization of God in life.
From the Brahmos he learned that the new generation of India made
a compromise between God and the world. Educated young men and
women were influenced more by the Western philosophers than by their
own prophets. But Sri Ramakrishna was not dismayed, for he saw in
this, too, the hand of God. And though he expounded to the Brahmos
all his ideas about God and austere religious disciplines, he bade them
accept from his teachings only as much as suited their tastes and
temperaments.

6

The Coming of the Disciples

The Master's Yearning for His Own Devotees

Contact with the Brahmos increased Sri Ramakrishna's longing to encounter aspirants who would be able to follow his teachings in their purest form. "There was no limit," he once declared, "to the longing I felt at that time."

> During the daytime I somehow managed to control it. The secular talk of the worldly minded was galling to me, and I would look wistfully to the day when my own beloved companions would come. I hoped to find solace in conversing with them and relating to them my own realizations. Every little incident would remind me of them, and thoughts of them wholly engrossed me. I was already arranging in my mind what I should say to one and give to another, and so on. But when the day would come to a close I would not be able to curb my feelings. The thought that another day had gone by, and they had not come, oppressed me. When, during the evening service, the temples rang with the sound of bells and conch shells, I would climb to the roof of the *kuthi* in the garden and, writhing in anguish of heart, cry at the top of my voice: "Come, my children! Oh, where are you? I cannot bear to live without you." A mother never longed so intensely for the sight of her child, nor a friend for his companions, nor a lover for his sweetheart, as I

Sri Ramakrishna
(standing in samadhi at Keshab Sen's house)

longed for them. Oh, it was indescribable! Shortly after
this period of yearning the devotees began to come.

In the year 1879 occasional writings about Sri Ramakrishna by the
Brahmos, in the Brahmo magazines, began to attract his future disciples from the educated middle-class Bengalis, and they continued to
come until 1884. But others, too, came, feeling the subtle power of his
attraction. They were an ever-shifting crowd of people of all castes and
creeds: Hindus and Brahmos, Vaishnavas and Saktas, the educated with
university degrees and the illiterate, old and young, maharajas and beggars, journalists and artists, pundits and devotees, philosophers and the
worldly minded, jnanis and yogis, men of action and men of faith,
virtuous women and prostitutes, officeholders and vagabonds, philanthropists and self-seekers, dramatists and drunkards, builders-up and
pullers-down. He gave to them all, without stint, from his illimitable
store of realization. No one went away empty-handed. He taught them
the lofty knowledge of the Vedanta and the soul-melting love of the
Purana. Twenty hours out of twenty-four he would speak without rest
or respite. He gave to all his sympathy and enlightenment, and he
touched them with that strange power of the soul that could not but
melt even the most hardened. And people understood him according
to their powers of comprehension.

The Master's Method of Teaching

But he remained as ever the willing instrument in the hand of God, the
child of the Divine Mother, totally untouched by the idea of being a
teacher. He used to say that three ideas—that he was a guru, a father,
and a master—pricked his flesh like thorns. Yet he was an extraordinary
teacher. He stirred his disciples' hearts more by a subtle influence than
by actions or words. He never claimed to be the founder of a religion

or the organizer of a sect. Yet he was a religious dynamo. He was the verifier of all religions and creeds. He was like an expert gardener, who prepares the soil and removes the weeds, knowing that the plants will grow because of the inherent power of the seeds, producing each its appropriate flowers and fruits. He never thrust his ideas on anybody. He understood people's limitations and worked on the principle that what is good for one may be bad for another. He had the unusual power of knowing the devotees' minds, even their inmost souls, at first sight. He accepted disciples with the full knowledge of their past tendencies and future possibilities. The life of evil did not frighten him, nor did religious squeamishness raise anybody in his estimation. He saw in everything the unerring finger of the Divine Mother. Even the light that leads astray was to him the light from God.

To those who became his intimate disciples, the Master was a friend, companion, and playmate. Even the chores of religious discipline would be lightened in his presence. The devotees would be so inebriated with pure joy in his company that they would have no time to ask themselves whether he was an incarnation, a perfect soul, or a yogi. His very presence was a great teaching; words were superfluous. In later years his disciples remarked that while they were with him they would regard him as a comrade, but afterward would tremble to think of their frivolities in the presence of such a great person. They had convincing proof that the Master could, by his mere wish, kindle in their hearts the love of God and give them his vision.

Through all this fun and frolic, this merriment and frivolity, he always kept before them the shining ideal of God-consciousness and the path of renunciation. He prescribed ascents steep or graded according to the powers of the climber. He permitted no compromise with the basic principles of purity. An aspirant had to keep his body, mind, senses, and soul unspotted; had to have a sincere love for God and an ever-mounting spirit of yearning. The rest would be done by the Mother.

His disciples were of two kinds: householders and young men, some of whom were later to become monks. There was also a small group of women devotees.

For the householders, Sri Ramakrishna did not prescribe the hard path of total renunciation. He wanted them to discharge their obligations to their families. Their renunciation was to be mental. Spiritual life could not be acquired by flying away from responsibilities. A married couple should live like brother and sister after the birth of one or two children, devoting their time to spiritual talk and contemplation. He encouraged the householders, saying that their life was, in a way, easier than that of the monk, since it was more advantageous to fight the enemy from inside a fortress than in an open field. He insisted, however, on their repairing into solitude every now and then to strengthen their devotion and faith in God through prayer, japa, and meditation. He prescribed for them the companionship of sadhus. He asked them to perform their worldly duties with one hand, while holding to God with the other, and to pray to God to make their duties fewer and fewer so that in the end they might cling to him with both hands. He would discourage in both the householders and the celibate youths any lukewarmness in their spiritual struggles. He would not ask them to follow indiscriminately the ideal of nonresistance, which ultimately makes a coward of the unwary.

But to the young men destined to be monks, he pointed out the steep path of renunciation, both external and internal. They must take the vow of absolute continence and eschew all thought of greed and lust. By the practice of continence, aspirants develop a subtle nerve through which they understand the deeper mysteries of God. For them, self-control is final, imperative, and absolute. The sannyasis are teachers of men, and their lives should be totally free from blemish. They must not even look at a picture that may awaken their animal passions. The Master selected his future monks from young men untouched by "woman and gold"* and plastic enough to be cast in his spiritual mold. When teaching them the path of renunciation and discrimination, he would not allow the householders to be anywhere near them.

Householder Devotees

Ram and Manomohan

The first two householder devotees to come to Dakshineswar were Ramchandra Dutta and Manomohan Mitra. A medical practitioner and chemist, Ram was skeptical about God and religion and never enjoyed peace of soul. He wanted tangible proof of God's existence. The Master said to him, "God really exists. You don't see the stars in the daytime, but that doesn't mean that the stars do not exist. There is butter in milk. But can anybody see it by merely looking at the milk? To get butter you must churn milk in a quiet and cool place. You cannot realize God by a mere wish; you must go through some mental disciplines." By degrees the Master awakened Ram's spirituality, and the latter became one of his foremost lay disciples. It was Ram who introduced Narendranath to Sri Ramakrishna. Narendra was a relative of Ram.

Manomohan at first met with considerable opposition from his wife and other relatives, who resented his visits to Dakshineswar. But in the end the unselfish love of the Master triumphed over worldly affection. It was Manomohan who brought Rakhal (Swami Brahmananda) to the Master.

Surendra

Suresh Mitra, a beloved disciple whom the Master often addressed as Surendra, had received an English education and held an important post in an English firm. Like many other educated young men of the time, he

---

* See footnote on p. 245.

prided himself on his atheism and led a Bohemian life. He was addicted to drinking. He cherished an exaggerated notion about man's free will. A victim of mental depression, he was brought to Sri Ramakrishna by Ramchandra Dutta. When he heard the Master asking a disciple to practice the virtue of self-surrender to God, he was impressed. But though he tried thenceforth to do so, he was unable to give up his old associates and his drinking. One day the Master said in his presence, "Well, when a man goes to an undesirable place, why doesn't he take the Divine Mother with him?" And to Surendra himself Sri Ramakrishna said, "Why should you drink wine as wine? Offer it to Kali, and then take it as her *prasad*, as consecrated drink. But see that you don't become intoxicated; you must not reel and your thoughts must not wander. At first you will feel ordinary excitement, but soon you will experience spiritual exaltation." Gradually Surendra's entire life was changed. The Master designated him as one of those commissioned by the Divine Mother to defray a great part of his expenses. Surendra's purse was always open for the Master's comfort.

Kedar

Kedarnath Chatterji was endowed with a spiritual temperament and had tried various paths of religion, some not very commendable. When he met the Master at Dakshineswar, he understood the true meaning of religion. It is said that the Master, weary of instructing devotees who were coming to him in great numbers for guidance, once prayed to the Goddess Kali, "Mother, I am tired of speaking to people. Please give power to Kedar, Girish, Ram, Vijay, and Mahendra to give them the preliminary instruction, so that just a little teaching from me will be enough." He was aware, however, of Kedar's lingering attachment to worldly things and often warned him about it.

Harish

Harish, a young man in affluent circumstances, renounced his family and took shelter with the Master, who loved him for his sincerity, singleness of purpose, and quiet nature. He spent his leisure time in prayer and meditation, turning a deaf ear to the entreaties and threats of his relatives. Referring to his undisturbed peace of mind, the Master would say, "Real men are dead to the world though living. Look at Harish. He is an example." When one day the Master asked him to be a little kind to his wife, Harish said, "You must excuse me on this point. This is not the place to show kindness. If I try to be sympathetic to her, there is a possibility of my forgetting the ideal and becoming entangled in the world."

Bhavanath

Bhavanath Chatterji visited the Master while he was still in his teens. His parents and relatives regarded Sri Ramakrishna as an insane person and tried their utmost to prevent him from becoming intimate with the Master. But the young boy was very stubborn and often spent nights at Dakshineswar. He was greatly attached to Narendra, and the Master encouraged their friendship. The very sight of him often awakened Sri Ramakrishna's spiritual emotion.

Balaram Bose

Balaram Bose came of a wealthy Vaishnava family. From his youth he had shown a deep religious temperament and had devoted his time to meditation, prayer, and the study of the Vaishnava scriptures. He was very much impressed by Sri Ramakrishna even at their first meeting. He asked Sri Ramakrishna whether God really existed and, if so, whether a man could realize him. The Master said, "God reveals himself to the devotee who thinks of him as his nearest and dearest. Because you do not draw response by praying to him once, you must not conclude that he does not exist. Pray to God, thinking of him as dearer than your very self. He is much attached to his devotees. He comes to a man even before he is sought. There is none more intimate and affectionate than God." Balaram had never before heard God spoken of in such forceful words; every one of the words seemed true to him. Under the Master's influence he outgrew the conventions of the Vaishnava worship and became one of the most beloved of the disciples. It was at his home that the Master slept whenever he spent a night in Calcutta.

Mahendra or M.

Mahendranath Gupta, known as "M.," arrived at Dakshineswar in February 1882. He belonged to the Brahmo Samaj and was headmaster of the Vidyasagar High School at Syambazar, Calcutta. At the very first sight the Master recognized him as one of his "marked" disciples. Mahendra recorded in his diary Sri Ramakrishna's conversations with his devotees. These are the first directly recorded words, in the spiritual history of the world, of a man recognized as belonging in the class of Buddha and Christ. The *Gospel of Sri Ramakrishna* is a translation of this diary. Mahendra was instrumental, through his personal contacts, in spreading the Master's message among many young and aspiring souls.

Nag Mahashay

Durgacharan Nag, also known as Nag Mahashay, was the ideal householder among the lay disciples of Sri Ramakrishna. He was the embodiment of the Master's ideal of life in the world, unstained by worldliness. In spite of his intense desire to become a sannyasi, Sri Ramakrishna asked him to live in the world in the spirit of a monk, and the disciple truly carried out this injunction. He was born of a poor family and even during his boyhood often sacrificed everything to lessen the sufferings of the needy. He married at an early age and after his wife's death married a second time to obey his father's command. But he once said to his wife, "Love on the physical level never lasts. He is indeed blessed who can give his love to God with his whole heart. Even a little attachment to the body endures for several births. So do not be attached to this cage of bone and flesh. Take shelter at the feet of the Mother and think of her alone. Thus your life here and hereafter will be ennobled." The Master spoke of him as a "blazing light." He received every word of Sri Ramakrishna in dead earnest. One day he heard the Master saying that it was difficult for doctors, lawyers, and brokers to make much progress in spirituality. Of doctors he said, "If the mind clings to the tiny drops of medicine, how can it conceive of the Infinite?" That was the end of Durgacharan's medical practice, and he threw his chest of medicines into the Ganges. Sri Ramakrishna assured him that he would not lack simple food and clothing. He bade him serve holy persons. On being asked where he would find real holy persons, the Master said that the sadhus themselves would seek his company. No sannyasi could have lived a more austere life than Durgacharan.

Girish Ghosh

Girish Chandra Ghosh was a born rebel against God, a skeptic, a Bohemian, a drunkard. He was the greatest Bengali dramatist of his time, the father of the modern Bengali stage. Like other young men he had imbibed all the vices of the West. He had plunged into a life of dissipation and had become convinced that religion was only a fraud. Materialistic philosophy he justified as enabling one to get at least a little fun out of life. But a series of reverses shocked him, and he became eager to solve the riddle of life. He had heard people say that in spiritual life the help of a guru was imperative and that the guru was to be regarded as God himself. But Girish was too well acquainted with human nature to see perfection in a man. His first meeting with Sri Ramakrishna did not impress him at all. He returned home feeling as if he had seen a freak at a circus, for the Master, in a semiconscious mood, had inquired whether it was evening, though the lamps were burning in the room. But their paths often crossed, and Girish could not avoid further encounters. The Master attended a performance in Girish's Star Theatre. On this occasion, too, Girish found nothing impressive about him. One day, however, Girish happened to see the Master dancing and singing with the devotees. He felt the contagion and wanted to join them, but restrained himself for fear of ridicule. Another day Sri Ramakrishna was about to give him spiritual instruction, when Girish said, "I don't want to listen to instructions. I have myself written many instructions. They are of no use to me. Please help me in a more tangible way if you can." This pleased the Master and he asked Girish to cultivate faith.

As time passed, Girish began to learn that the guru is the one who silently unfolds the disciple's inner life. He became a steadfast devotee of the Master. He often loaded the Master with insults, drank in his presence, and took liberties that astounded the other devotees. But the Master knew that at heart Girish was tender, faithful, and sincere. He would not allow Girish to give up the theater. And when a devotee asked him to tell Girish to give up drinking, he sternly replied, "That is none of your business. He who has taken charge of him will look after him. Girish is a devotee of heroic type. I tell you, drinking will not affect him." The Master knew that mere words could not induce a man to break deep-rooted habits, but that the silent influence of love worked miracles. Therefore he never asked him to give up alcohol, with the result that Girish himself eventually broke the habit. Sri Ramakrishna had strengthened Girish's resolution by allowing him to feel that he was absolutely free.

One day Girish felt depressed because he was unable to submit to any routine of spiritual discipline. In an exalted mood the Master said to him, "All right, give me your power of attorney. Henceforth I assume responsibility for you. You need not do anything." Girish heaved a sigh of relief. He felt happy to think that Sri Ramakrishna had assumed his spiritual responsibilities. But poor Girish could not then realize that he also, on his part, had to give up his freedom and make of himself a puppet in Sri Ramakrishna's hands. The Master began to discipline him according to this new attitude.

One day Girish said about a trifling matter, "Yes, I shall do this."

"No, no!" the Master corrected him. "You must not speak in that egotistic manner. You should say, 'God willing, I shall do it.'"

Girish understood. Thenceforth he tried to give up all idea of personal responsibility and surrender himself to the divine will. His mind began to dwell constantly on Sri Ramakrishna. This unconscious meditation in time chastened his turbulent spirit.

The householder devotees generally visited Sri Ramakrishna on Sunday afternoons and other holidays. Thus a brotherhood was gradually formed, and the Master encouraged their fraternal feeling. Now and then he would accept an invitation to a devotee's home, where other devotees would also be invited. Kirtan would be arranged, and they would spend hours in dance and devotional music. The Master would go into trances or open his heart in religious discourses and in the narration of his own spiritual experiences. Many people who could not go to Dakshineswar participated in these meetings and felt blessed. Such an occasion would be concluded with a sumptuous feast.

But it was in the company of his younger devotees, pure souls yet unstained by the touch of worldliness, that Sri Ramakrishna took greatest joy. Among the young men who later embraced the householder's life were Narayan, Paltu, the younger Naren, Tejchandra, and Purna. These visited the Master sometimes against strong opposition from home.

Purna

Purna was a lad of thirteen, whom Sri Ramakrishna described as an Isvarakoti, a soul born with special spiritual qualities. The Master said that Purna was the last of the group of brilliant devotees who, as he once had seen in a trance, would come to him for spiritual illumination. Purna said to Sri Ramakrishna during their second meeting, "You are God himself incarnated in flesh and blood." Such words coming from a mere youngster proved of what stuff the boy was made.

Mahimacharan and Pratap Hazra

Mahimacharan and Pratap Hazra were two devotees outstanding for their pretentiousness and idiosyncrasies. But the Master showed them his unfailing love and kindness, though he was aware of their short-comings. Mahimacharan Chakravarty had met the Master long before the arrival of the other disciples. He had had the intention of leading a spiritual life, but a strong desire to acquire name and fame was his weakness. He claimed to have been initiated by Totapuri and would say that he had been following the path of knowledge according to his guru's instructions. He possessed a large library of English and Sanskrit books. But though he pretended to have read them, most of the leaves were uncut. The Master knew all his limitations, yet enjoyed listening to him recite from the Vedas and other scriptures. He would always exhort Mahima to meditate on the meaning of the scriptural texts and to practice spiritual discipline.

Pratap Hazra, a middle-aged man, hailed from a village near Kamarpukur. He was not altogether unresponsive to religious feelings. On a moment's impulse he had left his home, aged mother, wife, and children and had found shelter in the temple garden at Dakshineswar, where he intended to lead a spiritual life. He loved to argue, and the Master often pointed him out as an example of barren argumentation. He was hypercritical of others and cherished an exaggerated notion of his own spiritual advancement. He was mischievous and often tried to upset the minds of the Master's young disciples, criticizing them for their happy and joyous life and asking them to devote their time to meditation. The Master teasingly compared Hazra to Jatila and Kutila, the two women who always created obstructions in Krishna's sport with the gopis, and said that Hazra lived at Dakshineswar to "thicken the plot" by adding complications.

Some Noted Men

Sri Ramakrishna also became acquainted with a number of people whose scholarship or wealth entitled them everywhere to respect. He had met, a few years before, Devendranath Tagore, famous all over Bengal for his wealth, scholarship, saintly character, and social position. But the Master found him disappointing, for, whereas Sri Ramakrishna expected of a saint complete renunciation of the world, Devendranath combined with his saintliness a life of enjoyment.

Sri Ramakrishna also met the great poet Michael Madhusudan, who had embraced Christianity "for the sake of his stomach." To him the Master could not impart instruction, for the Divine Mother "pressed his tongue." In addition he met Maharaja Jatindra Mohan Tagore, a titled aristocrat of Bengal; Kristodas Pal, the editor, social reformer, and patriot; Iswar Vidyasagar, the noted philanthropist and educator; Pundit Shashadhar, a great champion of Hindu orthodoxy; Aswini Kumar Dutta, a headmaster, moralist, and leader of Indian Nationalism; and Bankim Chatterji, a deputy magistrate, novelist, and essayist, and one of the fashioners of modern Bengali prose.

Sri Ramakrishna was not a man to be dazzled by outward show, glory, or eloquence. A pundit without discrimination he regarded as a mere straw. He would search people's hearts for the light of God, and if that was missing, he would have nothing to do with them.

Kristodas Pal

The Europeanized Kristodas Pal did not approve of the Master's emphasis on renunciation and said, "Sir, this cant of renunciation has almost ruined the country. It is for this reason that the Indians are a subject nation today. Doing good to others, bringing education to the door of the ignorant, and above all, improving the material conditions of the country— these should be our duty now. The cry of religion and renunciation would, on the contrary, only weaken us. You should advise the young men of Bengal to resort only to such acts as will uplift the country."

Sri Ramakrishna gave him a searching look and found no divine light within. "You man of poor understanding!" Sri Ramakrishna said sharply. "You dare to slight in these terms renunciation and piety, which our scriptures describe as the greatest of all virtues! After reading two pages of English you think you have come to know the world! You appear to think you are omniscient. Well, have you seen those tiny crabs that are born in the Ganges just when the rains set in? In this big universe you are even less significant than one of those small creatures. How dare you talk of *helping* the world? The Lord will look to that. You haven't the power in you to do it." After a pause, the Master continued, "Can you explain to me how you can work for others? I know what you mean by helping them. To feed a number of persons, to treat them when they are sick, to construct a road or dig a well—isn't that all? These are good deeds, no doubt, but how trifling in comparison with the vastness of the universe! How far can a man advance in this line? How many people can you save from famine? Malaria has ruined a whole province; what could you do to stop its onslaught? God alone looks after the world. Let a man first realize him. Let a man get the authority from God and be endowed with his power; then, and then alone, may he think of doing good to others. A man should first be purged of all egotism. Then alone will the Blissful Mother ask him to work for the world."

Sri Ramakrishna mistrusted philanthropy that presumed to pose as charity. He warned people against it. He saw in most acts of philanthropy nothing but egotism, vanity, a desire for glory, a barren excitement to kill the boredom of life, or an attempt to soothe a guilty conscience. True charity, he taught, is the result of love of God—service to man in a spirit of worship.

Monastic Disciples

The disciples whom the Master trained for monastic life were the following:

Narendranath Dutta (Swami Vivekananda)

Rakhal Chandra Ghosh (Swami Brahmananda)

Gopal Chandra Ghosh (Swami Advaitananda)

Baburam Ghosh (Swami Premananda)

Taraknath Ghoshal (Swami Shivananda)

Jogindranath Choudhury (Swami Jogananda)

Sashibhushan Chakravarty (Swami Ramakrishnananda)

Saratchandra Chakravarty (Swami Saradananda)

Latu (Swami Adbhutananda)

Nitya Niranjan Sen (Swami Niranjanananda)

Kaliprasad Chandra (Swami Abhedananda)

Harinath Chattopadhyaya (Swami Turiyananda)

Sarada Prasanna (Swami Trigunatitananda)

Gangadhar Ghatak (Swami Akhandananda)

Subodh Ghosh (Swami Subodhananda)

Hariprasanna Chatterji (Swami Vijnanananda)

Latu

The first of these young men to come to the Master was Latu. Born of obscure parents in Behar, he came to Calcutta in search of work and was engaged by Ramchandra Dutta as houseboy. Learning of the saintly Sri Ramakrishna, he visited the Master at Dakshineswar and was deeply touched by his cordiality. When he was about to leave, the Master asked him to take some money and return home in a boat or carriage. But

Latu declared he had a few pennies and jingled the coins in his pocket. Sri Ramakrishna later requested Ram to allow Latu to stay with him permanently. Under Sri Ramakrishna's guidance, Latu made great progress in meditation and was blessed with ecstatic visions, but all the efforts of the Master to give him a smattering of education failed. Latu was very fond of kirtan and other devotional songs but remained all his life illiterate.

Rakhal

Even before Rakhal's coming to Dakshineswar, the Master had had visions of him as his spiritual son and as a playmate of Krishna at Vrindavan. Rakhal Chandra Ghosh was born of wealthy parents. During his childhood he developed wonderful spiritual traits and used to play at worshiping gods and goddesses. In his teens he was married to a sister of Manomohan Mitra, from whom he first heard of the Master. His father objected to his association with Sri Ramakrishna but afterward was reassured to find that many celebrated people were visitors at Dakshineswar. The relationship between the Master and this beloved disciple was that of mother and child. Sri Ramakrishna allowed Rakhal many liberties denied to others. But he would not hesitate to chastise the boy for improper actions. At one time Rakhal felt a childlike jealousy because he found that other boys were receiving the Master's affection. He soon got over it and realized his guru as the guru of the whole universe. The Master was worried to hear of his marriage, but was relieved to find that his wife was a spiritual soul who would not be a hindrance to his progress.

The Elder Gopal

Gopal Chandra Ghosh came to Dakshineswar at a rather advanced age and was called the elder Gopal. He had lost his wife, and the Master assuaged his grief. Soon he renounced the world and devoted himself fully to meditation and prayer. Some years later Gopal gave the

Master the ocher cloths with which the latter initiated several of his disciples into monastic life.

Narendra

To spread his message to the four corners of the earth, Sri Ramakrishna needed a strong instrument. With his frail body and delicate limbs, he could not make great journeys across wide spaces. Such an instrument was found in Narendranath Dutta, his beloved Naren, later known to the world as Swami Vivekananda. Even before meeting Narendranath, the Master had seen him in a vision as a sage, immersed in meditation of the Absolute, who, at Sri Ramakrishna's request, had agreed to take human birth to assist him in his work.

Narendra was born in Calcutta on January 12, 1863, of an aristocratic *kayastha* family. His mother was steeped in the great Hindu epics, and his father, a distinguished attorney of the Calcutta High Court, was an agnostic, a friend of the poor, and a mocker of social conventions. Even in his boyhood and youth, Narendra possessed great physical courage and presence of mind, a vivid imagination, deep power of thought, keen intelligence, an extraordinary memory, a love of truth, a passion for purity, a spirit of independence, and a tender heart. An expert musician, he also acquired proficiency in physics, astronomy, mathematics, philosophy, history, and literature. He grew up into an extremely handsome young man. Even as a child he practiced meditation and showed great power of concentration. Though free and passionate in word and action, he took the vow of austere religious chastity and never allowed the fire of purity to be extinguished by the slightest defilement of body or soul.

In college he read the rationalistic Western philosophers of the nineteenth century, and his boyhood faith in God and religion was unsettled. He would not accept religion on mere faith; he wanted demonstration of God. But very soon his passionate nature discovered that mere universal reason was cold and bloodless. His emotional nature, dissatisfied with a mere abstraction, required concrete support to help him in the hours of temptation. He wanted an external power, a guru, who by embodying perfection in the flesh would still the commotion of his soul. Attracted by the magnetic personality of Keshab, he joined the Brahmo Samaj and became a singer in its choir. But in the Samaj he did not find the guru who could say that he had seen God.

In a state of mental conflict and torture of soul, Narendra came to Sri Ramakrishna at Dakshineswar. He was then eighteen years of age and had been in college two years. He entered the Master's room accompanied by some lighthearted friends. At Sri Ramakrishna's request he sang a few songs, pouring his whole soul into them, and the Master went into samadhi. A few minutes later Sri Ramakrishna suddenly left his seat, took Narendra by the hand, and led him to the screened veranda north of his room. They were alone. Addressing Narendra most tenderly, as if he were a friend of long acquaintance, the Master said, "Ah! You have come very late. Why have you been so unkind as to make me wait all these days? My ears are tired of hearing the futile words of worldly men. Oh, how I have longed to pour my spirit into the heart of someone fitted to receive my message!" He talked thus, sobbing all the time. Then, standing before Narendra with folded hands, he addressed him as Narayana, born on earth to remove the misery of humanity. Grasping Narendra's hand, he asked him to come again, alone, and very soon.

Narendra was startled. "What is this I have come to see?" he said to himself. "He must be stark mad. Why, I am the son of Viswanath Dutta. How dare he speak this way to me?"

When they returned to the room and Narendra heard the Master speaking to others, he was surprised to find in his words an inner logic, a striking sincerity, and a convincing proof of his spiritual nature. In answer to Narendra's question, "Sir, have you seen God?" the Master said, "Yes, I have seen God. I have seen him more tangibly than I see

you. I have talked to him more intimately than I am talking to you."
Continuing, the Master said, "But, my child, who wants to see God?
People shed jugs of tears for money, wife, and children. But if they would
weep for God for only one day, they would surely see him." Narendra
was amazed. These words he could not doubt. This was the first time he
had ever heard a man say that he had seen God. But he could not rec-
oncile these words of the Master with the scene that had taken place on
the veranda only a few minutes before. He concluded that Sri Ramakrishna was a monomaniac and returned home rather puzzled in mind.

During his second visit, about a month later, suddenly, at the touch
of the Master, Narendra felt overwhelmed and saw the walls of the room
and everything around him whirling and vanishing. "What are you
doing to me?" he cried in terror. "I have my father and mother at home."
He saw his own ego and the whole universe almost swallowed in a
nameless void. With a laugh the Master easily restored him. Narendra
thought he might have been hypnotized, but he could not understand
how a monomaniac could cast a spell over the mind of a strong person
like himself. He returned home more confused than ever, resolved to
be henceforth on his guard before this strange man.

But during his third visit Narendra fared no better. This time, at the
Master's touch, he lost consciousness entirely. While he was still in that
state, Sri Ramakrishna questioned him concerning his spiritual antecedents
and whereabouts, his mission in this world, and the duration of his mortal life. The answers confirmed what the Master himself had known and
inferred. Among other things, he came to know that Narendra was a sage
who had already attained perfection, and that the day he learned his
real nature he would give up his body in yoga, by an act of will.

A few more meetings completely removed from Narendra's mind
the last traces of the notion that Sri Ramakrishna might be a monomaniac or wily hypnotist. His integrity, purity, renunciation, and
unselfishness were beyond question. But Narendra could not accept a

man, an imperfect mortal, as his guru. As a member of the Brahmo Samaj, he could not believe that a human intermediary was necessary between man and God. Moreover, he openly laughed at Sri Ramakrishna's visions as hallucinations. Yet in the secret chamber of his heart he bore a great love for the Master.

Sri Ramakrishna was grateful to the Divine Mother for sending him one who doubted his own realizations. Often he asked Narendra to test him as the moneychangers test their coins. He laughed at Narendra's biting criticism of his spiritual experiences and samadhi. When at times Narendra's sharp words distressed him, the Divine Mother herself would console him, saying, "Why do you listen to him? In a few days he will believe your every word." He could hardly bear Narendra's absences. Often he would weep bitterly for the sight of him. Sometimes Narendra would find the Master's love embarrassing; and one day he sharply scolded him, warning him that such infatuation would soon draw him down to the level of its object. The Master was distressed and prayed to the Divine Mother. Then he said to Narendra, "You rogue, I won't listen to you anymore. Mother says that I love you because I see God in you, and the day I no longer see God in you I shall not be able to bear even the sight of you."

The Master wanted to train Narendra in the teachings of the non-dualistic Vedanta philosophy. But Narendra, because of his Brahmo upbringing, considered it wholly blasphemous to look on man as one with his Creator. One day at the temple garden he laughingly said to a friend, "How silly! This jug is God! This cup is God! Whatever we see is God! And we too are God! Nothing could be more absurd." Sri Ramakrishna came out of his room and gently touched him. Spellbound, he immediately perceived that everything in the world was indeed God. A new universe opened around him. Returning home in a dazed state, he found there too that the food, the plate, the eater himself, the people around him, were all God. When he walked in the street, he saw that the cabs, the horses, the streams of people, the buildings, were all Brahman.

He could hardly go about his day's business. His parents became anxious about him and thought him ill. And when the intensity of the experience abated a little, he saw the world as a dream. Walking in the public square, he would strike his head against the iron railings to know whether they were real. It took him a number of days to recover his normal self. He had a foretaste of the great experiences yet to come and realized that the words of the Vedanta were true.

At the beginning of 1884 Narendra's father suddenly died of heart failure, leaving the family in a state of utmost poverty. There were six or seven mouths to feed at home. Creditors were knocking at the door. Relatives who had accepted his father's unstinted kindness now became enemies, some even bringing suit to deprive Narendra of his ancestral home. Actually starving and barefoot, Narendra searched for a job, but without success. He began to doubt whether anywhere in the world there was such a thing as unselfish sympathy. Two rich women made evil proposals to him and promised to put an end to his distress; but he refused them with contempt.

Narendra began to talk of his doubt of the very existence of God. His friends thought he had become an atheist and piously circulated gossip adducing unmentionable motives for his unbelief. His moral character was maligned. Even some of the Master's disciples partly believed the gossip, and Narendra told these to their faces that only a coward believed in God through fear of suffering or hell. But he was distressed to think that Sri Ramakrishna, too, might believe these false reports. His pride revolted. He said to himself, "What does it matter? If a man's good name rests on such slender foundations, I don't care." But later on he was amazed to learn that the Master had never lost faith in him. To a disciple who complained about Narendra's degradation, Sri Ramakrishna replied, "Hush, you fool! The Mother has told me it can never be so. I won't look at you if you speak that way again."

The moment came when Narendra's distress reached its climax. He had gone the whole day without food. As he was returning home in the evening he could hardly lift his tired limbs. He sat down in front of a house in sheer exhaustion, too weak even to think. His mind began to wander. Then, suddenly, a divine power lifted the veil over his soul. He found the solution of the problem of the coexistence of divine justice and misery, the presence of suffering in the creation of a blissful providence. He felt bodily refreshed, his soul was bathed in peace, and he slept serenely.

Narendra now realized that he had a spiritual mission to fulfill. He resolved to renounce the world, as his grandfather had renounced it, and he came to Sri Ramakrishna for his blessing. But even before he had opened his mouth, the Master knew what was in his mind and wept bitterly at the thought of separation. "I know you cannot lead a worldly life," he said, "but for my sake live in the world as long as I live."

One day, soon after, Narendra requested Sri Ramakrishna to pray to the Divine Mother to remove his poverty. Sri Ramakrishna bade him pray to her himself, for she would certainly listen to his prayer. Narendra entered the shrine of Kali. As he stood before the image of the Mother, he beheld her as a living goddess, ready to give wisdom and liberation. Unable to ask her for petty worldly things, he prayed only for knowledge and renunciation, love and liberation. The Master rebuked him for his failure to ask the Divine Mother to remove his poverty and sent him back to the temple. But Narendra, standing in her presence, again forgot the purpose of his coming. Thrice he went to the temple at the bidding of the Master, and thrice he returned, having forgotten in her presence why he had come. He was wondering about it when it suddenly flashed in his mind that this was all the work of Sri Ramakrishna; so now he asked the Master himself to remove his poverty and was assured that his family would not lack simple food and clothing.

This was a very rich and significant experience for Narendra. It taught him that Sakti, the divine power, cannot be ignored in the world and that in the relative plane the need of worshiping a personal God is imperative. Sri Ramakrishna was overjoyed with the conversion. The next day, sitting almost on Narendra's lap, he said to a devotee, pointing first to himself, then to Narendra, "I see I am this, and again that. Really I feel no difference. A stick floating in the Ganges seems to divide the water; but in reality the water is one. Do you see my point? Well, whatever is, is the Mother—isn't that so?"

In later years Narendra would say, "Sri Ramakrishna was the only person who, from the time he met me, believed in me uniformly throughout. Even my mother and brothers did not. It was his unwavering trust and love for me that bound me to him forever. He alone knew how to love. Worldly people only make a show of love for selfish ends."

Tarak

Others destined to be monastic disciples of Sri Ramakrishna came to Dakshineswar. Taraknath Ghoshal had felt from his boyhood the noble desire to realize God. Keshab and the Brahmo Samaj had attracted him but proved inadequate. In 1882 he first met the Master at Ramchandra's house and was astonished to hear him talk about samadhi, a subject that had always fascinated him. And that evening he actually saw a manifestation of that superconscious state in the Master. Tarak became a frequent visitor at Dakshineswar and received the Master's grace in abundance. The young boy often felt ecstatic fervor in meditation. He also wept profusely while meditating on God. Sri Ramakrishna said to him, "God favors those who can weep for him. Tears shed for God wash away the sins of former births."

Baburam

Baburam Ghosh came to Dakshineswar accompanied by Rakhal, his classmate. The Master, as was often his custom, examined the boy's physiognomy and was satisfied about his latent spirituality. At the age of eight, Baburam had thought of leading a life of renunciation, in the company of a monk in a hut shut out from the public view by a thick wall of trees. The very sight of the Panchavati awakened in his heart that dream of boyhood. Baburam was tender in body and soul. The Master used to say that he was pure to his very bones. One day Hazra in his usual mischievous fashion advised Baburam and some of the other young boys to ask Sri Ramakrishna for some spiritual powers and not waste their life in mere gaiety and merriment. The Master, scenting mischief, called Baburam to his side and said, "What can you ask of me? Isn't everything that I have already yours? Yes, everything I have earned in the shape of realizations is for the sake of you all. So get rid of the idea of begging, which alienates by creating a distance. Rather realize your kinship with me and gain the key to all the treasures."

Niranjan

Nitya Niranjan Sen was a disciple of heroic type. He came to the Master when he was eighteen years old. He was a medium for a group of spiritualists. During his first visit, the Master said to him, "My boy, if you think always of ghosts you will become a ghost, and if you think of God you will become God. Now, which do you prefer?" Niranjan severed all connections with the spiritualists.

During his second visit the Master embraced him and said warmly, "Niranjan, my boy, the days are flitting away. When will you realize God? This life will be in vain if you do not realize Him. When will you devote your mind wholly to God?" Niranjan was surprised to see the Master's great anxiety for his spiritual welfare.

He was a young man endowed with unusual spiritual parts. He felt disdain for worldly pleasures and was totally guileless, like a child. But he had a violent temper. One day, as he was coming in a country boat to Dakshineswar, some of his fellow passengers began to speak ill of the Master. Finding his protest futile, Niranjan began to rock the boat, threatening to sink it in midstream. That silenced the offenders. When he reported the incident to the Master, he was rebuked for his inability to curb his anger.

Jogindra

Jogindranath, on the other hand, was gentle to a fault. One day, under circumstances very like those that had evoked Niranjan's anger, he curbed his temper and held his peace instead of threatening Sri Ramakrishna's abusers. The Master, learning of his conduct, scolded him roundly. Thus, to each the fault of the other was recommended as a virtue. The guru was striving to develop, in the first instance, composure, and in the second, mettle. The secret of his training was to build up, by a tactful recognition of the requirements of each given case, the character of the devotee.

Jogindranath Choudhury came of an aristocratic brahmin family of Dakshineswar. His father and relatives shared the popular mistrust of Sri Ramakrishna's sanity. At a very early age the boy developed religious tendencies, spending two or three hours daily in meditation, and his meeting with Sri Ramakrishna deepened his desire for the realization of God. He had a perfect horror of marriage. But at the earnest request of his mother he had had to yield, and he now believed that his spiritual future was doomed. So he kept himself away from the Master.

Sri Ramakrishna employed a ruse to bring Jogindra to him. As soon as the disciple entered the room, the Master rushed forward to meet the young man. Catching hold of the disciple's hand, he said, "What if you have married? Haven't I too married? What is there to be afraid of in that?" Touching his own chest he said, "If this [meaning himself] is propitious, then even a hundred thousand marriages cannot injure you. If you desire to lead a householder's life, then bring your wife here one day, and I shall see that she becomes a real companion in your spiritual progress. But if you want to lead a monastic life, then I shall eat up your attachment to the world." Jogindra was dumbfounded at these words. He received new strength, and his spirit of renunciation was reestablished.

Sashi and Sarat

Sashibhushan and Saratchandra Chakravarty were two cousins who came from a pious brahmin family of Calcutta. At an early age they had joined the Brahmo Samaj and had come under the influence of Keshab Sen. The Master said to them at their first meeting, "If bricks and tiles are burned after the trademark has been stamped on them, they retain the mark forever. Similarly, man should be stamped with God before entering the world. Then he will not become attached to worldliness." Fully aware of the future course of their life, he asked them not to marry. The Master asked Sashi whether he believed in God with form or in God without form. Sashi replied that he was not even sure about the existence of God, so he could not speak one way or the other. This frank answer very much pleased the Master.

Sarat's soul longed for the all-embracing realization of the Godhead. When the Master inquired whether there was any particular form of God he wished to see, the boy replied that he would like to see God in all the living beings of the world. "But," the Master demurred, "that is the last word in realization. One cannot have it at the very outset." Sarat stated calmly, "I won't be satisfied with anything short of that. I shall trudge on along the path till I attain that blessed state." Sri Ramakrishna was very much pleased.

Harinath

Harinath Chattopadhyaya had led the austere life of a brahmachari even from his early boyhood—bathing in the Ganges every day, cooking his own meals, waking before sunrise, and reciting the Gita from memory before leaving bed. He found in the Master the embodiment of the Vedanta scriptures. Aspiring to be a follower of the ascetic Sankara, he cherished a great hatred for women. One day he said to the Master that he could not allow even small girls to come near him. The Master scolded him and said, "You are talking like a fool. Why should you hate women? They are the manifestations of the Divine Mother. Regard them as your own mother, and you will never feel their evil influence. The more you hate them, the more you will fall into their snares." Hari said later that these words completely changed his attitude toward women.

The Master knew Hari's passion for Vedanta. But he did not wish any of his disciples to become dry ascetics or mere bookworms. So he asked Hari to practice Vedanta in life by giving up the unreal and following the Real. "But it is not so easy," Sri Ramakrishna said, "to realize the illusoriness of the world. Study alone does not help one very much. The grace of God is required. Mere personal effort is futile. A man is a tiny creature after all, with very limited powers. But he can achieve the impossible if he prays to God for his grace." Whereupon the Master sang a song in praise of grace. Hari was profoundly moved and shed tears. Later in life Hari achieved a wonderful synthesis of the ideals of the personal God and the impersonal Truth.

Gangadhar

Gangadhar Ghatak, Harinath's friend, also led the life of a strict brahmachari, eating vegetarian food cooked by his own hands and devoting himself to the study of the scriptures. He met the Master in 1884 and soon became a member of his inner circle. The Master praised his ascetic habit and attributed it to the spiritual disciplines of his past life. Gangadhar became a close companion of Narendra.

Hariprasanna

Hariprasanna Chatterji, a college student, visited the Master in the company of his friends Sashi and Sarat. Sri Ramakrishna showed him great favor by initiating him into spiritual life. As long as he lived, Hariprasanna remembered and observed the following drastic advice of the Master: "Even if a woman is pure as gold and rolls on the ground for love of God, it is dangerous for a monk ever to look at her."

Kali

Kaliprasad Chandra visited the Master toward the end of 1883. Given to the practice of meditation and the study of the scriptures, Kali was particularly interested in yoga. Feeling the need of a guru in spiritual life, he came to the Master and was accepted as a disciple. The young boy possessed a rational mind and often felt skeptical about the personal God. The Master said to him, "Your doubts will soon disappear. Others, too, have passed through such a state of mind. Look at Naren. He now weeps at the names of Radha and Krishna." Kali began to see visions of gods and goddesses. Very soon these disappeared and in meditation he experienced vastness, infinity, and the other attributes of the impersonal Brahman.

Subodh

Subodh Ghosh visited the Master in 1885. At the very first meeting Sri Ramakrishna said to him, "You will succeed. Mother says so. Those whom she sends here will certainly attain spirituality." During the second meeting, the Master wrote something on Subodh's tongue, stroked his body from the navel to the throat, and said, "Awake, Mother! Awake." He asked the boy to meditate. At once Subodh's latent spirituality was awakened. He felt a current rushing along the spinal column to the brain. Joy filled his soul.

Sarada

One more young man, Sarada Prasanna by name, completes the small band of the Master's disciples later to embrace the life of the wandering monk. With the exception of the elder Gopal, all of them were in their teens or slightly over. They came from middle-class Bengali families, and most of them were students in school or college. Their parents and relatives had envisaged for them bright worldly careers. They came to Sri Ramakrishna with pure bodies, vigorous minds, and uncontaminated souls. All were born with unusual spiritual attributes. Sri Ramakrishna accepted them, even at first sight, as his children, relatives, friends, and companions. His magic touch unfolded them. And later, each according to his measure reflected the life of the Master, becoming a torchbearer of his message across land and sea.

Woman Devotees

With his woman devotees Sri Ramakrishna established a very sweet relationship. He himself embodied the tender traits of a woman; he had dwelt on the highest plane of Truth, where there is not even the slightest trace of sex; and his innate purity evoked only the noblest emotion in men and women alike. His woman devotees often said, "We seldom looked on Sri Ramakrishna as a member of the male sex. We regarded him as one of us. We never felt any constraint before him. He was our best confidant." They loved him as their child, their friend, and their teacher. In spiritual discipline he advised them to renounce lust and greed and especially warned them not to fall into the snares of men.

Gopal Ma

Unsurpassed among the woman devotees of the Master in the richness of her devotion and spiritual experiences was Aghoremani Devi, an orthodox brahmin woman. Widowed at an early age, she had dedicated herself completely to spiritual pursuits. Gopala, the Baby Krishna, was her Ideal Deity, whom she worshiped following the vatsalya attitude of the Vaishnava religion, regarding him as her own child. Through him she satisfied her unassuaged maternal love, cooking for him, feeding him, bathing him, and putting him to bed. This sweet intimacy with Gopala won her the sobriquet of Gopal Ma, or Gopala's Mother. For forty years she had lived on the bank of the Ganges in a small, bare room, her only companions being a threadbare copy of the *Ramayana* and a bag containing her rosary. At the age of sixty, in 1884, she visited Sri Ramakrishna at Dakshineswar. During the second visit, as soon as the Master saw her, he said, "Oh, you have come! Give me something to eat." With great hesitation she gave him some ordinary sweets that she had purchased for him on the way. The Master ate them with relish and asked her to bring him simple curries or sweets prepared by her own hands. Gopal Ma thought him a queer kind of monk, for, instead of talking of God, he always asked for food. She did not want to visit him again, but an irresistible attraction brought her back to the temple garden. She carried with her some simple curries that she had cooked herself.

One early morning at three o'clock, about a year later, Gopal Ma was about to finish her daily devotions, when she was startled to find Sri Ramakrishna sitting on her left, with his right hand clenched, like the hand of the image of Gopala. She was amazed and caught hold of the hand, whereupon the figure vanished and in its place appeared the real Gopala, her Ideal Deity. She cried aloud with joy. Gopala begged her for butter. She pleaded her poverty and gave him some dry coconut candies. Gopala sat on her lap, snatched away her rosary, jumped on her shoulders, and moved all about the room. As soon as the day broke, she hastened to Dakshineswar like an insane woman. Of course Gopala accompanied her, resting his head on her shoulder. She clearly saw his tiny ruddy feet hanging over her breast. She entered Sri Ramakrishna's room. The Master had fallen into samadhi. Like a child, he sat on her lap, and she began to feed him with butter, cream, and other delicacies. After some time he regained consciousness and returned to his bed. But the mind of Gopal Ma was still roaming in another plane. She was steeped in bliss. She saw Gopala frequently entering the Master's body and again coming out of it. When she returned to her hut, still in a dazed condition, Gopala accompanied her.

She spent about two months in uninterrupted communion with God, the Baby Gopala never leaving her for a moment. Then the intensity of her vision was lessened; had it not been, her body would have perished. The Master spoke highly of her exalted spiritual condition and said that such vision of God was a rare thing for ordinary mortals. The fun-loving Master one day confronted the critical Narendranath with this simple-minded woman. No two could have presented a more striking contrast. The Master knew of Narendra's lofty contempt for all visions, and he asked the old lady to narrate her experiences to Narendra. With great hesitation she told him her story. Now and then she interrupted her maternal chatter to ask Narendra, "My son, I am a poor ignorant woman. I don't understand anything. You are so learned. Now tell me if these visions of Gopala are true." As Narendra listened to the story, he was profoundly moved. He said, "Yes, mother, they are quite true." Behind his cynicism Narendra, too, possessed a heart full of love and tenderness.

7

The Final Years

The March of Events

In 1881 Hriday was dismissed from service in the Kali temple for an act
of indiscretion and was ordered by the authorities never again to enter
the garden. In a way, the hand of the Divine Mother may be seen even
in this. Having taken care of Sri Ramakrishna during the stormy days of
his spiritual discipline, Hriday had come naturally to consider himself
the sole guardian of his uncle. None could approach the Master without his knowledge. And he would be extremely jealous if Sri Ramakrishna paid attention to anyone else. Hriday's removal made it possible
for the real devotees of the Master to approach him freely and live with
him in the temple garden.

During the weekends the householders, enjoying a respite from their
office duties, visited the Master. The meetings on Sunday afternoons
were of the nature of little festivals. Refreshments were often served. Professional musicians now and then sang devotional songs. The Master
and the devotees sang and danced, Sri Ramakrishna frequently going
into ecstatic moods. The happy memory of such a Sunday would linger
long in the minds of the devotees. Those whom the Master wanted for
special instruction he would ask to visit him on Tuesdays and Saturdays.
These days were particularly auspicious for the worship of Kali.

The young disciples destined to be monks, Sri Ramakrishna invited on weekdays, when the householders were not present. The training of the householders and of the future monks had to proceed along entirely different lines. Since M. generally visited the Master on weekends, the *Gospel of Sri Ramakrishna* does not contain much mention of the future monastic disciples.

Finally, there was a handful of fortunate disciples, householders as well as youngsters, who were privileged to spend nights with the Master in his room. They would see him get up early in the morning and walk up and down the room, singing in his sweet voice and tenderly communing with the Mother.

Injury to the Master's Arm

One day, in January 1884, the Master was going toward the pine grove when he went into a trance. He was alone. There was no one to support him or guide his footsteps. He fell to the ground and dislocated a bone in his left arm. This accident had a significant influence on his mind, the natural inclination of which was to soar above the consciousness of the body. The acute pain in the arm forced his mind to dwell on the body and on the world outside. But he saw even in this a divine purpose; for, with his mind compelled to dwell on the physical plane, he realized more than ever that he was an instrument in the hand of the Divine Mother who had a mission to fulfill through his human body and mind. He also distinctly found that in the phenomenal world, God manifests himself, in an inscrutable way, through diverse human beings, both good and evil. Thus he would speak of God in the guise of the wicked, God in the guise of the pious, God in the guise of the hypocrite, God in the guise of the lewd. He began to take a special delight in watching the divine play in the relative world. Sometimes the sweet human relationship with God would appear to him more appealing than the all-effacing knowledge of Brahman. Many a time he would pray, "Mother, don't make me unconscious through the knowledge of Brahman. Don't give me Brahmajnana, Mother. Am I not your child, and naturally timid? I must have my Mother. A million salutations to the knowledge of Brahman! Give it to those who want it." Again he prayed, "O Mother, let me remain in contact with men! Don't make me a dried-up ascetic. I want to enjoy your sport in the world." He was able to taste this very rich divine experience and enjoy the love of God and the company of his devotees because his mind, on account of the injury to his arm, was forced to come down to the consciousness of the body. Again, he would make fun of people who proclaimed him as a divine incarnation by pointing to his broken arm. He would say, "Have you ever heard of God breaking his arm?" It took the arm about five months to heal.

Beginning of His Illness

In April 1885 the Master's throat became inflamed. Prolonged conversation or absorption in samadhi, making the blood flow into the throat, would aggravate the pain. Yet when the annual Vaishnava festival was celebrated at Panihati, Sri Ramakrishna attended it against the doctor's advice. With a group of disciples he spent himself in music, dance, and ecstasy. The illness took a turn for the worse and was diagnosed as "clergyman's sore throat." The patient was cautioned against conversation and ecstasies. Though he followed the physician's directions regarding medicine and diet, he could neither control his trances nor withhold from seekers the solace of his advice. Sometimes, like a sulky child, he would complain to the Mother about the crowds, who gave him no rest day or night. He was overheard to say to her, "Why do you bring here all these worthless people, who are like milk diluted with five times its own quantity of water? My eyes are almost destroyed with blowing the fire to dry up the water. My health is gone. It is beyond my strength. Do it yourself, if you want it done. This [pointing to his own body] is but a perforated drum, and if you go on beating it day in and day out, how long will it last?"

But his large heart never turned anyone away. He said, "Let me be condemned to be born over and over again, even in the form of a dog, if I can be of help to a single soul." And he bore the pain, singing cheerfully, "Let the body be preoccupied with illness, but, O mind, dwell forever in God's Bliss!"

One night he had a hemorrhage of the throat. The doctor now diagnosed the illness as cancer. Narendra was the first to break this heartrending news to the disciples. Within three days the Master was removed to Calcutta for better treatment. At Balaram's house he remained a week until a suitable place could be found at Syampukur, in the northern section of Calcutta. During this week he dedicated himself practically without respite to the instruction of those beloved devotees who had been unable to visit him oftener at Dakshineswar. Discourses incessantly flowed from his tongue, and he often went into samadhi. Dr. Mahendra Sarkar, the celebrated homeopath of Calcutta, was invited to undertake his treatment.

Syampukur

In the beginning of September 1885, Sri Ramakrishna was moved to Syampukur. Here Narendra organized the young disciples to attend the Master day and night. At first the young disciples concealed the Master's illness from their guardians; but when it became more serious, they remained with him almost constantly, sweeping aside the objections of their relatives and devoting themselves wholeheartedly to the nursing of their beloved guru. These young men, under the watchful eyes of the Master and the leadership of Narendra, became the *antaranga* bhaktas, the devotees of Sri Ramakrishna's inner circle. They were privileged to witness many manifestations of the Master's divine powers. Narendra received instructions regarding the propagation of his message after his death.

The Holy Mother—so Sarada Devi had come to be affectionately known by Sri Ramakrishna's devotees—was brought from Dakshineswar to look after the general cooking and to prepare the special diet of the patient. The dwelling space being extremely limited, she had to adapt herself to cramped conditions. At three o'clock in the morning she would finish her bath in the Ganges and then enter a small covered place on the roof, where she spent the whole day cooking and praying. After eleven at night, when the visitors went away, she would come down to her small bedroom on the first floor to enjoy a few hours' sleep. Thus she spent three months, working hard, sleeping little, and praying constantly for the Master's recovery.

At Syampukur the devotees led an intense life. Their attendance on the Master was in itself a form of spiritual discipline. His mind was constantly soaring to an exalted plane of consciousness. Now and then they would catch the contagion of his spiritual fervor. They sought to divine the meaning of this illness of the Master, whom most of them had accepted as an incarnation of God. One group, headed by Girish with his robust optimism and great power of imagination, believed that the illness was a mere pretext to serve a deeper purpose. The Master had willed his illness in order to bring the devotees together and promote solidarity among them. As soon as this purpose was served, he would himself get rid of the disease. A second group thought that the Divine Mother, in whose hand the Master was an instrument, had brought about this illness to serve her own mysterious ends. But the young rationalists, led by Narendra, refused to ascribe a supernatural cause to a natural phenomenon. They believed that the Master's body, a material thing, was subject, like all other material things, to physical laws.

Growth, development, decay, and death were laws of nature to which the Master's body could not but respond. But though holding differing views, they all believed that it was to him alone that they must look for the attainment of their spiritual goal.

In spite of the physician's efforts and the prayers and nursing of the devotees, the illness rapidly progressed. The pain sometimes appeared to be unbearable. The Master lived only on liquid food, and his frail body was becoming a mere skeleton. Yet his face always radiated joy, and he continued to welcome the visitors pouring in to receive his blessing. When certain zealous devotees tried to keep the visitors away, they were told by Girish, "You cannot succeed in it; he has been born for this very purpose—to sacrifice himself for the redemption of others."

The more the body was devastated by illness, the more it became the habitation of the divine Spirit. Through its transparency the gods and goddesses began to shine with ever-increasing luminosity. On the day of the Kali Puja, the devotees clearly saw in him the manifestation of the Divine Mother.

It was noticed at this time that some of the devotees were making an unbridled display of their emotions. A number of them, particularly among the householders, began to cultivate, though at first unconsciously, the art of shedding tears, shaking the body, contorting the face, and going into trances, attempting thereby to imitate the Master. They began openly to declare Sri Ramakrishna a divine incarnation and to regard themselves as his chosen people, who could neglect religious disciplines with impunity. Narendra's penetrating eye soon sized up the situation. He found out that some of these external manifestations were being carefully practiced at home, while some were the outcome of malnutrition, mental weakness, or nervous debility. He mercilessly exposed the devotees who were pretending to have visions and asked all to develop a healthy religious spirit. Narendra sang inspiring songs for the younger devotees, read with them the *Imitation of Christ* and the Gita, and held before them the positive ideals of spirituality.

Last Days at Cossipore

When Sri Ramakrishna's illness showed signs of aggravation, the devotees, following the advice of Dr. Sarkar, rented a spacious garden house at Cossipore, in the northern suburbs of Calcutta. The Master was removed to this place on December 11, 1885.

It was at Cossipore that the curtain fell on the varied activities of the Master's life on the physical plane. His soul lingered in the body eight months more. It was the period of his great passion, a constant crucifixion of the body and the triumphant revelation of the Soul. Here one sees the humanity and divinity of the Master passing and repassing across a thin borderline. Every minute of those eight months was suffused with touching tenderness of heart and breathtaking elevation of spirit. Every word he uttered was full of pathos and sublimity.

It took the group only a few days to become adjusted to the new environment. The Holy Mother, assisted by Sri Ramakrishna's niece, Lakshmi Devi, and a few woman devotees, took charge of the cooking for the Master and his attendants. Surendra willingly bore the major portion of the expenses, other householders contributing according to their means. Twelve disciples were constant attendants of the Master: Narendra, Rakhal, Baburam, Niranjan, Jogin, Latu, Tarak, the elder Gopal, Kali, Sashi, Sarat, and the younger Gopal. Sarada, Harish, Hari, Gangadhar, and Tulasi visited the Master from time to time and practiced sadhana at home. Narendra, preparing for his law examination, brought his books to the garden house in order to continue his studies during the infrequent spare moments. He encouraged his brother disciples to intensify their meditation, scriptural studies, and other spiritual disciplines. They all forgot their relatives and their worldly duties.

Cossipore Garden House
(Sri Ramakrishna stayed in this house during his last days)

Among the attendants Sashi was the embodiment of service. He did not practice meditation, japa, or any of the other disciplines followed by his brother devotees. He was convinced that service to the guru was the only religion for him. He forgot food and rest and was ever ready at the Master's bedside.

Pundit Shashadhar one day suggested to the Master that the latter could remove the illness by concentrating his mind on the throat, the scriptures having declared that yogis had the power to cure themselves in that way. The Master rebuked the pundit. "For a scholar like you to make such a proposal!" he said. "How can I withdraw the mind from the lotus feet of God and turn it to this worthless cage of flesh and blood?"

"For our sake at least," begged Narendra and the other disciples.

"But," replied Sri Ramakrishna, "do you think I enjoy this suffering? I wish to recover, but that depends on the Mother."

Narendra: "Then please pray to her. She must listen to you."

Master: "But I cannot pray for my body."

Narendra: "You must do it, for our sake at least."

Master: "Very well, I shall try."

A few hours later the Master said to Narendra, "I said to her: 'Mother, I cannot swallow food because of my pain. Make it possible for me to eat a little.' She pointed you all out to me and said, 'What? You are eating enough through all these mouths. Isn't that so?' I was ashamed and could not utter another word." This dashed all the hopes of the devotees for the Master's recovery.

"I shall make the whole thing public before I go," the Master had said some time before. On January 1, 1886, he felt better and came down to the garden for a little stroll. It was about three o'clock in the afternoon. Some thirty lay disciples were in the hall or sitting about under the trees. Sri Ramakrishna said to Girish, "Well, Girish, what have you seen in me that you proclaim me before everybody as an incarnation of God?"

Girish was not a man to be taken by surprise. He knelt before the Master and said with folded hands, "What can an insignificant person like myself say about the One whose glory even sages like Vyasa and Valmiki could not adequately measure?"

The Master was profoundly moved. He said, "What more shall I say? I bless you all. Be illumined!" He fell into a spiritual mood. Hearing these words the devotees, one and all, became overwhelmed with emotion. They rushed to him and fell at his feet. He touched them all, and each received an appropriate benediction. Each of them, at the touch of the Master, experienced ineffable bliss. Some laughed, some wept, some sat down to meditate, some began to pray. Some saw light, some had visions of their Chosen Ideals, and some felt within their bodies the rush of spiritual power.

Narendra, consumed with a terrific fever for realization, complained to the Master that all the others had attained peace and that he alone was dissatisfied. The Master asked what he wanted. Narendra begged for samadhi, so that he might altogether forget the world for three or four days at a time. "You are a fool," the Master rebuked him. "There is a state even higher than that. Isn't it you who sings, 'All that exists art thou'? First of all, settle your family affairs and then come to me. You will experience a state even higher than samadhi."

The Master did not hide the fact that he wished to make Narendra his spiritual heir. Narendra was to continue the work after Sri Ramakrishna's passing. Sri Ramakrishna said to him, "I leave these young men in your charge. See that they develop their spirituality and do not return home." One day he asked the boys, in preparation for a monastic life, to beg their food from door to door without thought of caste. They hailed the Master's order and went out with begging bowls. A few days later he gave the ocher cloth of the sannyasi to each of them, including Girish, who was now second to none in his spirit of renunciation. Thus the Master himself laid the foundation of the future Ramakrishna Order of monks.

Sri Ramakrishna was sinking day by day. His diet was reduced to a minimum, and he found it almost impossible to swallow. He whispered to M., "I am bearing all this cheerfully, for otherwise you would be weeping. If you all say that it is better that the body should go rather than suffer this torture, I am willing." The next morning he said to his depressed disciples seated near the bed, "Do you know what I see? I see that God alone has become everything. Men and animals are only frameworks covered with skin, and it is he who is moving through their heads and limbs. I see that it is God himself who has become the block, the executioner, and the victim for the sacrifice." He fainted with emotion. Regaining partial consciousness, he said, "Now I have no pain. I am very well." Looking at Latu, he said, "There sits Latu resting his head on the palm of his hand. To me it is the Lord who is seated in that posture."

The words were tender and touching. Like a mother he caressed Narendra and Rakhal, gently stroking their faces. He said in a half whisper to M., "Had this body been allowed to last a little longer, many more souls would have been illumined." He paused a moment and then said, "But Mother has ordained otherwise. She will take me away lest, finding me guileless and foolish, people should take advantage of me and persuade me to bestow on them the rare gifts of spirituality." A few minutes later he touched his chest and said, "Here are two beings. One is she and the other is her devotee. It is the latter who broke his arm, and it is he again who is now ill. Do you understand me?" After a pause he added, "Alas! To whom shall I tell all this? Who will understand me?" "Pain," he consoled them, "is unavoidable as long as there is a body. The Lord takes on the body for the sake of his devotees."

Yet one is not sure whether the Master's soul actually was tortured by this agonizing disease. At least during his moments of spiritual exaltation—which became almost constant during the closing days of his life on earth—he lost all consciousness of the body, of illness and suffering. One of his attendants[1] said later on, "While Sri Ramakrishna lay sick he never actually suffered pain. He would often say, 'O mind! Forget the body, forget the sickness, and remain merged in Bliss.' No, he did not really suffer. At times he would be in a state when the thrill of joy was clearly manifested in his body. Even when he could not speak he would let us know in some way that there was no suffering, and this fact was clearly evident to all who watched him. People who did not understand him thought that his suffering was very great. What spiritual joy he transmitted to us at that time! Could such a thing have been possible if he had been suffering physically? It was during this period that he taught us again these truths: 'Brahman is always unattached. The three gunas are in it, but it is unaffected by them, just as the wind carries odor yet remains odorless. Brahman is infinite Being, infinite Wisdom, infinite Bliss. In it there exist no delusion, no misery, no disease, no death, no growth, no decay. The transcendental Being and the being within are one and the same. There is one indivisible absolute Existence.'"

The Holy Mother secretly went to a Siva temple across the Ganges to intercede with the deity for the Master's recovery. In a revelation she was told to prepare herself for the inevitable end.

One day when Narendra was on the ground floor, meditating, the Master was lying awake in his bed upstairs. In the depths of his meditation Narendra felt as though a lamp were burning at the back of his head. Suddenly he lost consciousness. It was the yearned-for, all-effacing experience of nirvikalpa samadhi, when the embodied soul realizes its unity with the Absolute. After a very long time he regained partial consciousness but was unable to find his body. He could see only his head. "Where is my body?" he cried. The elder Gopal entered the room and said, "Why, it is here, Naren!" But Narendra could not find it. Gopal, frightened, ran upstairs to the Master. Sri Ramakrishna only said, "Let him stay that way for a time. He has worried me long enough."

After another long period Narendra regained full consciousness. Bathed in peace, he went to the Master, who said, "Now the Mother has shown you everything. But this revelation will remain under lock and key, and I shall keep the key. When you have accomplished the Mother's, work you will find the treasure again."

Some days later, when Narendra was alone with the Master, Sri Ramakrishna looked at him and went into samadhi. Narendra felt the penetration of a subtle force and lost all outer consciousness. Regaining presently the normal mood, he found the Master weeping.

Sri Ramakrishna said to him, "Today I have given you my all and I am now only a poor fakir, possessing nothing. By this power you will do immense good in the world, and not until it is accomplished will you return." Henceforth the Master lived in the disciple.

Doubt, however, dies hard. After one or two days Narendra said to himself, "If in the midst of this racking physical pain he declares his Godhead, only then shall I accept him as an incarnation of God." He was alone by the bedside of the Master. It was a passing thought, but the Master smiled. Gathering his remaining strength, he distinctly said, "He who was Rama and Krishna is now, in this body, Ramakrishna— but not in your Vedantic sense." Narendra was stricken with shame.

Mahasamadhi

Sunday, August 15, 1886. The Master's pulse became irregular. The devotees stood by the bedside. Toward dusk Sri Ramakrishna had difficulty in breathing. A short time afterward he complained of hunger. A little liquid food was put into his mouth; some of it he swallowed, and the rest ran over his chin. Two attendants began to fan him. All at once he went into samadhi of a rather unusual type. The body became stiff. Sashi burst into tears. But after midnight the Master revived. He was now very hungry and helped himself to a bowl of porridge. He said he was strong again. He sat up against five or six pillows, which were supported by the body of Sashi, who was fanning him. Narendra took his feet on his lap and began to rub them. Again and again the Master repeated to him, "Take care of these boys." Then he asked to lie down. Three times, in ringing tones, he cried the name of Kali, his life's Beloved, and lay back. At two minutes past one o'clock there was a low sound in his throat and he fell a little to one side. A thrill passed over his body. His hair stood on end. His eyes became fixed on the tip of his nose. His face was lighted with a smile. The final ecstasy began. It was *mahasamadhi*, total absorption, from which his mind never returned. Narendra, unable to bear it, ran downstairs.

Dr. Sarkar arrived the following noon and pronounced that life had departed not more than half an hour before. At five o'clock the Master's body was brought downstairs, laid on a cot, dressed in ocher clothes, and decorated with sandal paste and flowers. A procession was formed. The passers-by wept as the body was taken to the cremation ground at the Baranagore Ghat on the Ganges.

While the devotees were returning to the garden house, carrying the urn with the sacred ashes, a calm resignation came to their souls and they cried, "Victory unto the guru!"

The Holy Mother was weeping in her room, not for her husband, but because she felt that Mother Kali had left her. As she was about to put on the marks of a Hindu widow, in a moment of revelation she heard the words of faith, "I have only passed from one room to another."

Appendix

Dhan Gopal Mukerji and His Intense Spiritual Longing

On Sunday, July 12, 1936, at age forty-seven, Dhan Gopal Mukerji died by taking his own life—a life that his son later described as one continuous search for the heart of Truth hidden within himself.

While to some eyes Dhan Gopal Mukerji experienced periods of mental depression, to others these moods were a symptom of his intense spiritual longing. His longing found its ultimate fulfillment in his discovery of Sri Ramakrishna, the Godman of nineteenth-century India. His spiritual yearning was intensified through his association with the great disciples of Sri Ramakrishna who became his spiritual teachers and guides. Mukerji received formal initiation into spiritual life from Swami Shivananda, a direct disciple of Sri Ramakrishna and president of the Ramakrishna Order from 1922 to 1934.

On July 12, the very day of his death, Dhan Gopal Mukerji wrote a letter to his spiritual confidante, Swami Akhandananda, another direct disciple of Sri Ramakrishna and president of the Ramakrishna Order from 1934 to 1937—a letter filled with profound and poignant emotion. This letter, which is presented below, gives us a glimpse into the mind of Dhan Gopal Mukerji during the final hours of his life.

In addition to the above-mentioned letter, this appendix includes several letters written to Jadu Gopal Mukherjee, the elder brother of Dhan Gopal Mukerji. Patty Mukerji, the wife of Dhan Gopal, tells Jadu that her husband "left his body in a moment of strength and not in weakness." Josephine MacLeod, the great devotee of Swami Vivekananda, writes, "Our Dhangopal has gone to join the great ones he so loved. His *nostalgie de Dieu* [love of God] took him over." Swami Nikhilananda, who was the spiritual leader of the Ramakrishna-Vivekananda Center of New York, and very close to Dhan Gopal Mukerji, expresses his belief that Mukerji had "some illumination in his meditation which induced him to put an end to his life." A close friend, Earl H. Brewster, says of Dhan Gopal Mukerji, "He always seemed to me like an incarnation of some young god, whose real home was not in this world; and now it is as though he had had to return to that brighter world from which he came."

Also included here is a 1933 letter from Dhan Gopal Mukerji to his brother, two letters to Dhan Gopal Mukerji from his guru, Swami Shivananda, and two excerpts from publications of the Ramakrishna Order.

These letters and reflections may offer us a way of understanding and finding meaning in the final act of one who played such a significant role in presenting Sri Ramakrishna to the world.

Dhan Gopal Mukerji to Swami Akhandananda
(translated from the Bengali)

D. G. Mukerji
325 East 72nd Street
New York
July 12, 1936

His Holiness
The Swami Akhandananda

Lord,

I prostrate millions of times at your holy feet. I just received your letter of June 17th. Received the ocher cloth you have sent me as a gift. I cannot understand why you never got my letter of thanks. I had written at length about that ocher and was certain about mailing it, yet it has gone astray. It is better to blame myself than blaming anyone else. You are aware how gratified I felt on receiving the ocher. Baba [Swami Shivananda] also had sent me an ocher. His footprint and that ocher are my support. Now the ocher from you has been added to it. Kindly send me a footprint of yours. Your letters are so surcharged with a divine feeling. By the contact of these letters, my mind is set to meditation. It is all your grace.

Now I come to the letter of June 17. You have written: "Do you want to become like Baba, or his worthy son?" What can I answer? Since that letter from you, an idea has dawned on me. I think, "I want to be a *sadhu* [holy man] like Baba." Now I realize that this thought is due to you. How else could my mind have such an idea? You have brought it.

For about a month my mind has been fiddling with the idea: "I have met many sadhus," listen to the tune of that fiddling, "but none like Baba. Baba most resembles Shri Shri Thakur [Sri Ramakrishna]. It is so hard to determine: Is he woman or man? He fully reflects both these

Dhan Gopal Mukerji

aspects. One has to become a sadhu like Baba." There is no end to this musing. Now I can understand whence came such waves of thinking to carry me up to the Lord. What a quality of waves, what beatific intention! Your grace keeps me fulfilled. Have grace on me. I am ready. I have no other choice than to become like Baba. I was born to become so. Have mercy to fulfill my birth. Have grace on me.

Just some words about Baba. When I came to this country in 1910 as a laborer, I struggled and suffered a lot. After two years I came across Abdul Baha, the Bahai Guru. I learned from him the truth about the power of prayer. During that suffering, not even a drop or two of tears did I shed for the Divine. But self-pity took the upper hand. At last I prayed to God for relief. Within one year since then, on reading Thibaut's translation of *Sankara Bhashya of Vedanta Sutra*, from July 1913 till November 1913 or thereabouts, I discovered the way. Putting an end to the livelihood of a laborer, I took to writing. Then Tantine [Josephine MacLeod], the elderly one, appeared when I got my B.A. in May 1914. The elderly one said to me that Swamiji [Swami Vivekananda] and Shri Shri Sankara were one. I said: "It sounds true." My uplift began after I had read *Vedanta Sutra* here and there. The elder one took me to Baba in 1922, when I met you. Baba's name, Shivananda, means Shiva, and Sankara too means Shiva, *Vande bodhamayam nityam gurum shankara-rupinam* [Salutation to the eternal guru, embodiment of knowledge, in the form of Sankara].

Among the sacred spots, I remember Tarakeshwar. I had been there in my childhood when I was twelve; my mind still rushes to that place. It was Baba's shrine. He is Shiva. I do not know who Sankara was, but I know that Baba is Shiva. He incarnated to bestow virtue and happiness to the earth. *Shivam kevalam bhashakam bhashakanam* [Shiva alone is the teacher and the teaching].

I want to be like him. I have to be his worthy child. Graciously fulfill these two wishes of mine. Have grace on me.

Where is Tarakeshwar—where my mind's eye perceives ever so many devotees fervently lying in prostration—and where is New York, sweltering in the hottest July 11th on record—and where is Sargachhi in all this? What can I write? It is midnight; 12th July 1936. I feel reborn with the newborn day.

Now tell me: who are you? Emperor of the spiritual realm, you are seated incognito at Sargachhi. If I come there, with my own eyes I could see Him in His physical form—and could see Baba, too.

In your letter you have asked me to reflect and reply. I find I am ready. I have reflected and made my decision. It is you who has decided, I am. I am a mere instrument.

I have given the answer you have prompted me to give. What strength do I have to send a reply to such a letter?

Have grace on me. Have grace on me. Lord, have grace on me. I am ready. I seek refuge, Lord. I seek refuge, Lord. I seek refuge.

My millions of prostrations at your holy feet.

Your Servant Dhangopal

P.S. A *dakshina* [offering] of $20 is enclosed with this letter

Patty Mukerji to Jadu Gopal Mukherjee

July 21, 1936

Dear Jadu:

On Sunday evening July twelfth your brother Dhan Gopal ended this life and reached the liberation he has so long yearned for. It would seem that he took his own life, but we know that what he did was the will of God and at the call of God. He left his body in a moment of strength and not in weakness.

That evening he had written a letter to India, to Swami Akhandananda, head of the Ramakrishna Mission. Swami Bodhananda [head of the Vedanta Society of New York] has translated it for us. It is so beautiful, so yearning for spiritual freedom, for life with God. It is clear to all of us that in the meditation that followed the writing of that letter, he had a realization—and he followed where it led.

We had his body cremated and shall some day bring his ashes to his beloved India.

Swami Bodhananda led a little service for those nearest to Dhan—Dhan did not need it for he was safe and happy with Ramakrishna and the Holy Mother. We who are left behind must not mourn but rejoice in his freedom and Peace.

For a long time now Dhan has fretted at the slavery of the body, of old habits and has yearned for quicker spiritual growth. During the last few months the separation of body and spirit and the expansion of the spirit has been clear to all.

Gopal is in Europe and my friends are sending me to join him there that together we may try to understand it all and get the blessing of Dhan's inspiration and teachings.

We must rejoice together.

With affectionate greetings
I am your sister
Patty

We shall be again in New York by September 1st.

Josephine MacLeod (Tantine)
[photograph presented to the author's son]
*"To Dhan Gopal II. from Tantine—J. MacLeod
Belur Jan. 27, 1939"*

Josephine MacLeod to Jadu Gopal Mukherjee

Helsinki
July 28, 1936

My dear Jadu:

Here I am in Finland—en route to Leningrad to stay with Lady Muriel Paget then I purpose being in India in the winter.

Our Dhangopal has gone to join the great ones he so loved. His *nostalgie de Dieu* [love of God] took him over—Patty is in London to join Gopal I hear. I've not seen her—as I left London the day she arrived July 22, 1936.

Write me to Hallscroft, Stratford-on-Avon please. You and I will only grow stronger in our friendship, with Dhan dead.

The Russian government has translated all of Romain Rolland's books into Russian—including his lives of Ramakrishna and Swamiji! It was Dhangopal's *The Face of Silence* that inspired him [Romain Rolland] to write these 2 great lives! Bless them both.

It was in 1914 I met Dhangopal in California! How steady he has been in his devotion to them—and how proud and glad he was when you threw in your lot with them and us.

How old is your boy now?

Always with love, "Tantine"
J. MacLeod

Swami Nikhilananda

Swami Nikhilananda to Jadu Gopal Mukherjee

Stockholm
August 21, 1936

My dear Jadu Gopal Babu,

Your kind letter has been received by me here today. I received only the other day, here, the sad news of your brother's passing away. I have no details about it except that he committed suicide by hanging himself in his room. Miss MacLeod has written to me to say that Dhan had left a letter to India.

Dhan Gopal has been one of my most intimate friends in New York. For the last three years we met each other very frequently—often two or three times a week. Whenever he felt mentally distressed, he ran to me. Besides he conducted services at our center several times. Our students cherish a great love for him.

Of late, I noticed a great change in him. He always asked me to talk about Sri Ramakrishna, Holy Mother and the other disciples of the Master. He would not relish any other talk. I have in my room a little Ganges water and Jagannath prasad. He always enjoyed these. When I met him last time before sailing for Europe for my vacation, I scolded him for neglecting his literary work and talking about religion. I admonished him to serve Sri Ramakrishna through literary activities. He said that everything else appeared to him as meaningless.

I believe he received some illumination in his meditation which induced him to put an end to his life. After that, he found life as a worthless entity. As Sri Ramakrishna used to say, nobody keeps the mould any more after the image is taken.

But I feel his death as a great personal loss. In him I have lost my own brother. He has been the Real Ambassador of India to the West. His book induced Romain Rolland to write his classical treatise on the great prophets of India. Dhan Gopal's death is being mourned by thousands of his admirers in every part of the world. Please accept my sincere condolence in your sad bereavement.

Yours sincerely,
Swami Nikhilananda

P.S. I think through meditation Dhan of late developed a very sensitive nature which could hardly stand the tough materialism of the West.

Earl H. Brewster to Jadu Gopal Mukherjee

Snow View Estate
Almora, U.P.
June 17, 1937

Dear Jadu,

(If I may be permitted to so address you—for it is always as "Jadu" that I think of you, as that I have heard you spoken of) Today came the enclosed letter from Tantine with the request that I forward it to you.

You have been so often in my thoughts since the sad death of Dhan, and I have wanted to write to you. I wish, better still, that I might have the privilege of seeing you. My deepest sympathy has gone to you. You know how close and dear Dhan was to me, and how greatly I miss his frequent and helpful letters. His departure is one of those mysteries which it is futile to try to explain: we simply have to accept it. He always seemed to me like an incarnation of some young god, whose real home was not in this world; and now it is as though he had had to return to that brighter world from which he came. He is spared such tragedy as old age and its illness brings to most of us. He was a most dear and wonderful friend—I am grateful to him, and to fate, for the precious relationship which existed between us. I must feel close to you also, being his brother.

When you find it convenient I would be very glad to have word from you, and news of your life, which I greatly hope is a well and happy one.

My daughter is married, and at present is living in the United States. My wife and I came to India the autumn of 1935, or early winter rather, and after a few months of travel settled down here, some three miles from Almora, higher in the mountains, where we live studying and painting, liking this part of the world very much. She would wish to join me in every good wish for your welfare and in deepest sympathy. Of course we remember so happily our meeting with you.

Ever sincerely yours
Earl H. Brewster

At the Feet of Swami Akhandananda

December 17, 1936

In the heart of Swami Akhandananda there was a very soft corner for Dhangopal Mukherji. Sometimes his feeling came out and expressed itself in words. A few months back, on hearing the news of his death, the Swami was moved to the core. A few days thereafter, Mukherji's letter came to him, in which he had written, "Very soon I will be going back and will attempt a biography of the Holy Mother in English and present it to the world." Every week his letters would come, scribbled in a childish handwriting. Even in seven or eight pages a letter would not be completed; at the end would be written, "to be continued." The letter would come to an end only after two or three installments.

Suddenly today Dhangopal became the topic of discussion. Baba (Swami Akhandananda) was speaking: They call his style "sparkling." They very much appreciate him there. They read his books, heard his lectures. This is not a matter of joke. How he went to America and

Dhan Gopal Mukerji

how he became a widely known man! How much faith he had in our Master! When it came to the Holy Mother, he would write that he was *Saranagata, Saranagata* (seeker of refuge). A whole letter would be filled up with saranagata. It was at my instance that he started writing in Bengali. When he met me at the time of Dada's (Swami Shivananda's) illness, he expressed his desire to write to me. I replied, "but it must be in Bengali." Thus it started.[1]

Dhan Gopal Mukherji to Jadu Gopal Mukherjee

325 E. 72nd St.
N. Y. City
August 12, 1933

Dear old man,

I have a great desire to come to India this winter in order to see you all. But I want to come determined to spend months in the Belur Math. *Sadhu Sanga* [holy company] is what I want to cultivate. Of course I should like to spend months with you. You too are a sannyasin. It is my hope to spend at least a year in India.

By the way, there is no doubt now that I want to find God. I am not interested in any more earthly things. It is not easy here. If you can send me any advice on meditation and prayer, do so.

Now that the political hubbub has died down, India ought to be pleasant. We are too old even to take Gandhi's latest failure to heart. Can you explain why he failed?

We are just turning the corner in America. The depression is giving place to elation. May God make this permanent!

All is well. Over here we are in good health and cheerful. May this letter find you the same.

Yours,
Dhan Gopal

Swami Shivananda to Dhan Gopal Mukherji

Sri Ramakrishna Math
Belur Math, Howrah India
August 29, 1929

My Dear Dhan Gopal,

Am so glad to learn from yours of the 22nd July that you are coming to India. Will Mrs. Mukherjee and the child come with you? We may be anxious to meet each other—but everything depends on Him. I am taking all necessary precautions—otherwise the body will make me suffer. To save myself from that humiliation, I do take necessary care. However we may try, He may show the way out of this cage to the soul at any moment. We believe this. Many a young man leaving this coil every moment—who might have been useful to the society—so how can we expect life for this body—unless be it His will.

Wherever we be—we are bound to meet again—when we have once met. Is it not His natural law? If it be here—well and good. If not that is also better.

Tantine also has informed me that she may come in the November next. But she may change her plan the moment before she sails. She has imbibed that freedom from Swamiji. Hope you received my letter—the previous one—which was in reply to your last one. May this find you well and free from rheumatism. With my affectionate good wishes and blessings,

Affably yours,
Shivananda

Swami Shivananda to Dhan Gopal Mukherji

Sri Ramakrishna Math
P. O. Belurmath, District Howrah, India
September 7, 1932

My dear Dhangopal,

Your affectionate letter of the 9th August received with much pleasure. Why shall you be my servant? Are you not the child of Sri Guru Maharaj [Sri Ramakrishna]? You are. You shall go to meet Him. Why as a lowly person, but with prince-like stateliness and with the love of a child. These are your birthright. That right is your passport. No other passports are necessary—quite unnecessary. You are as clean, pure and unpassionate as ever. The shining sun covered with cloud thinking that it has become cloudy. The sun identifying itself with the passing phase of cloudiness—forgetting its own inborn shining nature. Just so in your case. Forgetting that you are a prince, thinking yourself to be a commoner, low and passionate. Let all those passions and lies remain—do not devote to them a single moment of your thoughts. Think always you are the prince. Why shall you pray to Him to do away with evil thoughts and tendencies. Who told you that they are bad. Values we confer. Had they been unworthy of you—how can you through them and being stuffed with them get the glimpse of Him? If you have to pray at all, if you can rest satisfied with that. You are His child. Pray why He is not giving you that consciousness, consciousness of your eternal unity, sanity. Do it henceforth. Let passions come and go. They are like moving waves on the eternal face of existing calm and deep sea. They are existing for the moment—next moment going back to the surface of the sea. You are like an experienced mariner—do not get nervous, but keep your eyes fixed and compass set right toward the port.

About the books, glad that you are sending them. They ought to be in our library here. Akhilananda wrote me about you. So I asked him to write to you for the books. My intention was to establish contact between you two. You are all his children. If you all be known to each other will not that make me happy?

Vijoy has sailed for Argentina on the 18th August. He has reached safely Venice on the 29th August. He may stay for a month in Europe. If Tantine takes him to America—where she is going soon, you may meet.

Pooja is coming on. The greatest spiritual festival of the Bengalees. Worshiping the Motherhood! The aspect in which she comes to succor Her children. Year's pent up hope and expectations will be offered to Her. Grand conception!

I am, I mean the body, not so bad. Others at the Math doing well. May this find you, Gopal and Patty well. My blessings and best wishes to you all.

Affectionately ever yours,
Shivananda

At the Feet of Swami Shivananda

Dhan Gopal Mukherji, one of his disciples, who had been abroad for many years, came to Belur to see the Swami and at the sight of his broken condition burst into tears. The Swami consoled him, saying: "When Buddha was about to attain Pari-nirvana, final release from the body, Ananda was overwhelmed with grief. At this Buddha observed, 'Why are you weeping, Ananda? This life lasts for fifty, sixty or at the most a hundred years. I am about to attain Eternal Life.'"[2]

Notes

Introduction

1. The word *devotee* is generally used to denote one devoted to God, a worshiper of the personal God, or a follower of the path of love. A devotee of Sri Ramakrishna is one who is devoted to Sri Ramakrishna and follows his teachings. The word *disciple*, when used in connection with Sri Ramakrishna, refers to one who had been initiated into spiritual life by Sri Ramakrishna and who regarded him as his guru.

The Face of Silence

Chapter 2

1. Mahendranath Gupta, "M.," the chronicler of *The Gospel of Sri Ramakrishna.*

Chapter 4

1. *Tat* or *That* signifies Ultimate Reality, or Brahman.
2. Among the contemporary biographies of Holy Mother, Sri Sarada Devi, the reader may see Swami Nikhilananda, *Holy Mother: Being the Life of Sri Sarada Devi, Wife of Sri Ramakrishna, and Helpmate in His Mission* (New York: Ramakrishna-Vivekananda Center, 1962)

and Swami Nikhilananda, trans., Swami Adiswarananda, ed., *Sri Sarada Devi, The Holy Mother: Her Teachings and Conversations* (Woodstock, Vt.: SkyLight Paths Publishing, 2004).

Chapter 7

1. William Ewart Gladstone (1809–1898), four-time prime minister of Great Britain.

Chapter 8

1. Bal Gangadhar Tilak (1856–1920).

Sri Ramakrishna

Chapter 2

1. Romain Rolland, *Prophets of the New India*, trans. E. F. Malcolm-Smith (London: Cassell & Co., 1930), p. 11.

2. No definite information is available as to the origin of this name. Most probably it was given by Mathur Babu, as Ramlal, Sri Ramakrishna's nephew, has said, quoting the authority of his uncle himself.

3. Hriday's mother was the daughter of Sri Ramakrishna's aunt (Khudiram's sister). Such a degree of relationship is termed in Bengal that of a "distant nephew."

Chapter 4

1. Romain Rolland, *Prophets of the New India*, pp. 38–39.

2. This version of the incident is taken from the biography of Sri Ramakrishna by Swami Saradananda, one of the Master's direct disciples.

3. This expression is used to translate the Bengali word denoting a rich man's country house set in a garden.

Chapter 7

    1. Latu, later known as Swami Adbhutananda.

Appendix

1. From *Prabuddha Bharata: Awakened India* (Calcutta: Advaita Ashrama, August 1976), p. 329. *Prabuddha Bharata* is an English-language monthly journal on religion and philosophy, founded by Swami Vivekananda in 1896 and published by the Ramakrishna Order.

2. From Swami Vividishananda, *A Man of God* (Mylapore, Madras: Sri Ramakrishna Math, 1968), pp. 342–43.

Glossary

Advaita Vedanta Nonduality; a school of Vedanta philosophy, declaring the oneness of God, soul, and universe.

anahata sabda Another name for Om.

Ananda Bliss.

antaranga Belonging to the inner circle; generally used with reference to an intimate disciple.

arati Worship of the deity accompanied by the waving of lights.

Atman Self or soul; denotes also the Supreme Soul, which, according to the Advaita Vedanta, is one with the individual soul.

avatar Incarnation of God.

bel A tree whose leaves are sacred to Siva; also the fruit of the same tree.

Benares The holiest of all places of pilgrimage for Hindus and noted for the temple of Visvanath; modern-day Varanasi.

Bhagavad Gita An important Hindu scripture, part of the *Mahabharata* epic, containing the teachings of Sri Krishna.

Bhagavan (*Lit.*, One endowed with the six attributes, viz. infinite treasures, strength, glory, splendor, knowledge, and renunciation) An epithet of the Godhead; also the personal God of the devotee.

Bhagavata A sacred book of the Hindus, especially of the Vaishnavas, dealing with the life of Sri Krishna.

bhakta A follower of the path of bhakti, divine love; a worshiper of the personal God.

bhakti Love of God; single-minded devotion to one's Chosen Ideal.

bhava Existence; feeling; emotion; ecstasy; samadhi; also denotes any one of the five attitudes that a dualistic worshiper assumes toward God.

Bhavatarini (*Lit.*, The Savior of the Universe) A name of the Divine Mother.

brahmachari A religious student devoted to the practice of spiritual discipline; a celibate belonging to the first stage of life.

brahmacharya The first of the four stages of life: the life of an unmarried student.

Brahmajnana The knowledge of Brahman.

Brahmajnanin A knower of Brahman.

Brahman The Absolute; the Supreme Reality of the Vedanta philosophy.

brahmin The highest caste in Hindu society.

Brahmo Samaj A theistic organization of India, founded by Raja Rammohan Roy.

Chaitanya, Sri A prophet born in 1485 CE who lived at Navadvip, Bengal, and emphasized the path of divine love for the realization of God; he is also known as Gauranga, Gaur, Gora, or Nimai.

Dakshineswar The suburb of Calcutta wherein is situated the Kali temple of Rani Rasmani, in which Sri Ramakrishna stayed for the greater part of his life.

Dvaita The philosophy of Dualism.

fakir Beggar; often a religious mendicant.

Gaya An important place of pilgrimage where Hindus from all parts of India go to perform the obsequies of their ancestors, the belief being that rites performed at Gaya release the souls of the dead from all obstructions to higher evolution.

Gauranga See **Chaitanya, Sri.**

Gayatri The presiding deity of the Gayatri, a sacred verse of the Vedas.

ghat Bathing-place on a lake or river.

Gita See **Bhagavad Gita.**

Gopala The Baby Krishna.

gopis The milkmaids of Vrindavan, playmates of Sri Krishna.

Gora See **Chaitanya, Sri.**

guna One of the three basic modifications of nature. According to the Samkhya philosophy, Prakriti (nature), in contrast with Purusha (soul), consists of three gunas (qualities or strands) known as sattva, rajas, and tamas. Sattva stands for balance or wisdom, rajas for activity or restlessness, and tamas for inertia or dullness.

Hanuman The great monkey devotee of Rama, mentioned in the *Ramayana.*

Ishta The Chosen Ideal, Spiritual Ideal, or Ideal Deity of the devotee.

Isvarakoti A perfected soul born with a special message for humanity. "An incarnation of God or one born with some of the characteristics of an incarnation is called an Isvarakoti." (Sri Ramakrishna)

Jagannath The Lord of the Universe; a name of Vishnu.

Janaka, King One of the ideal kings in Hindu mythology and the father of Sita. Sri Ramakrishna often described him as the ideal householder, who combined yoga with enjoyment of the world.

japa Repetition of God's name.

jnana Knowledge of God arrived at through reasoning and discrimination; also denotes the process of reasoning by which the ultimate Truth is attained. The word is generally used to denote the knowledge by which one is aware of one's identity with Brahman.

jnani One who follows the path of knowledge and discrimination to realize God; generally used to denote a nondualist.

Kali A name of the Divine Mother; the presiding deity of the Dakshineswar temple.

Kaliyuga The last of the four long ages of Hindu mythology, namely, Krita, Treta, Dvapara, and Kali. Their order of succession is according to the degree of degeneration of spirituality and righteousness in them. The present age is Kali, the most degenerate, and owing to the general lowering of standards in it, even a little spiritual practice is supposed to lead to great results.

karma (1) Action in general; duty. (2) The law of cause and effect.

karma-yoga (*Lit.,* Union with God through action) The path by which the aspirant seeks to realize God through work without attachment.

kayastha One of the subsidiary castes in Bengal.

kirtan Devotional music, often accompanied by dancing.

Krishna One of the Ideal Deities of the Vaishnavas, regarded by the Hindus as a divine incarnation.

kundalini (*Lit.*, the serpent power) The spiritual energy lying coiled up, or dormant, at the base of the spine in all individuals. When awakened through spiritual practice, it rises through the spinal column, passes through various centers, chakras, and at last reaches the brain, whereupon the yogi experiences samadhi.

kuthi The bungalow in the Dakshineswar temple garden where the proprietors and their guests stayed while visiting Dakshineswar.

lila The divine play; the Relative. The creation is often explained by the Vaishnavas as the lila of God, a conception that introduces elements of spontaneity and freedom into the universe. As a philosophical term, the Lila (the Relative) is the correlative of the Nitya (the Absolute).

Mahabharata A celebrated Hindu epic.

mahabhava The most ecstatic love of God.

maharaj (*Lit.*, great king) A title of respect used to address Indian holy men, either instead of the name or following the first name.

maharaja Emperor; king.

mantra A sacred word or mystic syllable in Sanskrit, used in japa.

Master, the An honorific name for Sri Ramakrishna.

maya Ignorance obscuring the vision of God; the cosmic illusion on account of which the One appears as many, the Absolute as the relative; it is also used to denote attachment.

nahabat Music tower.

natmandir A spacious hall supported by pillars in front of a temple, meant for devotional music, religious assemblies, and the like.

neti (*Lit.*, "not this") The negative process of discrimination, advocated by the followers of the nondualistic Vedanta.

Nimai See **Chaitanya, Sri.**

nirvikalpa samadhi The highest state of samadhi, in which the aspirant realizes his total oneness with Brahman.

Nyaya Indian logic; one of the six systems of orthodox Hindu philosophy, founded by Gautama.

Panchavati A grove of five sacred trees planted by Sri Ramakrishna in the temple garden of Dakshineswar for his practice of spiritual discipline.

paramahamsa One belonging to the highest order of sannyasins.

Patanjali The author of the Yoga system, one of the six systems of orthodox Hindu philosophy, dealing with concentration and its methods, control of the mind, and similar matters.

Prakriti Primordial Nature, which, in association with Purusha, creates the universe. It is one of the categories of the Samkhya philosophy.

pranayama Control of breath; one of the disciplines of yoga.

prasad Food or anything else that has been offered to the deity. Devotees consider it sanctifying to partake of it.

prema Ecstatic love, divine love of the most intense kind.

puja Ritualistic worship.

Purana(s) Books of Hindu mythology.

Purusha (*Lit.*, a man) A term of the Samkhya philosophy, denoting the eternal Conscious Principle; the universe evolves from the union of Prakriti and Purusha. The word also denotes the soul and the Absolute.

Radha Sri Krishna's most intimate companion among the gopis of Vrindavan.

Radhakanta (*Lit.*, the Consort of Radha) A name of Sri Krishna.

Radhika Same as Radha.

Raghuvir A name of Rama; the family deity of Sri Ramakrishna.

rajas The principle of activity or restlessness. See **guna.**

rajasic Pertaining to, or possessed of, rajas.

Rama The hero of the *Ramayana*, regarded by the Hindus as a divine incarnation.

Ramachandra Same as Rama.

Ramanuja A famous saint and philosopher of southern India, the founder of the school of Qualified Nondualism (1017–1137 CE).

Ramayana A famous Hindu epic.

rishi A seer of Truth; the name is also applied to the pure souls to whom were revealed the words of the Vedas.

rudraksha Beads made from rudraksha seeds, used for rosaries.

sadhana Spiritual discipline.

sadhu Holy man; a term generally used with reference to a monk.

Sahasrara The thousand-petaled lotus, or highest plane of realization, beyond the sixth center of consciousness, at the crown of the head.

Sakta A worshiper of Sakti, the Divine Mother, according to the Tantra philosophy.

Sakti Power, generally the creative power of Brahman; a name of the Divine Mother.

samadhi Ecstasy, trance, communion with God.

Sankara A name of Siva; also short for Sankaracharya, the great Vedantist philosopher.

Sankaracharya One of the greatest philosophers of India, an exponent of Advaita Vedanta (788–820 CE).

sannyas The monastic life; the last of the four stages of life.

sannyasin A Hindu monk.

Satchidananda (*Lit.*, Existence-Knowledge-Bliss Absolute) A name of Brahman, the Ultimate Reality.

sattva The principle of balance or wisdom. See **guna.**

sattvic Pertaining to, or possessed of, sattva.

Sita The wife of Rama.

Siva The destroyer God; the third person of the Hindu Trinity, the other two being Brahma and Vishnu.

Sivaratri An all-night vigil dedicated to Siva and observed by worship, meditation, and fasting.

Sri (*Lit.*, blessed or holy) A prefix used with names or the titles of certain scriptures. It serves as an honorific title before the name of a deity or holy man.

sudra The fourth caste in Hindu society.

Sushumna The central nadi, or nerve, situated within the spinal column from the base of the spine to the brain. It is the point of harmony between the ida to the left of the spinal column and the pingala to the right. The sushumna, through which the awakened spiritual energy (kundalini) rises, is described as the pathway to Brahman.

tamas The principle of inertia or dullness. See **guna.**

tamasic Pertaining to, or possessed of, tamas.

Tantra A system of religious philosophy in which the Divine Mother, or Power, is the Ultimate Reality; also the scriptures dealing with this philosophy.

Upanishad(s) Scriptures that contain the inner or mystic teachings of the Vedas, dealing with the ultimate Truth and its realization.

Vaishnava (*Lit.,* follower of Vishnu) A member of the well-known dualistic sect of that name, generally the followers of Sri Chaitanya in Bengal and of Ramanuja and Madhva in south India.

Valmiki The author of the *Ramayana.*

Vedanta One of the six systems of orthodox philosophy, formulated by Vyasa.

Veda(s) The most sacred scriptures of the Hindus.

vijnana Special Knowledge of the Absolute, by which one affirms the universe and sees it as the manifestation of Brahman.

vijnani One endowed with vijnana.

Vishnu The preserver God; the second of the Hindu Trinity, the other two being Brahma and Siva; the personal God of the Vaishnavas.

Visishtadvaita The philosophy of Qualified Nondualism.

Vrindavan A town on the bank of the Jamuna river associated with Sri Krishna's childhood.

Vyasa The compiler of the Vedas and father of Sukadeva.

Yoga (1) One of the six systems of orthodox Hindu philosophy, the Yoga system of Patanjali. (2) Union of the individual soul with the Universal Soul. (3) The method by which to realize union through control of mind and concentration.

Credits

Grateful acknowledgment is given for permission to use material from the following sources:

The Face of Silence by Dhan Gopal Mukerji, 1926, used by permission of Ramakrishna-Vivekananda Center of New York.

From *The Gospel of Sri Ramakrishna* translated by Swami Nikhilananda, © 1942, used by permission of the publisher, Ramakrishna-Vivekananda Center of New York.

"Sri Ramakrishna and His God-Consciousness" by Swami Adiswarananda, from *Vedanta Kesari*, 1985, used by permission of the publisher, Sri Ramakrishna Math, Madras, India.

About the Authors

Dhan Gopal Mukerji (1890–1936) was one of the earliest émigrés from India to America. A prolific writer and lecturer, he was an important figure in creating a bridge of understanding between America and India. His poetic biography, *The Face of Silence*, was the first book written in English to introduce Sri Ramakrishna and his teachings to America and the West.

Swami Nikhilananda (1895–1973), a direct disciple of Holy Mother Sri Sarada Devi, was a distinguished monk of the Ramakrishna Order of India and a major figure in introducing the teachings of Yoga and Vedanta to America and the West. A gifted writer, he is noted for his beautiful and scholarly translations of the spiritual literature of India. Among his books are *Sri Sarada Devi, The Holy Mother: Her Teachings and Conversations* (SkyLight Paths) and his translation into English from the original Bengali of *The Gospel of Sri Ramakrishna*, a work that has made the immortal words of this great prophet of the nineteenth century available to countless readers throughout the world. He founded the Ramakrishna-Vivekananda Center of New York in 1933 and was its spiritual leader until his death in 1973.

About the Editor

Swami Adiswarananda, a senior monk of the Ramakrishna Order of India, is the Minister and Spiritual Leader of the Ramakrishna-Vivekananda Center of New York. Born in 1925 in West Bengal, India, Swami received his undergraduate and Master's degrees from the University of Calcutta. He joined the monastic order of Sri Ramakrishna in 1954 and was ordained a monk in 1963. Before being sent by the Ramakrishna Order to its New York center in 1968, he taught religious subjects in one of the premier colleges of the Order and was later editor of *Prabuddha Bharata: Awakened India,* the English-language monthly journal on religion and philosophy published by the Order. Swami is a frequent lecturer at colleges, universities, and other religious, educational, and cultural institutions, and his writings appear regularly in many scholarly journals on religion and philosophy. He is the author of *The Spiritual Quest and the Way of Yoga: The Goal, the Journey and the Milestones; The Vedanta Way to Peace and Happiness* and *Meditation and Its Practices: A Definitive Guide to Techniques and Traditions of Meditation in Yoga and Vedanta* (all SkyLight Paths). He is also the editor of *Sri Sarada Devi, The Holy Mother: Her Teachings and Conversations* (SkyLight Paths).

About SKYLIGHT PATHS Publishing

SkyLight Paths Publishing is creating a place where people of different spiritual traditions come together for challenge and inspiration, a place where we can help each other understand the mystery that lies at the heart of our existence.

Through spirituality, our religious beliefs are increasingly becoming a part of our lives—rather than *apart* from our lives. While many of us may be more interested than ever in spiritual growth, we may be less firmly planted in traditional religion. Yet, we do want to deepen our relationship to the sacred, to learn from our own as well as from other faith traditions, and to practice in new ways.

SkyLight Paths sees both believers and seekers as a community that increasingly transcends traditional boundaries of religion and denomination—people wanting to learn from each other, *walking together, finding the way.*

For your information and convenience, at the back of this book we have provided a list of other SkyLight Paths books you might find interesting and useful. They cover the following subjects:

Buddhism / Zen	Gnosticism	Mysticism
Catholicism	Hinduism /	Poetry
Children's Books	Vedanta	Prayer
Christianity	Inspiration	Religious Etiquette
Comparative	Islam / Sufism	Retirement
Religion	Judaism / Kabbalah /	Spiritual Biography
Current Events	Enneagram	Spiritual Direction
Earth-Based	Meditation	Spirituality
Spirituality	Midrash Fiction	Women's Interest
Global Spiritual	Monasticism	Worship
Perspectives		

Or phone, fax, mail or e-mail to: SKYLIGHT PATHS Publishing
Sunset Farm Offices, Route 4 • P.O. Box 237 • Woodstock, Vermont 05091
Tel: (802) 457-4000 • Fax: (802) 457-4004 • www.skylightpaths.com
Credit card orders: (800) 962-4544 (8:30AM–5:30PM ET Monday–Friday)
Generous discounts on quantity orders. SATISFACTION GUARANTEED. Prices subject to change.

Spiritual Practice

Divining the Body
Reclaim the Holiness of Your Physical Self *by Jan Phillips*
A practical and inspiring guidebook for connecting the body and soul in spiritual practice. Leads you into a milieu of reverence, mystery, and delight, helping you discover a redeemed sense of self.
8 x 8, 256 pp, Quality PB, ISBN 1-59473-080-6 **$16.99**

Finding Time for the Timeless
Spirituality in the Workweek *by John McQuiston II*
Simple, refreshing stories that provide you with examples of how you can refocus and enrich your daily life using prayer or meditation, ritual, and other forms of spiritual practice. 5½ x 6½, 208 pp, HC, ISBN 1-59473-035-0 **$17.99**

The Gospel of Thomas: A Guidebook for Spiritual Practice
by Ron Miller; Translations by Stevan Davies
An innovative guide to bring a new spiritual classic into daily life. Offers a way to translate the wisdom of the Gospel of Thomas into daily practice, manifesting in your life the same consciousness revealed in Jesus of Nazareth. Written for readers of all religious backgrounds, this guidebook will help you to apply Jesus's wisdom to your own life and to the world around you.
6 x 9, 160 pp, Quality PB, ISBN 1-59473-047-4 **$14.99**

The Knitting Way: A Guide to Spiritual Self-Discovery
by Linda Skolnik and Janice MacDaniels
Through sharing stories, hands-on explorations, and daily cultivation, Skolnik and MacDaniels help you see beyond the surface of a simple craft in order to discover ways in which nuances of knitting can apply to the larger scheme of life and spirituality. Includes original knitting patterns.
7 x 9, 240 pp, Quality PB, ISBN 1-59473-079-2 **$16.99**

Earth, Water, Fire, and Air: Essential Ways of Connecting to Spirit
by Cait Johnson 6 x 9, 224 pp, HC, ISBN 1-893361-65-9 **$19.95**

Forty Days to Begin a Spiritual Life
Today's Most Inspiring Teachers Help You on Your Way
Edited by Maura Shaw and the Editors at SkyLight Paths; Foreword by Dan Wakefield
7 x 9, 144 pp, Quality PB, ISBN 1-893361-48-9 **$16.95**

Labyrinths from the Outside In
Walking to Spiritual Insight—A Beginner's Guide
by Donna Schaper and Carole Ann Camp
6 x 9, 208 pp, b/w illus. and photographs, Quality PB, ISBN 1-893361-18-7 **$16.95**

Practicing the Sacred Art of Listening: A Guide to Enrich Your Relationships and Kindle Your Spiritual Life—The Listening Center Workshop
by Kay Lindahl 8 x 8, 176 pp, Quality PB, ISBN 1-893361-85-3 **$16.95**

The Sacred Art of Bowing: Preparing to Practice
by Andi Young 5½ x 8½, 128 pp, b/w illus., Quality PB, ISBN 1-893361-82-9 **$14.95**

The Sacred Art of Chant: Preparing to Practice
by Ana Hernandez 5½ x 8½, 192 pp, Quality PB, ISBN 1-59473-036-9 **$15.99**

The Sacred Art of Fasting: Preparing to Practice
by Thomas Ryan, CSP 5½ x 8½, 192 pp, Quality PB, ISBN 1-59473-078-4 **$15.99**

The Sacred Art of Listening: Forty Reflections for Cultivating a Spiritual Practice
by Kay Lindahl; Illustrations by Amy Schnapper
8 x 8, 160 pp, Illus., Quality PB, ISBN 1-893361-44-6 **$16.99**

Sacred Speech: A Practical Guide for Keeping Spirit in Your Speech
by Rev. Donna Schaper 6 x 9, 176 pp, Quality PB, ISBN 1-59473-068-7 **$15.99**;
HC, ISBN 1-893361-74-8 **$21.95**

Kabbalah from Jewish Lights Publishing

Ehyeh: A Kabbalah for Tomorrow *by Dr. Arthur Green*
6 x 9, 224 pp, Quality PB, ISBN 1-58023-213-2 **$16.99;** HC, ISBN 1-58023-125-X **$21.95**

The Enneagram and Kabbalah: Reading Your Soul *by Rabbi Howard A. Addison*
6 x 9, 176 pp, Quality PB, ISBN 1-58023-001-6 **$15.95**

Finding Joy: A Practical Spiritual Guide to Happiness *by Dannel I. Schwartz with Mark Hass*
6 x 9, 192 pp, Quality PB, ISBN 1-58023-009-1 **$14.95;** HC, ISBN 1-879045-53-2 **$19.95**

The Gift of Kabbalah: Discovering the Secrets of Heaven, Renewing Your Life on Earth
by Tamar Frankiel, Ph.D.
6 x 9, 256 pp, Quality PB, ISBN 1-58023-141-1 **$16.95;** HC, ISBN 1-58023-108-X **$21.95**

Zohar: Annotated & Explained
Translation and annotation by Dr. Daniel C. Matt. Foreword by Andrew Harvey
5½ x 8½, 160 pp, Quality PB, ISBN 1-893361-51-9 **$15.99**

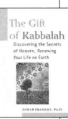

Meditation / Prayer

Prayers to an Evolutionary God
by William Cleary; Afterword by Diarmuid O'Murchu
How is it possible to pray when God is dislocated from heaven, dispersed all around us, and more of a creative force than an all-knowing father? Inspired by the spiritual and scientific teachings of Diarmuid O'Murchu and Teilhard de Chardin, Cleary reveals that religion and science can be combined to create an expanding view of the universe—an evolutionary faith.
6 x 9, 208 pp, HC, ISBN 1-59473-006-7 **$21.99**

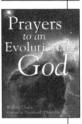

The Song of Songs: A Spiritual Commentary
by M. Basil Pennington, OCSO; Illustrations by Phillip Ratner
Join M. Basil Pennington as he ruminates on the Bible's most challenging mystical text. You will follow a path into the Songs that weaves through his inspired words and the evocative drawings of Jewish artist Phillip Ratner—a path that reveals your own humanity and leads to the deepest delight of your soul.
6 x 9, 160 pp, HC, 14 b/w illus., ISBN 1-59473-004-0 **$19.99**

Women of Color Pray: Voices of Strength, Faith, Healing, Hope, and Courage   *Edited and with Introductions by Christal M. Jackson*
Through these prayers, poetry, lyrics, meditations and affirmations, you will share in the strong and undeniable connection women of color share with God. It will challenge you to explore new ways of prayerful expression.
5 x 7¼, 208 pp, Quality PB, ISBN 1-59473-077-6 **$15.99**

The Art of Public Prayer, 2nd Edition: Not for Clergy Only
by Lawrence A. Hoffman   6 x 9, 288 pp, Quality PB, ISBN 1-893361-06-3 **$18.95**

Finding Grace at the Center: The Beginning of Centering Prayer
by M. Basil Pennington, ocso, Thomas Keating, ocso, and Thomas E. Clarke, sj
5 x 7¼, 112 pp, HC, ISBN 1-893361-69-1 **$14.95**

A Heart of Stillness: A Complete Guide to Learning the Art of Meditation
by David A. Cooper   5½ x 8½, 272 pp, Quality PB, ISBN 1-893361-03-9 **$16.95**

Meditation without Gurus: A Guide to the Heart of Practice
by Clark Strand   5½ x 8½, 192 pp, Quality PB, ISBN 1-893361-93-4 **$16.95**

Praying with Our Hands: Twenty-One Practices of Embodied Prayer from the
World's Spiritual Traditions   *by Jon M. Sweeney; Photographs by Jennifer J. Wilson; Foreword by
Mother Tessa Bielecki; Afterword by Taitetsu Unno, PhD*
8 x 8, 96 pp, 22 duotone photographs, Quality PB, ISBN 1-893361-16-0 **$16.95**

Silence, Simplicity & Solitude: A Complete Guide to Spiritual Retreat at Home
by David A. Cooper   5½ x 8½, 336 pp, Quality PB, ISBN 1-893361-04-7 **$16.95**

Three Gates to Meditation Practice: A Personal Journey into Sufism, Buddhism,
and Judaism   *by David A. Cooper*   5½ x 8½, 240 pp, Quality PB, ISBN 1-893361-22-5 **$16.95**

Women Pray: Voices through the Ages, from Many Faiths, Cultures, and Traditions
Edited and with introductions by Monica Furlong
5 x 7¼, 256 pp, Quality PB, ISBN 1-59473-071-7 **$15.99;**
Deluxe HC with ribbon marker, ISBN 1-893361-25-X **$19.95**

Spirituality

Autumn: A Spiritual Biography of the Season
Edited by Gary Schmidt and Susan M. Felch; Illustrations by Mary Azarian
Autumn is a season of fruition and harvest, of thanksgiving and celebration of abundance and goodness of the earth. But it is also a season that starkly and realistically encourages us to see the limitations of our time. Warm and poignant pieces by Wendell Berry, David James Duncan, Robert Frost, A. Bartlett Giamatti, Kimiko Hahn, P. D. James, Julian of Norwich, Garret Keizer, Tracy Kidder, Anne Lamott, May Sarton, and many others rejoice in autumn as a time of preparation and reflection. 6 x 9, 320 pp, 5 b/w illus., HC, ISBN 1-59473-005-9 **$22.99**

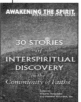

Awakening the Spirit, Inspiring the Soul
30 Stories of Interspiritual Discovery in the Community of Faiths
Edited by Brother Wayne Teasdale and Martha Howard, MD; Foreword by Joan Borysenko, PhD
Thirty original spiritual mini-biographies that showcase the varied ways that people come to faith—and what that means—in today's multi-religious world.
6 x 9, 224 pp, HC, ISBN 1-59473-039-3 **$21.99**

Winter: A Spiritual Biography of the Season
Edited by Gary Schmidt and Susan M. Felch; Illustrations by Barry Moser
Delves into the varied feelings that winter conjures in us, calling up both the barrenness and the beauty of the natural world in wintertime. Includes selections by Will Campbell, Rachel Carson, Annie Dillard, Donald Hall, Ron Hansen, Jane Kenyon, Jamaica Kincaid, Barry Lopez, Kathleen Norris, John Updike, E. B. White, and many others. "This outstanding anthology features top-flight nature and spirituality writers on the fierce, inexorable season of winter.... Remarkably lively and warm, despite the icy subject." —*Publishers Weekly* Starred Review
6 x 9, 288 pp, 6 b/w illus., Deluxe PB w/flaps, ISBN 1-893361-92-6 **$18.95**; HC, ISBN 1-893361-53-5 **$21.95**

The Alphabet of Paradise: An A–Z of Spirituality for Everyday Life
by Howard Cooper 5 x 7¾, 224 pp, Quality PB, ISBN 1-893361-80-2 **$16.95**

Creating a Spiritual Retirement: A Guide to the Unseen Possibilities in Our Lives
by Molly Srode 6 x 9, 208 pp, b/w photos, Quality PB, ISBN 1-59473-050-42 **$14.99**; HC, ISBN 1-893361-75-6 **$19.95**

The Geography of Faith: Underground Conversations on Religious, Political and Social Change by Daniel Berrigan and Robert Coles; Updated introduction and afterword by the authors 6 x 9, 224 pp, Quality PB, ISBN 1-893361-40-3 **$16.95**

God Lives in Glass: Reflections of God for Adults through the Eyes of Children
by Robert J. Landy, PhD; Foreword by Sandy Eisenberg Sasso
7 x 6, 64 pp, HC, Full-color illus., ISBN 1-893361-30-6 **$12.95**

God Within: Our Spiritual Future—As Told by Today's New Adults Edited by Jon M.
Sweeney and the Editors at SkyLight Paths 6 x 9, 176 pp, Quality PB, ISBN 1-893361-15-2 **$14.95**

Jewish Spirituality: A Brief Introduction for Christians by Lawrence Kushner
5½ x 8½, 112 pp, Quality PB, ISBN 1-58023-150-0 **$12.95** (a Jewish Lights book)

A Jewish Understanding of the New Testament
by Rabbi Samuel Sandmel; New preface by Rabbi David Sandmel
5½ x 8½, 384 pp, Quality PB, ISBN 1-59473-048-2 **$19.99**

Journeys of Simplicity: Traveling Light with Thomas Merton, Basho, Edward Abbey,
Annie Dillard & Others by Philip Harnden 5 x 7¼, 128 pp, HC, ISBN 1-893361-76-4 **$16.95**

Keeping Spiritual Balance As We Grow Older: More than 65 Creative Ways to
Use Purpose, Prayer, and the Power of Spirit to Build a Meaningful Retirement
by Molly and Bernie Srode 8 x 8, 224 pp, Quality PB, ISBN 1-59473-042-3 **$16.99**

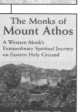

The Monks of Mount Athos: A Western Monk's Extraordinary Spiritual Journey on
Eastern Holy Ground by M. Basil Pennington, ocso; Foreword by Archimandrite Dionysios
6 x 9, 256 pp, 10+ b/w line drawings, Quality PB, ISBN 1-893361-78-0 **$18.95**

One God Clapping: The Spiritual Path of a Zen Rabbi by Alan Lew with Sherrill Jaffe
5½ x 8½, 336 pp, Quality PB, ISBN 1-58023-115-2 **$16.95** (a Jewish Lights book)

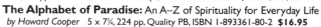

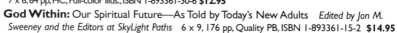

Spirituality

Prayer for People Who Think Too Much
A Guide to Everyday, Anywhere Prayer from the World's Faith Traditions   by Mitch Finley
5½ x 8½, 224 pp, Quality PB, ISBN 1-893361-21-7   **$16.95**; HC, ISBN 1-893361-00-4   **$21.95**

The Shaman's Quest: Journeys in an Ancient Spiritual Practice
by Nevill Drury; with a Basic Introduction to Shamanism by Tom Cowan
5½ x 8½, 208 pp, Quality PB, ISBN 1-893361-68-3   **$16.95**

Show Me Your Way: The Complete Guide to Exploring Interfaith Spiritual Direction
by Howard A. Addison   5½ x 8½, 240 pp, Quality PB, ISBN 1-893361-41-1   **$16.95**;
HC, ISBN 1-893361-12-8 **$21.95**

Spirituality 101: The Indispensable Guide to Keeping—or Finding—Your Spiritual Life
on Campus   by Harriet L. Schwartz, with contributions from college students at nearly thirty cam-
puses across the United States   6 x 9, 272 pp, Quality PB, ISBN 1-59473-000-8 **$16.99**

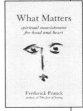

Spiritually Incorrect: Finding God in All the Wrong Places
by Dan Wakefield; Illus. by Marian DelVecchio
5½ x 8½, 192 pp, b/w illus., HC, ISBN 1-893361-88-8   **$21.95**

Spiritual Manifestos: Visions for Renewed Religious Life in America from Young
Spiritual Leaders of Many Faiths   Edited by Niles Elliot Goldstein; Preface by Martin E. Marty
6 x 9, 256 pp, HC, ISBN 1-893361-09-8   **$21.95**

A Walk with Four Spiritual Guides: Krishna, Buddha, Jesus, and Ramakrishna
by Andrew Harvey   5½ x 8½, 192 pp, 10 b/w photos & illus., HC, ISBN 1-893361-73-X   **$21.95**

What Matters: Spiritual Nourishment for Head and Heart
by Frederick Franck   5 x 7¼, 144 pp, 50+ b/w illus., HC, ISBN 1-59473-013-X   **$16.99**

Who Is My God?, 2nd Edition
An Innovative Guide to Finding Your Spiritual Identity
Created by the Editors at SkyLight Paths   6 x 9, 160 pp, Quality PB, ISBN 1-59473-014-8   **$15.99**

Spirituality—A Week Inside

Come and Sit: A Week Inside Meditation Centers
by Marcia Z. Nelson; Foreword by Wayne Teasdale
The insider's guide to meditation in a variety of different spiritual traditions.
Traveling through Buddhist, Hindu, Christian, Jewish, and Sufi traditions, this essential guide takes you to different meditation centers to meet the teachers and students
and learn about the practices, demystifying the meditation experience.
6 x 9, 224 pp, b/w photographs, Quality PB, ISBN 1-893361-35-7   **$16.95**

Lighting the Lamp of Wisdom: A Week Inside a Yoga Ashram
by John Ittner; Foreword by Dr. David Frawley
This insider's guide to Hindu spiritual life takes you into a typical week of retreat
inside a yoga ashram to demystify the experience and show you what to expect
from your own visit. Includes a discussion of worship services, meditation and yoga
classes, chanting and music, work practice, and more.   6 x 9, 192 pp, b/w photographs,
Quality PB, ISBN 1-893361-52-7   **$15.95**; HC, ISBN 1-893361-37-3   **$24.95**

Making a Heart for God: A Week Inside a Catholic Monastery
by Dianne Aprile; Foreword by Brother Patrick Hart, ocso
This essential guide to experiencing life in a Catholic monastery takes you to
the Abbey of Gethsemani—the Trappist monastery in Kentucky that was home
to author Thomas Merton—to explore the details. "More balanced and infor-
mative than the popular *The Cloister Walk* by Kathleen Norris." —*Choice:
Current Reviews for Academic Libraries*   6 x 9, 224 pp, b/w photographs, Quality PB,
ISBN 1-893361-49-7   **$16.95**; HC, ISBN 1-893361-14-4 **$21.95**

Waking Up: A Week Inside a Zen Monastery
by Jack Maguire; Foreword by John Daido Loori, Roshi
An essential guide to what it's like to spend a week inside a Zen Buddhist monastery.
6 x 9, 224 pp, b/w photographs, Quality PB, ISBN 1-893361-55-1   **$16.95**;
HC, ISBN 1-893361-13-6   **$21.95**

Sacred Texts—SkyLight Illuminations Series
Andrew Harvey, series editor

Offers today's spiritual seeker an enjoyable entry into the great classic texts of the world's spiritual traditions. Each classic is presented in an accessible translation, with facing pages of guided commentary from experts, giving you the keys you need to understand the history, context, and meaning of the text. This series enables readers of all backgrounds to experience and understand classic spiritual texts directly, and to make them a part of their lives. Andrew Harvey writes the foreword to each volume, an insightful, personal introduction to each classic.

Bhagavad Gita
Annotated & Explained
Translation by Shri Purohit Swami; Annotation by Kendra Crossen Burroughs
"The very best Gita for first-time readers." —Ken Wilber. Millions of people turn daily to India's most beloved holy book, whose universal appeal has made it popular with non-Hindus and Hindus alike. This edition introduces you to the characters, explains references and philosophical terms, shares the interpretations of famous spiritual leaders and scholars, and more.
5½ x 8½, 192 pp, Quality PB, ISBN 1-893361-28-4 **$16.95**

Dhammapada
Annotated & Explained
Translation by Max Müller and revised by Jack Maguire; Annotation by Jack Maguire
The Dhammapada—believed to have been spoken by the Buddha himself over 2,500 years ago—contain most of Buddhism's central teachings. This timeless text concisely and inspirationally portrays the route a person travels as he or she advances toward enlightenment and describes the fundamental role of mental conditioning in making us who we are.
5½ x 8½, 160 pp, b/w photographs, Quality PB, ISBN 1-893361-42-X **$14.95**

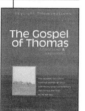

The Gospel of Thomas
Annotated & Explained
Translation and annotation by Stevan Davies
Discovered in 1945, this collection of aphoristic sayings sheds new light on the origins of Christianity and the intriguing figure of Jesus, portraying the Kingdom of God as a present fact about the world, rather than a future promise or future threat.
5½ x 8½, 192 pp, Quality PB, ISBN 1-893361-45-4 **$16.95**

Hasidic Tales
Annotated & Explained
Translation and annotation by Rabbi Rami Shapiro
Introduces the legendary tales of the impassioned Hasidic rabbis, which demonstrate the spiritual power of unabashed joy, offer lessons for leading a holy life, and remind us that the Divine can be found in the everyday.
5½ x 8½, 240 pp, Quality PB, ISBN 1-893361-86-1 **$16.95**

The Hebrew Prophets
Selections Annotated & Explained
Translation and annotation by Rabbi Rami Shapiro
Focuses on the central themes covered by all the Hebrew prophets: moving from ignorance to wisdom, injustice to justice, cruelty to compassion, and despair to joy, and challenges us to engage in justice, kindness, and humility in every aspect of our lives.
5½ x 8½, 224 pp, Quality PB, ISBN 1-59473-037-7 **$16.99**